USER INTERFACE EVALUATION

EVALUATION

A STRUCTURED APPROACH

LANGUAGES AND INFORMATION SYSTEMS*

Series Editor: Shi-Kuo Chang
University of Pittsburgh
Pittsburgh, Pennsylvania
and Knowledge Systems Institute
Skokie, Illinois

*Series was formerly entitled:
MANAGEMENT AND INFORMATION SYSTEMS

HUMAN–MACHINE INTERACTIVE SYSTEMS
Edited by Allen Klinger

LANGUAGES FOR AUTOMATION
Edited by Shi-Kuo Chang

MANAGEMENT AND OFFICE INFORMATION SYSTEMS
Edited by Shi-Kuo Chang

USER INTERFACE DESIGN: A Structured Approach
Siegfried Treu

USER INTERFACE EVALUATION: A Structured Approach
Siegfried Treu

VISUAL LANGUAGES
Edited by Shi-Kuo Chang, Tadao Ichikawa, and Panos A. Ligomenides

VISUAL LANGUAGES AND APPLICATIONS
Edited by Tadao Ichikawa, Erland Jungert, and Robert R. Korfhage

VISUAL LANGUAGES AND VISUAL PROGRAMMING
Edited by Shi-Kuo Chang

USER INTERFACE EVALUATION
A STRUCTURED APPROACH

Siegfried Treu
University of Pittsburgh
Pittsburgh, Pennsylvania

SPRINGER SCIENCE+BUSINESS MEDIA, LLC

Library of Congress Cataloging-in-Publication Data

Treu, Siegfried.
    User interface evaluation : a structured approach / Siegfried
Treu.
        p.   cm. -- (Languages and information systems)
    Includes bibliographical references and index.
    ISBN 978-1-4613-6081-0   ISBN 978-1-4615-2536-3 (eBook)
    DOI 10.1007/978-1-4615-2536-3
    1. User interfaces (Computer systems)   I. Title. II. Series.
QA76.9.U83T75 1994
004.2'4--dc20   94-25688
                                                             CIP

PUBLISHER CREDITS

A number of figures and tables have been reprinted herein, mostly in revised form, from published papers. In such cases, written permission from the publishers is acknowledged in the corresponding figure captions and table footnotes. In addition, various portions of text from published papers have been extracted and usually updated and revised extensively. Publisher permission for such usage is more conveniently summarized at this point. Kind permission was granted by each of the following:

- *Academic Press*, London, UK: for selections of text from each of: Treu (1992), used in Chapters 4, 10, and 12; Treu (1990), used in Chapter 11
- *ACM Press*, New York: for selections of text from Abrams and Treu (1977), used in Chapter 5
- *Taylor & Francis Ltd.*, Hants, UK: for selections of text from Mullins and Treu (1991), used in Chapter 9

ISBN 978-1-4613-6081-0

©1994 Springer Science+Business Media New York
Originally published by Plenum Press, New York in 1994

To my invaluable wife, Erika,

      and our entire, wonderful family –

      present and future.

Fame and fortune are fleeting; but,

a family, secure in structure and in loving

      support for every member, provides a

genuine, lasting measure of success.

PREFACE

Methodology for human–computer interface (HCI) design has been presented in the companion book (Treu, 1994) and in numerous other publications cited in that book. Included are the myriad design factors, features, principles, and guidelines that must be understood and utilized by the interface designer in making design decisions. The resulting products, whether in interim (e.g., prototype) or in operational forms, are subject to evaluation.

This book addresses the topic of interface measurement and evaluation. Like its companion volume, it develops methodology that is purposely *systematic* and *comprehensive*. Within an organized framework (implied by the right half of Fig. P1 on page xii), the material encompasses the major considerations that should enter any attempt to evaluate user interfaces, especially when the evaluation is to be as objective as reasonably possible. As for HCI design, it is not feasible to include the details on all considerations that are relevant to an interdisciplinary specialty like HCI evaluation. But numerous pointers to the literature are included. The reader is encouraged to pursue them.

As shown in Fig. P1, this book consists of four parts. The introductory part summarizes the background, status, and literature of HCI evaluation, with emphasis on contrasting it with HCI design on each of those subjects. Included also is a chapter that gives a capsule overview of structured design methodology (Treu, 1994) and of how some of its elements carry over to evaluation methodology.

Part II contains three chapters presenting materials deemed prerequisite to the development and use of methodology for objective measurement and evaluation of user interfaces. The major topics are:

- Tools and techniques, such as for data collection, experimental design, and statistical analysis (Chapter 3)
- Patterns within the user–computer interface that enable various types of measurement to be carried out (Chapter 4)
- Basic measures, or metrics or statistical formulas, that are variously dependent on such patterns and that become influential (along with more advanced measures) in different types of and methods for evaluation (Chapter 5)

The patterns, called "interface structures," which are defined in Chapter 4, are consistent with the aim of being systematic and comprehensive. As is true of the companion volume, this book has a pervasive theme: *structure*. Interface structures provide an underlying foundation by focusing on the conceptual, logical, and physical patterns that are significant to both the user model and the computer model in the dual-model relationship forming the core of HCI. This material is fairly new and different in the HCI arena, although it is largely based on knowledge representation systems that are well known in other areas (Treu, 1992).

If such interface structures are supportive of HCI evaluation, as suggested in this book, they must surely also pertain to HCI design. This fact is borne out by many references (in the companion book and in other resources) to the needs for and uses of structure. However, for several reasons, the detailed treatment of interface structures was included in this book. Given the choice, the measurement of HCI performance is more critically dependent on the recognition and use of structure than is HCI design. As the HCI area advances, however, the design side will hopefully be viewed as increasingly dependent on the explicit, up-front introjection of structure, as opposed to the currently prevalent practice of ending up with various implicit structures, or with structures that resulted by default or in ad hoc ways.

While the companion book is concerned with "How to design something," this book focuses on "How well does it work?" and "What factors make it work that way?" Part III presents the methodology for answering such questions. The relevant terminology and evaluative aspects are defined in Chapter 6. Then, in Chapter 7, the basic measures of Chapter 5 and the underlying patterns of Chapter 4 are utilized for purposes of constructing new measures. Particularly important is the need to tailor measures that specifically address, or represent, the different evaluative aspects of interest to the evaluator. Such measures are subsequently employed, within the context of evaluation methodology, to assess how the interface design actually performs in relation to (1) current needs and expectations and/or (2) originally specified design principles. The latter, after all, reflect the designer's goals for the interface (Treu, 1994). It should be possible to determine whether those goals have in fact been reached.

In Chapter 8, evaluation approaches are distinguished, and a number of illustrative studies found in the literature are briefly described and characterized according to their commonalities and differences. This is followed by definition of a measures-based evaluation method and by discussion of how the results of its use must be interpreted. Then a selected set of evaluation studies is profiled with regard to the methods and measures that they employed, and the chapter ends with an overview of how the benefits (to an organization) of evaluative results and the changes they might indicate are also subject to evaluation. Chapter 8 is the culmination of the evaluation methodology built up in the first seven chapters.

Finally, in Part IV, several special and more advanced topics relating to interface evaluation are addressed. Chapter 9 considers how various kinds of stress can affect users of computers, and how such stress may be correlated with a user's level of satisfaction. Relevant definitions, models, and measurement techniques are discussed. Chapter 10 deals with structure-based forms of visualization at the interface. Visualization is defined to have two distinctive but interrelated meanings. Then, a partitioning into "visualizable spaces" is introduced and illustrated. Chapter 11 elaborates on the topic of interaction techniques and styles to portray the range of mental involvements (or efforts), including visualizations, that are imposed on users in HCI. Direct and indirect manipulation as well as virtual reality options are included. Finally, the specification of user-oriented structures and the evaluation of their utility are considered in Chapter 12.

As was also stated in the Preface of the companion book on design (Treu, 1994), this book is significantly based on (1) definitions, (2) models, (3) categorizations and taxonomies, (4) structures, (5) methods and techniques, (6) references to the literature, and (7) a conceptual framework to encompass all of the above. The last of these is consistent with a goal resulting from a recent workshop on the topic of teaching HCI (Gasen and Aiken, 1993). Also, "multidisciplinary integration" was one of the workshop themes. It is certainly reflected by the material on evaluation presented in this book.

The evaluation methodology developed should be applicable to any interface design. While the book does report some comparisons of current evaluation methods (e.g., in Chapter 8) and also compares several interface features (e.g., interaction styles, in Chapter 11), it is not intended to be a source (or catalogue) of performance information about different named products. Such data are deliberately outside the scope of this book.

Accordingly, its primary objectives are to develop interface evaluation methodology and to guide the reader in using that methodology. A bias exists in favor of the objective, measures-based method of evaluation. However, the reader will find that other, more subjective methods are also included and considered as appropriate under various circumstances.

The methodology is designed also to work on either existing interfaces or new, original designs. In either case, the object of evaluation may range from consisting of the entire interface system (including user, application software, and interface software/hardware) to involving only some part or module of that system. In other words, the scope of evaluation is variable.

This book can be utilized as a reference or a text. Its organization (see

Contents), subject index, and bibliography should be useful in either case. In addition, the exercises appended to chapters are designed to enhance its use as a text.

With the assumption that students have already taken a course in HCI design, this volume can serve as the text for a follow-up course, for either graduate or undergraduate students. For undergraduate purposes, the advanced topics in Part IV should be used only very selectively. On the other hand, the material in Part II (especially in Chapters 3 and 5) and Part III (especially Chapters 7 and 8) can be elaborated and supplemented considerably. Projects involving the construction of innovative measures and their use within clearly delimited and controlled evaluation studies can make the course more interesting and challenging for students. In graduate-level coursework, a project can also include some of the more advanced topics (e.g., specification and subsequent comparison of visualized objects in different spaces of definition).

An alternative to having a two-course, design–evaluation sequence in HCI is to combine the coverage into one course. However, for undergraduate purposes this is definitely not recommended; it is likely to lead to coverage that is too superficial and selective. On the other hand, that option may be reasonable for a graduate-level offering. Although it may not be possible to cover in depth all topics pertaining to both design and evaluation, the instructor can set priorities and address in detail only those that are considered to be most important.

SIEGFRIED TREU

Pittsburgh, Pennsylvania

ACKNOWLEDGMENTS

The prototype interface systems that were designed and implemented by Pete Sanderson, Paul Mullins, Sherman Tyler, and Rick Bournique, respectively, as parts of their Ph.D. dissertations, were acknowledged in the HCI design volume (Treu, 1994). Each prototype also had to undergo the scrutiny of some form of evaluation, as indicated in this book. The fine contributions made by these very capable former graduate students are very much appreciated.

Also, the work reflected by this book was made possible, in part, by the research support provided to me since 1985 by the National Science Foundation (NSF Grant DCR-850562) and by the NCR Corporation, Cambridge, Ohio. Furthermore, it represents the opportunities I was given in earlier years to become intimately involved in the design and conduct of system/interface evaluation studies. Especially noteworthy are the periods of time I spent at the Goodyear Aerospace Corporation, in Akron, Ohio, with John T. Welch as my main colleague, and at the Institute for Computer Science and Technology of the National Bureau of Standards (now NIST), in Washington, D.C., with Bob Blanc, Tom Pyke, Marshall Abrams, and Robbie Rosenthal as my principal colleagues. Their assistance and support are gratefully acknowledged.

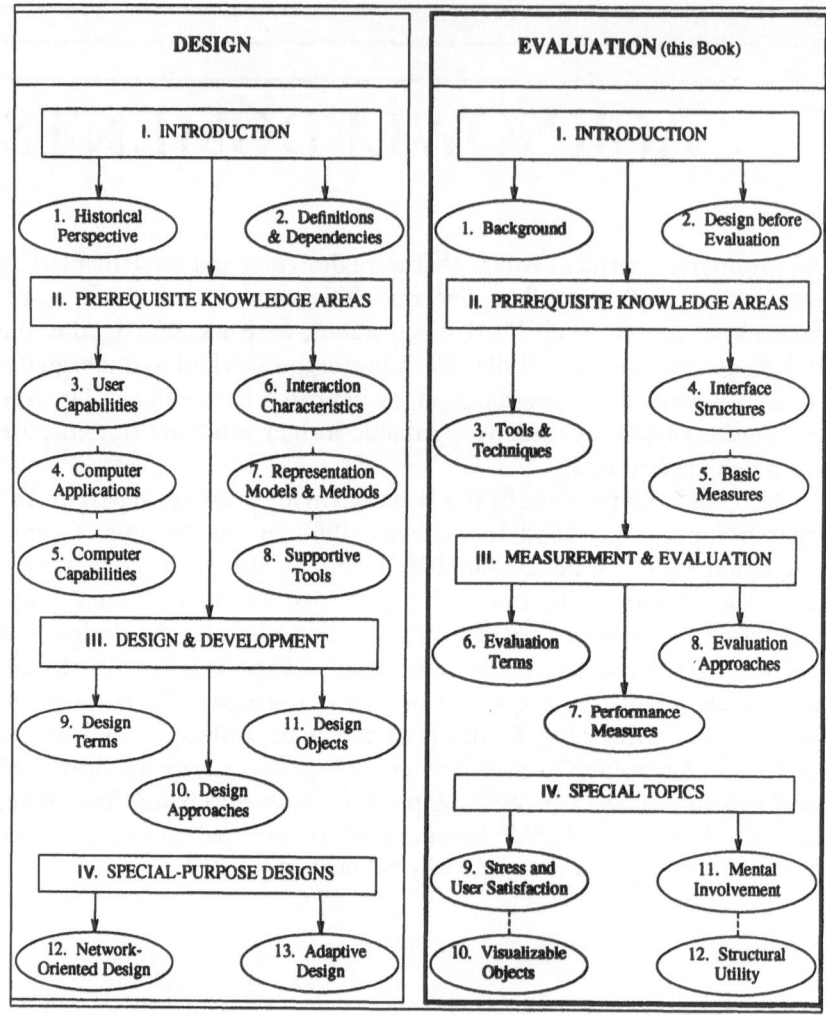

FIGURE P1. Organizations of Design and Evaluation books.

CONTENTS

PART IV
SPECIAL TOPICS

INTRODUCTION

This two-chapter part provides background for the study of human–computer interface (HCI) evaluation. Chapter 1 presents a perspective on how evaluation relates to design. It also gives an overview of the historical background of HCI evaluation and the literature that has appeared on that topic. Emphasis is on comparing the amount of attention paid to evaluation with that paid to design. Then, in Chapter 2, the major terms that represent the methodology for HCI design, and their relationships, are described in capsule forms. This is to ensure that the reader has at least a summary of the design methodology, when references are made to it in subsequent chapters. Finally, Chapter 2 outlines the places or time-points at which evaluation can/should be invoked, relative to the design process and to the products of design.

BACKGROUND AND STATUS

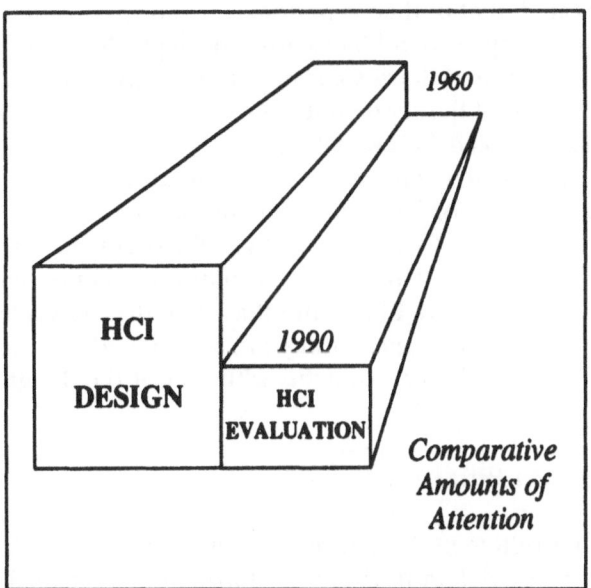

Comparative Amounts of Attention

1.1. Overview

People evaluate other people's appearances, behaviors, and performances. For examples, teachers evaluate students, students evaluate teachers, teachers may evaluate other teachers, and students may even evaluate each other. But evaluation is also applied by people to any "objects" that are somehow subject to being experienced or used. The objects may vary greatly, both in the ways in which they were created and in the characteristics that resulted. They may include the home in which one lives, the car that one drives, the movie that one watches, the zoo that one visits, the job that one holds, and, yes, the computer that one uses on the job or at home.

Evaluation can take on many different forms. It can be very informal in nature, or it can be very systematic and rigorous; its results can be subjective, objective, or both in some combination. Our purpose in this book is to develop methodology for evaluating the human–computer interface, or HCI, and the associated, dynamic human–computer interaction. For simplicity, the latter is labeled HCI also. The entire user–computer "system" or any part of it may be evaluated. Section 1.2 presents a perspective on the objects and objectives of evaluation that are possible and important.

With regard to the objects of evaluation, we presuppose that they were somehow created, that is, they were designed and specified and/or implemented in some way. Section 1.3 discusses the dependency of HCI evaluation on HCI design and draws some important distinctions between those two phases. Several of the key definitions used in design are also applicable to and, hence, adopted for evaluation.

It is interesting to compare the backgrounds of HCI evaluation and HCI design, in terms of interest shown and progress made over the last three decades. Section 1.4 gives a portrait of the current status of HCI evaluation methodology. Finally, this introductory chapter characterizes the publications in the HCI literature that are either in whole or in part dedicated to evaluation. Some writings are highlighted and the Bibliography is contrasted in size and contents with that of the design literature.

1.2. Evaluation Perspective

Computer system performance has been evaluated for a long time. A considerable methodology has been developed just for it (e.g., Kant, 1992). In the early years of batch processing computers, "benchmark" programs were selected and then executed while carrying out appropriate measurements (e.g., CPU cycles, disk accesses) for later analysis. The advent of time-sharing computer systems required more complicated approaches. Under carefully controlled system conditions, predefined, interactive scenarios were used to "drive" the system from a set of terminals, while measuring system performance.

Such evaluation efforts shared an important characteristic: primary emphasis was on the "internal performance" of the computer. This emphasis suggests the "object–objective" pairing of the first entry in Table 1.1. By evaluating the computer in a manner independent of how the results might impact the user, a study has limited value for HCI. Although that type of evaluation is obviously of interest to designers of computer hardware and software, it is in itself not very relevant to the human user engaged in HCI. Unless he or she can actually notice any effects of internal functioning on externally observable behavior, the computer-

TABLE 1.1
Major Evaluation Objects and Objectives

	Evaluation object(s)	Evaluation objective
1	**C:** Computer Interface, Hardware, Software	Determination of user-independent performance
2	**U:** User	Determination of computer-independent performance
3	U ← C	Determining the implications of computer performance on the user
4	U → C	Determining implications (demands) of user performance on the computer
5	U ↔ C	User–computer performance: the combined system with interdependence

internal side may just as soon remain hidden. This is particularly true of the kind of user who is *not* very computer-knowledgeable. However, whenever externally visible behavior (e.g., response time) deteriorates or improves significantly, the user, regardless of computer-oriented level of expertise, is likely to notice and be affected.

An analogous argument can be made in favor of not merely studying human characteristics and performance in and of themselves, independently of interaction with computers. This option is implied by the second entry in Table 1.1. Our knowledge of human capabilities may thereby be extended, and it may supply useful inputs to both HCI design and evaluation. But most important in HCI evaluation is to relate the human capabilities and limitations specifically to the requirements they impose on computer technology, and vice versa.

The point of the above discussion is to motivate a perspective on the kinds of evaluation that are possible and meaningful. We should be able to evaluate both computers and users independently, as suggested by Entries 1 and 2 of Table 1.1. If for no other reason, we can thereby gain further insights into their respective information processing talents. But we should pay special attention to evaluating the two main objects *in the context of HCI*. That is, we want to be able to determine:

- Implications of the computer system (hardware and software) performance on the user and on his/her interaction with the computer
- Implications of the computer interface (hardware: display, input devices, etc.) performance on the user and HCI
- Implications of the computer's interactive software features (techniques, styles, etc.) and dynamics (including communication speed) on the user and HCI
- Implications of the application software performance (enabled by the above-implied computer facilities) on the user and HCI

The above-indicated "objects" of evaluation, including the computer-internal hardware and software and the user-visible hardware and software, seem to suggest that we only are interested in the following "objective" in evaluation: what are their implications for the "services" rendered to the interactive user? Indeed that is a very high-priority objective. It is indicated by Entry 3 of Table 1.1. It basically treats the user as a consumer of computer services; it tacitly assumes that the consumer is always right (i.e., not subject to criticism). Evaluation methodology can then be restricted to determining how well a system is serving the indicated needs or wants of a particular user or user population.

For such purposes, the user population to be targeted must be clearly defined and understood. Figure 1.1 distinguishes the single user from the collective user model that can be employed. Computer services can be evaluated from an individualistic standpoint, focusing on how well every single user is served. Resulting data can then be analyzed in cumulative ways. Alternatively, the services provided by a computer can be assessed with regard to the welfare, or the "common good," of a group of users, such as the employees within a department. Perhaps management decides on the type of computer service that is (or should be) satisfactory for everyone. The choice of focus has a bearing on the type of user (e.g., "idiosyncratic," "stereotypical," "average") who is to be the beneficiary of the services rendered.

However, the above-characterized, consumer-oriented approach is

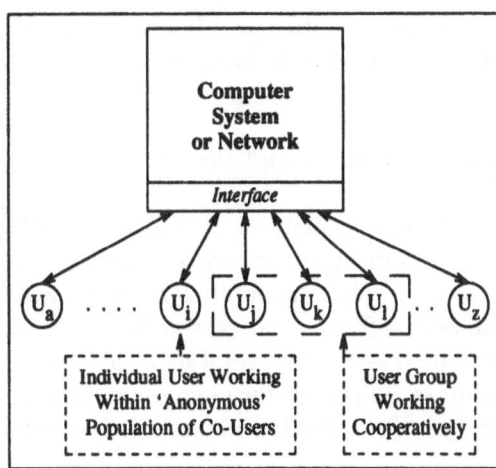

FIGURE 1.1. Individual and group users in total user population.

very one-sided and really not adequate, if we are interested in thorough evaluation of HCI. The user's role and responsibility must, in general, also be taken into account:

- Implications of the user characteristics (including knowledge, preparedness, etc.) and the user's interactive behavior on the computer system (hardware, software, interactive tools, etc.) and on HCI

These implications can be viewed as "demands" imposed on the computer (fourth entry of Table 1.1). On the other hand, they can be interpreted as presenting user strengths and weaknesses that can/should be reinforced and/or ameliorated by the capabilities of the computer. Adding the user to the list of potential evaluation objects, and considering his/her capabilities and limitations as meaningful evaluative results that can be shown to affect HCI performance, extends our evaluation perspective significantly.

It leads us to take the next step of treating the human–computer pair as a symmetric system or partnership (Treu, 1994, Chapter 2). This is suggested by Entry 5 in Table 1.1. The methodology we want to develop should be capable of supporting any one of the five "object + objective" combinations outlined in Table 1.1. The chapters in Parts II and III are designed to be supportive of this goal.

In addition, a higher-level goal can be identified. After determining the performance of computer and/or user (the major evaluative objects), independently or in conjunction, it is desirable to assess the effects of such performance on the organizational unit in which the objects are (or are planned to be) situated. While this type of evaluation is beyond the scope of this book, it is briefly characterized at the end of Chapter 8.

1.3. Evaluation and Design

To have something to evaluate in HCI, we need to have that something properly described (or specified) and available in some form of existence. This means that it must have been designed and/or implemented before it can reasonably serve as an object of evaluation. We already referred to several such "objects" in the previous section. It makes sense to utilize the very generic definition employed for designing HCI objects (Treu, 1994) and adapt it for evaluation purposes:

Definition 1.1 **Object**: an information entity represented at any level of specificity or generality; any entity that is defined in physical, logical, or conceptual form and that is either static or dynamic in its behavior and/or appearance; any unit of knowledge.

Although the objects that we are most likely to want to evaluate have either a real existence (e.g., a computer, a user) or are represented within some kind of (logical) specification or model, the definition of the term "object" is intentionally broader than those choices would imply. It also encompasses objects that are conceptualized for specialized evaluations, such as in the comparison of visualized object representations (mental pictures) with those that are actually displayed and viewed at the interface. This topic is addressed in later chapters (Part IV).

Evaluation is very dependent on design. That is, the methodology developed and utilized must naturally relate to the results and constituents of the design process. Thus, the user (or user model) who (or which) was a design target, in the sense that the HCI design was to serve the needs and wants of such a user, now becomes a target of the evaluation. After all, it may not be fair to evaluate a computer interface with respect to some user (type) whose needs were not targeted during design. On the other hand, a very good design may go beyond satisfying only the originally stipulated requirements, thereby extending the user population that can be served.

Definition 1.2. **Target user**: the human user, or category of human users, included directly in an interface evaluation; the user who personally interacts with the interface to be evaluated; the user who is being represented for purposes of evaluation.

The user (U) to be targeted is one major module (object) in an HCI evaluation. Depending on the type of evaluation carried out, the user may be real or be modeled to represent real user(s). In addition, a computer-based application (A) module is required.

Definition 1.3. **Target application**: the computer application that is defined and implemented to support the work of interest to the target user (Definition 1.2); the application that is being represented (or modeled) for purposes of evaluation.

Third, to make a target application available for evaluation, a computer/interface (I) module is essential.

Definition 1.4. **Target computer**: the (type of) computer that provides the platform and environment for the target application (Definition 1.3) for interaction with the target user (Definition 1.2); the computer that is being represented (or modeled) for purposes of evaluation.

Definitions 1.2 through 1.4 represent the three major modules, U, A, and I, which supply the enabling and constraining design factors (called U-factors, A-factors, and I-factors) during the HCI design process (Treu, 1994). They are used as important inputs to design decisions, as summarized in the next chapter.

At this point, it is useful to adapt, for inclusion in HCI evaluation terminology, two more definitions that are obviously prominent in HCI design methodology. They involve the "HCI" acronym in its "interface" and "interaction" interpretations, respectively:

Definition 1.5. **Human–computer interface**: the physical surface and facilities, between human user and computer, providing the medium through which they can connect and interact; the physical (visual, audio, tactile) means, methods, and patterns that support human–computer interaction.

Definition 1.6. **Human–computer interaction**: the combination of physical, logical, conceptual, and language-based actions between a human user and a computer, toward achieving some purpose.

Both versions of HCI are composite "objects" of evaluation, as implied by Entry 5 of Table 1.1. HCI evaluation methodology should exhibit attributes that are analogous to those advocated for design methodology (Treu, 1994):

- *Systematic*: providing for clear organization and process in carrying out the evaluation
- *Objective*: producing evaluative results that are based on measurable, confirmable data, when possible, while utilizing subjective data only when necessary or appropriate

- *Comprehensive*: enabling evaluation of the composite HCI, if desired, while also permitting *selective* evaluation of only those parts or those features that are of interest
- *Accountable*: by clearing recording and revealing the means, methods, sources, criteria, rationales, etc. that were employed in arriving at evaluative conclusions.

These methodological attributes are reflected both in the prerequisite knowledge areas described in Part II and in the evaluation terminology, measures, and methods defined and developed in Part III.

1.4. Progress and Status

In the technology-dominated period of the 1960s, formal evaluation of human–computer interfaces was very limited in scope. Various response time studies (mentioned in Chapter 5) are indicative. But these were application-specific attempts at evaluation. For example, a review of the literature on information storage and retrieval (IS&R) systems at that time found the following five test and evaluation methods (Treu, 1967a) employed for that application. Both retrospective and current awareness searches (queries) were involved:

1. Operational *query-file search-system response* procedure, leading to analysis of the responses in terms of such measures as "precision" and "recall." In other words, the system was evaluated with regard to performance in its primary purpose: retrieving as much and as relevant information as possible in response to a user's query.
2. *Out-of-system-service context* procedure, to assess any part or aspect of the system independently, i.e., outside of the service function inherent to the first method. For example, the comparative effectiveness of different surrogate versions (e.g., abstracts and sets of index terms) of stored documents could be tested, regardless of how many might be retrieved in response to a particular query.
3. *Questionnaire and interview* techniques, to determine user requirements and levels of user satisfaction with the IS&R system and its services.
4. *Observation of functioning system*, in its operational environment, to determine system workloads and effects of system components and staff performance.
5. *System modeling and simulation*, based on an approximate representation (model) of the entire system, or part of it, in operation.

What can we deduce from the above, for the particular application involved? The user's judgment on how well the system was doing its operational job (retrieving relevant information) was important to the first method. Also, application-oriented user needs and satisfaction were determined via questionnaires and interviews. Otherwise, the remaining methods were principally designed to evaluate "the system," including its components and staff. There was virtually no interest in evaluating the visible user interface *per se*. This was related in part to the fact that interactive interfaces to information retrieval systems were not yet commonly available to most users. The user interface was loosely equivalent to enabling the user to somehow (e.g., by intermediary) get out of the computer (enough of) what he/she wanted. Delay times, from request to response, lasting hours and even days were not uncommon and often were viewed as satisfactory. Interface evaluation for the IS&R application was, therefore, more about having success in obtaining relevant information than about the details of user interaction with an information system in real time.

Even after interactive user interfaces became more widely available, their designs were pursued for years with relatively little attention to systematic evaluation. Indeed, there was evidence in a number of forums (e.g., Treu, 1977) of open resistance to formal evaluations of interface designs. Through the 1970s and into the early 1980s, the prevailing attitude of HCI investigators seemed to be: let us design interesting and neat interfaces and let evaluation take care of itself; if people like the products, they will acquire or emulate them and use them; that was good enough evaluation!

But, in more recent years, the importance of HCI evaluation has been recognized and gained much more attention. This is confirmed by the illustrative studies outlined in Chapter 8. It is also reflected by the growing although still limited literature characterized in the next section. At the present time, we have a number of tools and techniques available to support efforts at systematic, objective, and comprehensive types of evaluation. Included are the topics of *experimental design* and *statistical analysis*, which have been acquired from other disciplines and adapted to HCI. Relevant tools and techniques are outlined in Chapter 3. It is obviously not feasible in this book to describe them in great detail. Instead, the reader is referred to useful resources found in the literature.

Such material constitutes one of the knowledge areas (Part II) that are deemed prerequisite to successful development and/or utilization of HCI evaluation methodology (in Parts III and IV). Other such knowledge areas are the basic and (mostly) well-known performance measures, described in

Chapter 5. They are needed to provide certain kinds of inputs to evaluative judgments. Many such measures are dependent on patterns, called *interface structures* (Chapter 4), which are evident in HCI. Those structures can also stimulate and support the evaluator in the design and construction of more complex performance measures, thereby enabling more substantive and interesting types of evaluation. This is illustrated in Chapter 7.

While progress has been made and continues to be made, the state-of-the-art of HCI evaluation is not as yet very advanced. In view of the interdisciplinary nature of HCI, this is understandable. HCI is very difficult, both in its design and in its evaluation. However, the current state is also explainable by the relatively low level of attention paid to HCI evaluation, when compared with design. Both phases are in need of much more research and development. But evaluation has lagged behind and is expected to challenge HCI researchers for many years to come.

1.5. Literature

The literature on HCI evaluation can be compared with that of HCI design by looking at the bibliographies of this book and its companion (Treu, 1994). A total of over 425 different publications were selected and referenced in the two books combined. Of that total number, approximately 75% were deemed relevant to the coverage of HCI design, while less than 50% were either in whole or in part pertinent to HCI evaluation. Thus, about 100 publications are listed in both bibliographies.

The above-indicated sample was of course selected with typical author bias, generally favoring the types of publications that would either support or contrast the coverages planned for both topics. Also, the sample naturally leans toward more recent publications. Only about 15% or so date to the 1970s or earlier, and many of those represent historical milestones and lasting resources. But if we assume that the total sample of over 425 is reasonably representative of the entire HCI literature, it is clear that evaluation-oriented studies are not nearly as numerous and extensive as are the studies involving the design and building of interfaces.

That conclusion can also be drawn from scanning the titles of all the publications for key terms suggesting HCI design and/or evaluation. Terms such as "design," "specification," "development," "building," and "software engineering" appear among the sample titles nearly twice as often as terms like "evaluation," "measurement," "comparison," "experiment," and "performance." However, the majority of titles do not contain any such obvious clues. Hence, this kind of simple analysis is not only too superficial but also incomplete. Ultimately, one must judge a publication as relevant based on review of its contents.

Any historical perspective on HCI naturally should encompass both design and evaluation (e.g., Treu, 1994, Chapter 1). But, consistent with above-suggested conclusions, the increasing numbers of journals, books, and also conference proceedings have given little *special* attention to the evaluation side. The regular journals that are in place (e.g., *International Journal of Man–Machine Studies*, renamed in 1994 to *International Journal of Human–Computer Studies*) and the regular conferences (e.g., CHI) of course include evaluation-oriented papers to the extent that they are submitted *and* considered worthy of publication. However, the increasing numbers of books that have appeared in recent years typically either

1. *Imply evaluation* by stipulating design principles and guidelines that should be followed in order to achieve good design (i.e., a design that could stand up to rigorous testing and evaluation), or
2. Include a chapter or two of *selected coverage* on evaluation, normally as it relates to or fits into the design process.

There is nothing wrong with the above; they serve useful purposes. But they indicate that evaluation coverage seems to be limited in scope and secondary in importance. Examples of the first, above-outlined option are the books by Norman and Draper (1986) and Brown (1988). Examples of the second option are Thimbleby (1990), containing a chapter entitled "Easy to use?"; Shneiderman (1992), containing a chapter on "Response Time and Display Rate" and also a chapter on "Iterative Design, Testing, and Evaluation"; and Preece (1993), containing a chapter on "Evaluation."

Books that are among the exceptions, in that they are dedicated more extensively to some kind of evaluation, are those of Spence (1985), addressing the testing and evaluation of "computer usability," and Duffy *et al.* (1993), focusing on both design and evaluation of "on-line help."

Finally, the book edited by Baecker and Buxton (1987) should be mentioned. Its collection of reprint articles is organized into 14 chapters. Only one chapter (containing two reprints) explicitly addresses the evaluation of user interfaces. Nevertheless that volume is very useful, for purposes of both HCI design and HCI evaluation.

Exercises

1.1. In Section 1.1, it is suggested that computer users really don't care about computer-internal performance unless it is externally noticeable in some ways. Do you agree? Why? Identify three computer-internal performance features that are likely to be noticed by users; likewise, list three that probably will not be noticed. Explain each one.

1.2. With regard to Entry 3 of Table 1.1, describe six different computer performance features (based in software and/or hardware) that are likely to affect *user performance*.

1.3. Repeat Exercise 1.2, but focus on the reverse (Entry 4 of Table 1.1): user performance affecting *computer performance*.

1.4. One of the most prevalent excuses in our modern society is "the computer made me do it." The computer tends to be blamed for most everything. Is that really fair? Write a brief essay on the issue of who is more likely to be at fault when problems arise in computer-based information systems and networks: the computer or the user (or the human designer)?

1.5. Notice that in each of Definitions 1.2, 1.3, and 1.4, the possibility of using a model (of user, application, computer) is allowed. Why is that necessary?

1.6. Consider the two meanings of the acronym HCI (Definitions 1.5 and 1.6). For evaluation purposes, should the "interface" version essentially represent hardware objects, while the "interaction" version represents the dynamics of what humans do with computers? Or is that an oversimplification? Explain.

1.7. Read Draper and Norman (1985) to determine how many topics or points discussed pertain more to HCI evaluation than to HCI design. Does your answer support or contradict the suggestion that the study of HCI should be viewed as "interface engineering"?

1.8. Read Shneiderman (1992) and write a general summary of the contents of the two chapters pertaining to evaluation.

1.9. Scan the collections of reprints compiled by Baecker and Buxton (1987) and write general summaries of those papers/parts that pertain to evaluation.

1.10. The interaction of humans with machines, including various types of equipment in factories, has been a subject of evaluation for many years. Terms like "human factors" resulted from it. Write an essay to characterize the differences between human–computer interaction and human interaction with any machine, including any computer-assisted equipment. Discuss the implications of those differences on how the major alternatives might be evaluated.

DESIGN BEFORE EVALUATION

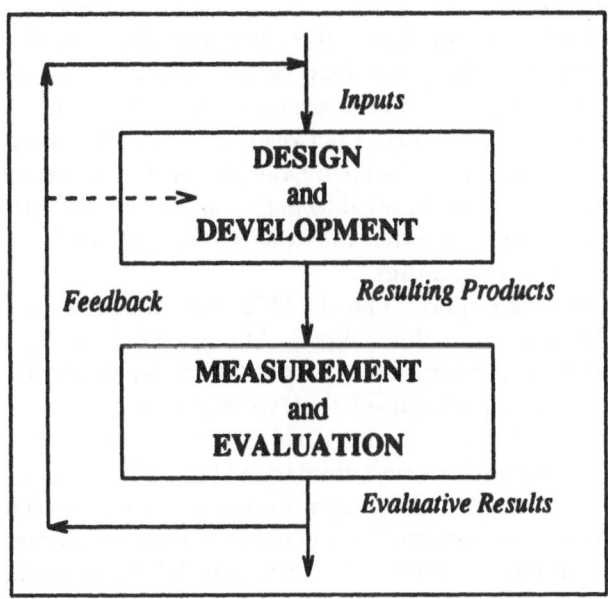

2.1. Overview

To evaluate something, we must have that something available in some form—subject to being observed, tested, measured, etc., as desirable and appropriate. The object of evaluation may or may not be in its completed or final representation or state of existence. It may only be partially implemented, with other modules, functionalities, and refinements yet to be added; or it may be implemented on a trial basis, as a prototype. Further, it may not be implemented in any form, but only exist in terms of a detailed description or model, or as a specification for implementation. Finally, the object of evaluation may in fact be a product that is complete and operational.

Regardless of its stage of development, the HCI object that we want to be able to evaluate must already reflect some history of design activity.

Accordingly, this chapter is entitled "Design *before* Evaluation." However, this does not mean that the evaluator is necessarily informed of the details of the design method employed. Indeed, such information may be unavailable for a variety of reasons, including the likelihood (in years past) that designers made no attempts at systematic recordings of design methodology, especially the rationales behind their design decisions.

It can be argued that it is preferable for the HCI evaluator not to be cognizant of the design rationales, lest they somehow unduly influence the direction of evaluation methodology. That may be true in certain types of evaluation studies, particularly when the objectives are to determine whether levels of performance may exceed initial design goals or may somehow be contrary to them. However, ultimately it becomes useful to be able to explain the assessed HCI performance with reference to the goals and constraints that were faced by the designer. For example, if the computer interface is determined to perform poorly for a certain type of user, it is good to know whether the designer was purposely not trying to serve the needs of such a user.

In general, it is important for the HCI evaluator to be knowledgeable not only of evaluation methodology; he/she should also be quite familiar with methodology of design. Knowledge of the latter should, therefore, be viewed as a major prerequisite to HCI evaluation, *in addition* to the prerequisite knowledge areas described in the chapters of Part II. However, the design material is only summarized here, while making reference to its extensive coverage in the companion book (Treu, 1994). This chapter, therefore, represents a kind of bridge between the two volumes. It gives a capsule view of the major considerations and definitions encountered in design, but it does so with emphasis on relationships to and implications for evaluation.

Section 2.2 outlines the major categories of design factors that are used as inputs to design decisions. Section 2.3 defines and lists a variety of design principles, which are interpreted to be the equivalents of design goals. They also are inputs to design decisions. Then, Section 2.4, describes the kinds of design features that must be understood and utilized by the designer to achieve the design goals according to specified design principles, while fully taking the enabling or constraining effects of the specified design factors into account. The design features represent the outcomes or results of design decisions.

As already implied above, cause-and-effect and input-to-output paradigms are very prevalent in structured approaches to HCI design. Such patterns are broadly described, in Section 2.5, as significant constituents of the framework for design methodology.

Finally, in Section 2.6, we return to the question implied at the outset of this chapter: When is evaluation relevant and applicable? Before, during, or after design? We characterize the points in the design and development stages at which evaluation methodology can be invoked.

2.2. *Design Factors*

A special type of "factors analysis" is pertinent to HCI design. It involves the identification, prioritization, comparison, weighting, selection, and utilization of factors that somehow influence the design.

Definition 2.1 **Design factor**: an element or characteristic that is causal in nature, either enabling or constraining the attainment of a design goal.

The realistic capabilities and limitations of each of the user (Definition 1.2), the computer-based application (Definition 1.3), and the computer (Definition 1.4), especially with regard to its user interface, become factors that the designer must recognize and take into account. This takes a lot of knowledge and skill on the part of the designer. He/she must be able to distinguish the factors that are important from those that are not, in the context of trying to attain the design goals that have been set. Resulting factors are then used as inputs to design decisions.

Once the selected design factors have served their purpose of influencing the design, in ways that are either enabling or constraining, they may seem to disappear from sight. In fact, that is not true. They become embedded in the design and carry implications for the evaluation phase in at least two ways:

- *Delimiting performance*: if certain design factors were identified as reflecting the capabilities and limitations inherent to the major HCI modules (user, application, computer/interface), then it stands to reason that those factors will naturally delimit resulting performance. Hence, during HCI evaluation, various design factors may also become evident as performance factors, that is, as factors that directly affect the evaluative results.

- *Explaining features*: because design factors, in general, not only include observable or measuring capabilities (e.g., interaction speed) but also choices (e.g., expressed user preferences), they can later be used to explain why a particular design feature (among available alternatives) was included in a design. Thus, during HCI evaluation, the knowledge that a feature (e.g., an interaction technique) was purposely selected during design (e.g., to compensate for certain limiting factors) can be useful.

HCI design factors, therefore, are seen as potentially carrying through to the assessments of HCI performance. Following are summary descriptions of the design factors pertaining to each of the user (U-factors), application (A-factors), and computer interface (I-factors). For each of these modules, the factors can be categorized into the general groupings shown in Fig. 2.1. In addition, there are miscellaneous design factors that do not involve substantive capabilities as such, but are nevertheless influential. Illustrative are administrative limits that are imposed, such as restrictions on design costs. Such factors must at least be acknowledged here, although we do not discuss them further.

User Factors

The factual data (Fig. 2.1) about an individual user or a user group either are specific to the particular target users involved in a design or are generally known and accepted characteristics of such users. These data can be stratified into the following subgroupings (Treu, 1994, Chapter 3):

- *Background* factors, e.g., experience, skills
- *Physiological/Physical* factors, e.g., vision, dexterity
- *Psychological/Cognitive* factors, e.g., memory, understanding
- *Application Interest and Use* factors, e.g., choices, goals, frequency

In addition, any such factors are subject to being confirmed, counteracted, or contrasted by either user opinions (e.g., expressed preferences) or relevant performance data, obtained for/about the target user(s) in question.

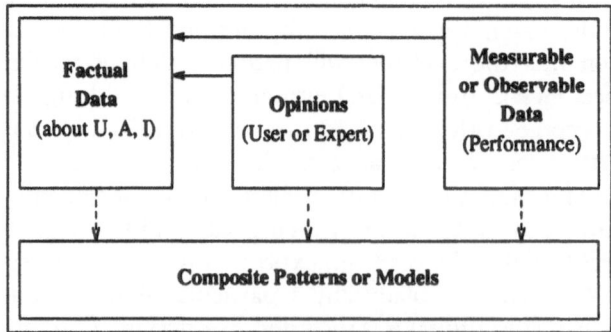

FIGURE 2.1. Groupings of design factors.

Third, various meaningful approaches have been developed for composing higher-level representations or models of users, either individually or collectively oriented. These models are, in effect, converted into design factors that can certainly influence subsequent design decisions. They tend to be dependent on some subset of (lower-level) user factors, with selected values attributed to the parameters involved. They may also be coupled with some organizational paradigm (e.g., a metaphor). Examples of such models are the definition of a "user type" (e.g., experienced, average) and the construction of a "mental model" to be reinforced in a design.

Application Factors

A computer-based application must be analyzed into its constituent tasks and task patterns before the interface to it can be designed in a systematic, user-oriented manner. The design factors that reflect the nature and complexity of the application can be grouped as follows (Treu, 1994, Chapter 4):

- *Impacts on COMPUTER*, dichotomized into required data storage and processing support
- *Impacts on USER*, dichotomized into required (human) memory and mental processing support
- *Interaction* factors, with regard to necessary facilities for *user input* and *computer output*
- *Status and Purpose* factors, e.g., whether the application already exists or is planned

Again, as for the U-factors, the A-factors are subject to being confirmed, contrasted, or even replaced as a result of expert opinions and also because of observations and testing of the computer-based, user-oriented performance of the target application. Figure 2.1 is indicative.

Third, various subsets of A-factors can be used to create composite, application-specific factors to influence HCI design. Included are high-level structures that represent the states, tasks, and paths through an application domain. Also relevant here are the multiapplication and multimedia combinations.

Computer/Interface Factors

This category of factors, called I-factors, represents the third major module involved in HCI design. The factual data (Fig. 2.1) about the computer must reflect whether and how it can be supportive of the application(s) (A-factors) that must reside within it and that must be accessible to the user (U-factors) across the interface, in accordance with whatever performance stipulations are made. These I-factors can be stratified as follows (Treu, 1994, Chapter 5):

- *Software* factors, in terms of programming languages, operating systems, environments
- *Hardware/Physical* factors, including CPU speed, storage capacity, architecture
- *Interface* factors, in terms of both software (e.g., interaction language) and hardware (e.g., interactive tools)
- *Application Suitability* factors, to represent the type(s) of application for which the computer is/not well suited

As for U-factors and A-factors, the I-factors may be counterbalanced by expert opinions and by results of performance tests specifically designed with the target user and/or target application in mind. Also, the I-factors can include higher-level composites, such as special configurations (e.g., multidisplay interfaces) and networks of computers to be accessed via the user interface.

It is noteworthy that each of the above-summarized categories of factors (U-factors, A-factors, and I-factors) already subsumes performance data. This means that each major module is subject to being evaluated and having such data used in design. Thus, even before design factors are used as inputs to an HCI design process, the need for obtaining evaluative kinds of information is already indicated. This fact is reiterated in Section 2.6.

2.3. Design Principles

The HCI literature uses "design principle" in a great variety of ways. Seemingly, it can mean any number of different terms, like design guideline, design feature, design purpose, and others. In the interest of being consistent in our interpretation of how design principles may apply to any and all of the major HCI modules (U, A, I), we use the following definition.

Definition 2.2. **Design principle**: a fundamental truth or belief about a design; a rule explaining the expected behavior or appearance of a design object; a rule of action or conduct for a design object; a design goal.

In comprehensive HCI design, we must specify and adhere to sets of design principles that are user-oriented, application-oriented, and computer-oriented, respectively. The latter two are particularly dependent on well-known software engineering principles. Thus, for example, if the interface software is to satisfy the principle of modularity, the designer should ensure that the interface is specified accordingly, i.e., to be modular. The details of the implementation as such do not matter; it is important that the goal of modularity in the interface software be achieved by whatever means (software tools and techniques) available. Modularity is the goal.

By analogy, suppose that a selected, user-oriented principle is specified for HCI design. An example is consistency. Rendering the interface consistent (e.g., in the actions expected of the user) then becomes the equivalent of a design goal. It may not matter which design features (e.g., interaction techniques) are used, as long as the specified goal is met.

Design principles are also inputs to design decision-making, as are design factors. They obviously must be used to guide the designer throughout the design process, toward attaining the goals that have been established. But design principles also can play a very significant role in the evaluation phase. This of course assumes that they were recorded during the design phase and subsequently recalled for reference during evaluation.

Because of their importance to evaluation, a list of user-oriented design principles, expressed in adjectival form (Treu, 1994), is repeated in Table 2.1. A number of references to the labeled entries are made in later chapters of this book.

2.4. Design Features

The outcomes or results of the designer's decision-making are called design features.

Definition 2.3. **Design feature**: a characteristic in content, appearance, or behavior of a design object, or in the representation of an object with regard to one of those characteristics.

Features represent not only what the user sees and experiences at the interface, but also those characteristics of a design that are variously supportive. They fall into the following general groupings (Treu, 1994, Chapters 6–8):

- *Interaction techniques and styles*, e.g., menu-based, DMI; various levels of feature details are included in this grouping
- *Superimposed models*, to provide organizational paradigms (e.g., extended BNF for interaction language), especially to contain, surround, structure, accentuate, etc., the features employed and/or observed by the users

TABLE 2.1
User-Oriented Design Principles

I.D.	Adjective: desirable characteristic	Qualified **object** or intended **purpose**
P1	Accessible	To enable user interaction via the interface
P2	Accurate, correct	With regard to values of objects output
P3	Adaptable	Interface is changeable
P4	Adaptive	Interface adapts to user
P5	Aesthetically pleasing	In color, appearance, . . .
P6	Associative	Providing explicit and implicit association links among objects
P7	Clear, concise	In choice and meaning of vocabulary and other objects used in interaction
P8	Comfortable	Making user feel at ease (see also P34, P39)
P9	Compatible	With specified user factors
P10	Complete, comprehensive	In functional capabilities . . .
P11	Congenial	Agreeable, suitable, . . .
P12	Consistent	In commands, spatial location, . . .
P13	Context-providing	In surrounding layers of support for the user
P14	Continuous	In interactive behavior, and output of changing objects
P15	Controllable	Providing user override, . . .
P16	Correctable	When errors occur
P17	Error-preventing or -minimizing	To avoid the need to correct errors (P16)
P18	Expressive	To enable clear, concise communication
P19	Extendible	To add other functions, commands, . . .
P20	Facilitative	Making it easy to use, learn, get things done
P21	Fail-safe	When user commits mistakes, serious consequences are precluded
P22	Feedback-providing	Acknowledging user input, and informing the user of current state
P23	Flexible	In interface layout, devices, scrolling, . . .
P24	Forgiving	After the user makes mistakes or takes other undesirable actions
P25	Helpful	With error messages, explanations, feedback (P22), tutorials, . . .
P26	Learnable	With respect to user capabilities and limitations
P27	Meaningful	Use of mnemonics, logical actions, . . .
P28	Memory-supporting	To supplement or obviate user memory
P29	Network-oriented	To give the user a network perspective
P30	Nonoverwhelming	In display density, action choices
P31	Organized or structured	In interaction language, display layout, functions, state transitions, . . .
P32	Powerful	To support more complex tasks
P33	Precise, exact	In relative positioning of objects, . . .
P34	Recoverable	From undesirable actions and states
P35	Responsive in content	With respect to information in system response
P36	Responsive in time	With respect to system time taken to respond

TABLE 2.1
User-Oriented Design Principles (*continued*)

I.D.	Adjective: desirable characteristic	Qualified **object** or intended **purpose**
P37	Reliable	In advice, performance, . . .
P38	Simple or simplified	To avoid unnecessary complexity
P39	Stress-reducing or -minimizing	With regard to user stress
P40	Unambiguous	Similar to P7
P41	Unconstraining	To encourage or enable learning
P42	Uniform	In available functions, . . . (see also P12)
P43	Understandable	In phraseology, expectations, . . .
P44	Usable	Toward achieving desired goals
P45	Versatile	Offering different input devices, . . .
P46	Visualizable, conceivable	Reinforcing conceptualization, imagination, and viewing of objects

- *Other supportive models and techniques,* e.g., pertaining to the organization of the interface software, which are of greater direct interest
  to designers than to users

The design features can be further distinguished with regard to their
effects on the major dimensions of HCI (e.g., in information content,
structure, behavior, appearance). They then become subject to evaluation
as indicated by Fig. 2.2. The evaluation of specific features is carried out
either *with* or *without* reference to the design principles (if any) that were
the goals during the design process. If the principles used are not known
or not revealed, the evaluation phase obviously cannot relate to them. In
that case, or in any case, evaluation methodology must be able to accommodate the assessment of HCI performance with respect to other criteria,
including the priorities and principles that are presently deemed desirable.

2.5. Methodological Summary

The capsule discussions (above) of design factors, principles, and
features have already implied a general, cause-and-effect pattern applicable to HCI design. That pattern is also depicted in Fig. 2.3 and serves as a
kind of high-level template for decision-making schematics that the designer must construct, in order to reach decisions on which features are to
be selected and specified. Thus, a schematic graph may contain several,
selected design factors in separate nodes, which are connected (by arrows)
to a decision-making box, in which the applicable design principle(s) and
other inputs (e.g., design criteria) are utilized to render a decision on

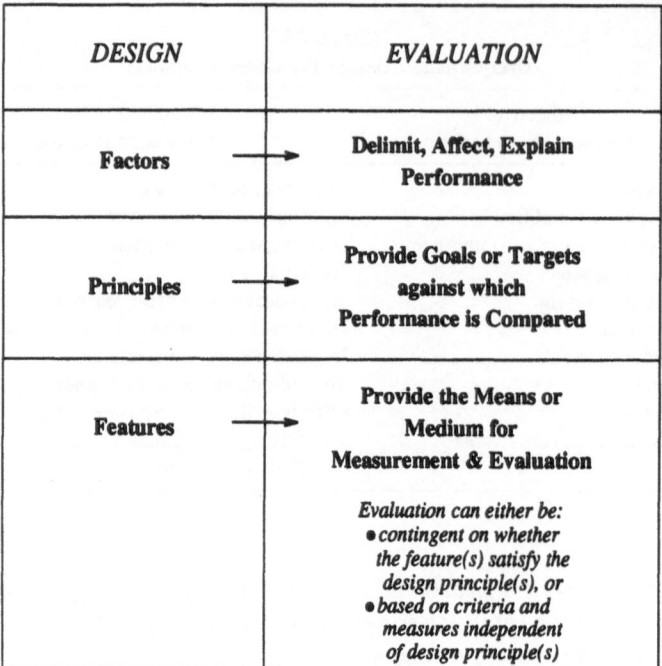

DESIGN	EVALUATION
Factors $\longrightarrow$	**Delimit, Affect, Explain Performance**
Principles $\longrightarrow$	**Provide Goals or Targets against which Performance is Compared**
Features $\longrightarrow$	**Provide the Means or Medium for Measurement & Evaluation** *Evaluation can either be:* • *contingent on whether the feature(s) satisfy the design principle(s), or* • *based on criteria and measures independent of design principle(s)*

FIGURE 2.2. Design-to-evaluation carryover.

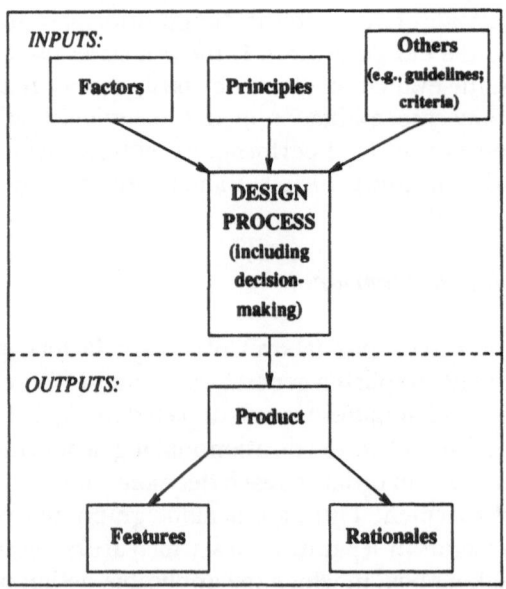

FIGURE 2.3. Cause-and-effect design pattern.

which design feature(s) is(are) indicated. Such a schematic can, in turn, be collapsed into one node to become a design factor within a higher-level decision-making schematic. Alternatively, it may have to be refined to lower levels of detail, depending on the granularity and complexity of the design feature currently under consideration (Treu, 1994).

In addition to the set of features that must result from the HCI design process, it is important for us to highlight the need to also output and record the rationales used in support of design decisions. When these are not known, valuable information is lost, not only to interested designers but also to evaluators who may want to relate to those rationales (including specified design principles) during the evaluation process.

Design → Evaluation → Design

The design product and its features (Fig. 2.3) become the principal objects of evaluation that are of interest to us in this book. The product need not yet be in final, implemented form; it can be partially implemented or be a prototype, or even a simulation model of a planned, hypothetical design. Thus, evaluation can take place at various preliminary or interim points during the design process, as is emphasized in the next section. In any case, however, some concrete design product or some kind of representation of the product is needed in order to carry out an evaluation of it.

Unlike the design process (which produces some kind of interface design), evaluation does not create any interface object directly. Instead, it assesses the design "outcome" as it currently exists, including any observable, measurable features, as well as the designer's rationale behind those features, if that is available. Such an assessment can and should influence design. The results should provide significant inputs to (re-)design decisions. With appropriate feedback loops and depending on whether the evaluative results are positive or negative, they should cause design iterations and changes in design specifications. In that sense, HCI evaluation also ends up in a cause-and-effect relationship with interface design. This fact is accentuated by the performance factors (Figure 2.1) that represent the user, application software, and computer interface, respectively, in the design process.

2.6.   Evaluation Invocations

We cannot here duplicate the detailed descriptions of the general HCI design method presented in the companion book. However, we can accentuate the facts that

- Evaluation can/should occur *after* design, that is, after something concrete has been designed (as discussed in Section 2.1), and
- Evaluation can be invoked at a number of places or timepoints *during* the design process, or it can be supportive of that process.

The possible "invocations" of evaluation can be extracted from a general, cause-and-effect design method and outlined as follows:

1. *Preliminary Feasibility Analysis*, carried out during the preparation phase of design, considering any tentative *specifications* of HCI design features and attempting to predict or project their suitability for intended design purposes; included is the need to obtain performance data and opinions about the major HCI modules, for use as design factors.
2. *Analysis of Design Features*, as initially proposed in response to the applicable set of design factors (for each of the U, A, and I modules and their combinations), while guided by specified design principles; this analysis can lead to prediction or projection on whether a feature will satisfactorily meet a design goal.
3. *Analysis of Implications of Proposed Design Features* on each of the major modules (U, A, I), to determine whether selected changes in those modules (e.g., user training; or expanded functionality of application software) might suggest modifications of the design features, thereby perhaps facilitating or enhancing the design; this suggests the use of interim, evaluative information to drive the further iterations in design.
4. *Analysis of Design Validity and Performance*, based on design specifications resulting from previous steps in the design method; this is carried out prior to or instead of a full, operational implementation of the design; accordingly, preliminary instantiations of the design (e.g., simulation studies and prototypes) become involved.
5. *Testing and Evaluation of HCI Product*, after it has been fully implemented.

The first three points at which evaluation may be invoked require special-purpose methods. Their objects of evaluation are only specifications for or models of the planned HCI design. Hence, some kind of limited simulation study may be called for. The models (e.g., of the planned, target users) may be in different stages of detail or specificity. Consequently, while some meaningful and concrete design evidence may already be available, the design is not concrete enough to be subject to more rigorous approaches to evaluation.

The fourth point, however, suggests that a more substantial evaluation can take place. Examples are the use of formal simulation experiments and/or prototype implementation, in each case followed by assessment of performance of the simulation model or the prototype, respectively.

Finally, the fifth, above-outlined point at which evaluation may be invoked is after the HCI design has been implemented in operational form. This is the kind of evaluation that is most likely to come to mind, in view of the many computer interfaces in existence and the increasing interest in determining their comparative levels of performance. However, the other types of evaluation are also important. In particular, the practice of implementing prototype interfaces and then evaluating them, prior to full implementation, is becoming increasingly prevalent and recommended.

The methodology for HCI evaluation, as portrayed in Part III of this book, following coverage in Part II of the several other prerequisite knowledge areas (besides HCI design) with which the evaluator should be familiar, is designed to accommodate a wide variety of different evaluation objects and objectives.

Exercises

2.1. With regard to user design factors, select one factor from each of the four subgroupings outlined in the text, and describe how each can potentially affect HCI performance.

2.2. Repeat Exercise 2.1 for application design factors.

2.3. Repeat Exercise 2.1 for computer/interface design factors.

2.4. Look up the definitions of "principle" and "goal" in an ordinary dictionary. Do you consider it reasonable to treat them as equivalent for HCI design purposes? Present a case for or against this equivalence.

2.5. According to Section 2.4 and Fig. 2.2, design features in effect become "objects" of evaluation. They end up representing the major HCI component objects (user, application, computer) in what they do and how they do it in interaction with each other. Does that mean that a design feature (e.g., an interaction technique) *once it undergoes evaluation* becomes a feature that is labeled (e.g., with some performance attribute, such as good, bad, etc.)? Diagram and describe the cause-and-effect relationship that it implies for the HCI design-to-evaluation sequence. (Note: The design outputs in Fig. 2.3 can feed directly into the evaluation phase.)

2.6. If design principles provide "targets" for performance evaluation, as indicated in Fig. 2.2, each one should inherently suggest something about the kind of performance results that it calls for. Select six principles from Table 2.1 that seem to require an evaluation based on *quantitative* considerations. Explain your choices and the general types of evaluative data that might be necessary for each.

2.7. Repeat Exercise 2.6 but for six principles that seem to require *qualitative* considerations and data.

2.8. Repeat Exercise 2.6 but for six principles that seem ambiguous or difficult to categorize according to types of evaluative data required. Explain.

2.9. Locate a software engineering book in your library. Find a description on the general topic of "software development life cycle." Where in that cycle does evaluation enter in? Should that be any different for HCI evaluation? Compare the two situations and describe the results.

2.10. In computer science courses, a lot of emphasis is placed on designing software in a systematic, structured manner. Further, before implementing any software that has been specified in various abstract ways, it is important to have an understanding of the "efficiency" of the algorithms to be utilized. That efficiency is expressed at a high level, using the big-O notation, but it is meaningful nevertheless. Based on your understanding of that topic as well as of the topic of HCI design, can you imagine an analogous high-level formulation for the efficiency of/in human–computer interaction? Try to construct a broad model of HCI that might enable the use of something like the big-O notation.

PREREQUISITE KNOWLEDGE AREAS

The evaluators of HCI should, first and foremost, understand the design of HCI, as summarized in Part I. But then, they must also become knowledgeable in other topical areas that are deemed *prerequisite* to use of evaluation methodology. Chapter 3 covers the very important sources, techniques, and tools necessary for collection, measurement, and analysis of evaluative data. Included are overviews of experimental designs and of statistical analysis techniques. Chapter 4 provides a structural basis for the measurement of various characteristics that represent HCI objects. This is done by means of "interface structures." It is followed by introduction, in Chapter 5, of several sets of well-known measures that use those structures and that are prominent in current evaluation studies.

PREREQUISITE KNOWLEDGE AREAS

SUPPORTIVE TOOLS
AND TECHNIQUES

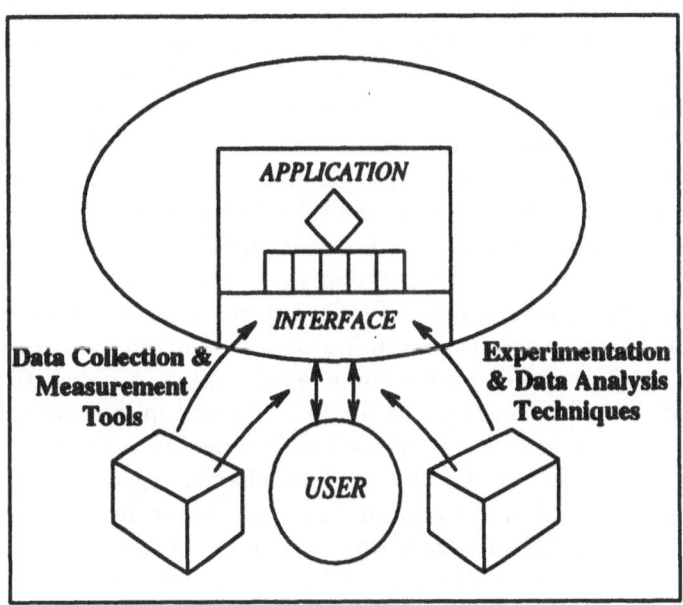

3.1. Overview

It was suggested in Chapter 2 that one important prerequisite to HCI evaluation is to understand HCI design. Now in Part II of this book, several other prerequisite areas are described. This chapter considers the major techniques and tools that are necessary to support both measurement and evaluation of HCI.

Some of the material used in design methodology, such as the models for representing the interface and its constituents and behavior (Treu, 1994, Chapters 7 and 8), now becomes useful in providing structure and direction for the evaluation. As part of the planning for a particular evaluation study, the evaluator must decide which supportive tools and techniques might be most appropriate and effective. To that end, it can be very helpful to know what was done during the design phase. But the evaluator must know much more than that.

Sections 3.2 and 3.3, respectively, outline the sources and the techniques available for collecting and measuring relevant data. Section 3.4 indicates some of the supportive tools that can be employed in actually doing the collecting. But some of the sources and techniques require special attention. One such category of tools or instruments is modeled in Section 3.5. It is designed for carrying out quantitative measurements.

Another special category of supportive tools and techniques becomes relevant when the HCI evaluation effort is to involve experimentation. Depending on the nature of the planned evaluation, each of the data collection sources, techniques, and tools may differ significantly. The evaluator must make choices and understand when and how to apply them. If the results of data collection efforts, including those involving measurement, are to be credible and reliable, they must be enveloped by appropriate methodology. This has been described extensively in the sizable and growing literature pertaining to experimental design. Because of the interdisciplinary nature of HCI, any experimentation encompassing both human users (representing user psychology) and computers (representing computer science and engineering) must necessarily relate to empirical evaluation methods that have evolved in the corresponding disciplines. An overview is developed in Section 3.6. It includes a high-level procedure that ties the topics of this chapter together.

But, even if all of the indicated sources, means, tools, devices, and experimental designs are taken into account, the evaluation outcome will be lacking if the collected/measured data are not properly analyzed. It is easy to gather reams of data, but it is another matter to know what to do with them once you have them. This means that statistical analysis techniques must not only be well understood but must also be contingent on (or appropriate for) the experimental organization (Section 3.6) and, then, be used to guide the actual data collection (Sections 3.2 and 3.3). In addition, they must be employed effectively, preferably with the help of already existing and reliable analysis software. The topic is addressed in Section 3.7.

Finally, the combination of simulation methodology and experimental design techniques is discussed in Section 3.8. It provides an overview of one means for evaluating a design that is represented by a model.

3.2. Data Collection/Measurement Sources

Among the responsibilities facing evaluators are decisions on the purpose and objectives of an evaluation, on the type of evaluation, and, subsequently, on the kinds of quantitative and qualitative performance measures and other indicators that should become parts of the evaluative evidence. All of these will be discussed in preparation for the general evaluation method recommended in Chapter 8. After making such decisions, the *sources* of required data and the *techniques* and *tools* for collecting them must be understood and determined. The techniques and tools are characterized in the next several sections. The sources generally fall into the following categories:

1. *Persons*, including
   - *Target users* (Definition 1.2), who may be utilized as sources *before*, *during*, or *after* interaction with the computer, depending on the evaluation objectives involved. They are the most desirable candidates to serve as "experimental subjects" (i.e., as HCI objects represented by variables in an experiment).
   - *Surrogate users*, e.g., who attempt to carry out or emulate the goal-oriented roles of target users for purposes of either (1) personally evaluating the interface and/or (2) being measured or observed; if necessary, the latter option can include service as experimental subjects.
   - *User associates* (e.g., manager, colleague), able to provide information about organizational goals in using computers, tasks assigned to users, expectations of users, etc.
   - *Designers*, with information about the design methodology used, including design principles, factors, features, criteria, rationales, etc.
   - *Developers and implementors*, with detailed technical knowledge about implementation tools and techniques and about how an interface design was (or should be) implemented.
   - (Experimental) *observers*, qualified to obtain evidence through direct observations and recordings about selected features and aspects of HCI performance.
   - *Analysts and evaluators*, with detailed knowledge of evaluation methodology, including experimental design, and how to analyze, interpret, etc., evaluative data.
   - *HCI experts*, able to supply factual data about HCI design and evaluation, to conduct formal tests and experiments, and to serve as specialists on evaluation teams, e.g., to test an interface by conducting "cognitive walk-throughs."
2. *Computers*, including
   - *Target computers* (Definition 1.3), which may be utilized in a manner analogous to target users. Two or more computers

may be involved in distributed, network-based HCI applications. In HCI experimentation, they are objects represented by selected variables that can be either manipulated (controlled) or measured.

- *Intermediary computer* or *software module*, designed to be "inserted" between target user and target computer, to carry out data collection (within user–computer transactions) and measurement, as well as to enable a human observer to experiment with HCI in real time.
- *Alternative or baseline computer*, to provide the ability (or data) for comparative performance evaluation.

3. *User* **and** *Computer*, in conjunction, including

- *Interaction scenarios* or *protocols* representing the sequences of interactive transactions carried out between user and computer in real time. An intermediary computer/module (2 above) can serve as the collection source or agent. Because the interaction scenario, as recorded and measured, reflects the details of an HCI design, it, in turn, becomes a data source that provides the means for evaluating different design features. For example, alternative interaction techniques can serve as features (HCI objects) to be represented by one parameter (independent variable) in an experiment designed to determine how selected user-based variables (e.g., think time) and/ or selected computer-based variables (e.g., response time) might be affected.
- *Projected, prescribed interactions*, or interaction models, e.g., based on analyses carried out by HCI experts (1 above) who can identify interactive patterns deemed most appropriate or desirable. Results can be used in comparisons against the patterns that are actually employed.

4. *Documentation*, including

- *Manuals and other publications*, describing technical details of the target computer, interface, application software, etc.
- *Administrative records*, which are not confidential or to which access has been properly authorized (with user agreement), about user characteristics, types of computer usage, frequency of use, etc.
- *HCI literature*, to obtain generally acknowledged characteristics of humans and computers in their roles as information processors, including various guidelines, thresholds, etc., on desirable HCI designs.

5. *Theories* and *Models*, developed to represent HCI objects (e.g., user,

computer, their interaction) in terms of their characteristics (limiting and enabling factors) including behaviors. Theoretical models can be used for comparative purposes by skilled analysts. Simulation of valid models can supply useful performance data. However, the latter data source tends to be of greater interest within the HCI design cycle than during a subsequent evaluation phase.

Some redundancies are evident in the above list of sources. For example, some of the information about the user–computer combination (3 above) can be obtained from HCI experts (in 1). But the user + computer conjunction highlights the need to collect data about their direct interaction, in contrast to only relying on knowledge about their separate, individualistic performances.

In addition, various other combinations of data sources may be useful. The sources collectively are not only expected to supply the evaluative data themselves, but also various other data (e.g., thresholds) that can be used for evaluative decision-making.

3.3. Data Collection/Measurement Techniques

Given the potential sources of evaluative data, how should the data collection actually be carried out? Appropriate techniques and methods are necessary. They can be characterized in different ways. Following they are outlined with emphasis on (1) the type of data collection technique and (2) responsibility for data accuracy.

1. *Questionnaires*, specifically designed to elicit from the user, or other human source of data, written or typed answers that can be analyzed, either quantitatively or qualitatively. Results can produce the input values for variables in selected measures (or other indicators) of performance and for data groupings in experimental designs. Questionnaires can be:
   • Conventional versions (e.g., Chin *et al.*, 1988)
   • On-line, real-time versions (e.g., Treu, 1972)
   The person being questioned or prompted (on-line) to respond is responsible for the accuracy of the answers. This assumes that the questionnaire is designed in a reliable manner, using carefully constructed and unambiguous questions posed in systematic, logical patterns. In the case of on-line, real-time questioning, the timing of questions (or prompts) must correspond to the interactive events and phases or functions currently experienced by the user.

2. *Interviews*, representing a more dynamic and also more variable form of questioning users, and other human sources of data, than is available through the traditional written/printed questionnaire. Results are very much contingent on the skills of the interviewer, including whether he/she (a) structures the interview based on a preplanned strategy and pattern of (written) questions used for guidance or (b) conducts the interview in an unstructured, free-wheeling format. Responsibility for data accuracy lies both with the interviewee (in the answers given) and with the interviewer (based on care taken in asking the necessary questions and in correct recording of the answers).

3. *Observations* of user and computer in interaction, made by qualified persons (in the list of sources, Section 3.2), focusing on observable features and performance during HCI. The resulting data may reflect occurrences of critical events as well as judgments about them. In this technique, the persons doing the observation and recording, who may include target users themselves, are responsible for the accuracy of the data. Manual recording also applies to the human sources who complete questionnaires (1 above) and who conduct interviews (2 above).

4. *Inspections* of the user–computer interface, made by experts acting as (surrogate) users, focusing on observable features and their performance, including the detection of specific problems. Characteristics of this technique are similar to those of Technique 3, except that the observers are directly involved by pretending to be users.

5. *Monitoring, measurement, and recording* of user and computer in interaction, either
   • Triggered under software/hardware control, or
   • Directed by a human observer who has software support.
   In these cases, data accuracy is contingent on having reliable software/hardware. The first version requires suitable computer-based monitoring support (e.g., Kant, 1992). The second version of this technique involves the preprogrammed stimulation of users to react, whenever certain conditions are met (Treu, 1972). It can be controlled and complemented by an on-line experimenter able to observe (unobtrusively) what the user is doing and able to introduce both changes in functionality and prompts (stimuli) to the user in real time. This technique is mentioned again in conjunction with measurement devices in Section 3.5. Another example is the use of dialog monitoring described by Hanusa (1983). It involves graphical interaction.

6. *Audio* and/or *Visual Recording*, to record verbal protocols and/or nonverbal behaviors. As pointed out in Section 3.4, such recording devices may be used as alternative or supplementary means for the data collected via the other techniques in this list. In this technique, data accuracy depends on the clarity, angle, etc., of the recording. Of course, the real problems arise in the analysis and interpretation of such recordings. As is well known (e.g., from instant replays in professional sports), the information on record, even if clearly visible, is not necessarily unambiguous.

7. *Simulation* of valid models of user, computer, or their combination. It can be useful for obtaining evaluative data and is included in this list for sake of completeness. But, as previously stated, it tends to be more relevant to the HCI design phase when trying to decide whether an interface design is worthy of implementation.

8. *Analysis* of observed, inspected, monitored, or otherwise represented HCI performance in comparison against theoretical models. The analyst is responsible for the accuracy of resulting information.

9. *Testing* of users and computers, either separately or in their interaction. It must be organized and directed by qualified persons (in the list of sources, Section 3.2). This method can subsume a subset of the techniques listed, or it can be supplemented by them.

In general, some subset of the above is required for an evaluation. For example, a combination of Techniques 1 and 5 was used to evaluate the network-based text editors employed by graduate students serving as experimental subjects (Treu, 1975b). The techniques may have to be supplemented by searches for relevant data that may be available in documentation, one of the data sources included in the previous section. The choice of techniques depends on which (types of) data are essential to feed into (1) any specified measures and other indicators of performance and (2) any experimental design organization to be applied. But they also depend on how the users, who become involved in HCI evaluation, might perceive the techniques to be employed. User perceptions can influence interest and willingness to participate cooperatively in such studies.

An evaluation team may be faced with the following realistic task: to recruit real users (current or prospective) to serve as experimental subjects. How can this be done? Many computer users (other than graduate students!) are disinclined to be drafted into providing such services. They prefer not to be bothered, not wanting to "waste their time," especially when they are faced with real-world pressures on the job. Thus, short of requesting management intervention, the evaluators may have to consider the data collection technique deemed (by the potential subjects) to be most acceptable and least disruptive.

As shown in Fig. 3.1, the different data collection techniques can generally be categorized along two dimensions affecting users. They are either passive or active in nature, and they involve either obtrusive or unobtrusive techniques. Depending on which combination the evaluators select, the user serving as an evaluative data source may (1) spend more or less time (dedicated to the evaluation), (2) be more or less disrupted in his/her regular work responsibilities, (3) be more or less responsible for data accuracy, and (4) be more or less satisfied with the evaluation process and the benefits it might produce.

We must of course acknowledge that evaluator decisions on which data collection techniques and tools to employ for obtaining data from/about target users must not only be influenced by user preferences. The effectiveness of the collection technique must also be taken into account and may have to take priority. Thus, while the user may prefer unobtrusive monitoring of the interaction, the evaluator may have to ask him/her specific questions, either via questionnaire or interview. Or, while the user may like to give a brief interview and then be done as an experimental subject, the evaluator may need to conduct formal measurements, to ensure that any user-supplied performance factors can indeed by verified.

Throughout this section (and also the previous section), emphasis has been on the *means* for achieving the *end* of evaluating HCI in some manner. The detailed specification or prescription of the techniques must necessarily depend on what, exactly, is to be evaluated and how that is to be

A User Would Judge It To Be:	OBTRUSIVE	UNOBTRUSIVE
PASSIVE	• Await User Complaints and Suggestions	• Monitor and Record HCI Dialogues • Simulation • Analysis
ACTIVE	• Questionnaires • Interviews • Observations • Testing	• Observations • Measurement • Stimulation • Testing

FIGURE 3.1. Data collection techniques affecting users.

accomplished, that is, with respect to what evaluation criteria and evaluative aspects. These topics are addressed in detail in Part III. The specific kinds and formats of questions to be asked (in questionnaires and interviews), the particular kinds of observations to be made (using observation techniques), and the specific types of data to be measured (using monitoring and measurement techniques) for inclusion in performance measures and experimental designs, all must result from the clear stipulation of evaluation purpose, objectives, and scope. Consequently, the specific tools that can support the data collection techniques, to be applied to selected sources of data, can be determined. These tools are outlined in the next two sections.

3.4. Supportive Collection Devices

A decision to use one of the data collection techniques (previous section) is only one step; now the evaluator is faced with having to implement that technique for actual use. What kinds of tools are available to support this effort?

The design and construction of questionnaires as well as of the formats and guidelines to be used in formal interviews and observations, must be specifically tailored to the types of questions, critical incidents, etc., that are generated within the evaluation methodology. Literature on their designs tends to refer to their existence and utilization. But it normally does not display them in detail (for length limitations), nor discuss them extensively.

Some kind of physical "device" as such is not relevant, except in the sense that any questionnaire may be defined as a hard-copy (or on-line) document that is organized to solicit user answers in the blank spaces provided. The notion of an existing, model tool (e.g., in hardware or software) is generally not applicable. However, that assertion can be contradicted if either (1) the evaluators are willing to adopt someone else's questionnaire (e.g., that of Chin et al., 1988), as it already exists, or (2) the tool idea is extended to include the use of a general text formatting/editing system that can obviously facilitate the preparation of a questionnaire, including its composition based on questions selected from a variety of other evaluators' questionnaires.

In any case, the questions asked (in questionnaires or interviews) should be suitably tailored to the population of users to be targeted. Also, the answers, whether they be quantitative or qualitative in nature, should be conducive to the type of analysis that is planned. To ensure that these conditions are met, experience and knowledge (e.g., about published formats, guidelines, etc.) are very important. There are no "tools" to replace such qualifications.

However, some special-purpose tools do exist to support the conducts of questionnaires, interviews, and observations. The use of on-line questionnaires was already mentioned. In that case, the tool is the software-controlled presentation of questions, including iterations as necessary, leading to the recording of answers for subsequent analysis. This question-and-answer technique can resemble various forms of computer-assisted tutoring or learning.

In addition, there are audiovisual tools that can be employed very effectively. Options include:

- An interviewer or observer is located in a separate room, set up with either a one-way or two-way audiovisual connection to the user, who is interacting with a computer; the technique can be either *obtrusive* (e.g., by interrupting and asking the user incident-specific questions) or *unobtrusive* (e.g., with the user unaware of being observed).
- An audiovisual recording is made of an entire interview or observation session, for purposes of later analysis, possibly in correlation with software-controlled recordings of interactive scenarios. The user may or may not be aware of being recorded at any particular time, but he/she should certainly have given permission to do so.

Because of the significant differences that exist among HCI users, the popularity of using audiovisual means to capture their behaviors and performances is not surprising. However, the task of utilizing such exhaustive records in evaluation studies can be enormous. For that and other reasons, it is desirable, when possible and appropriate, to isolate and measure only specific factors representing the objects of interest. Of course that means that other factors that might influence results must be separated out or somehow be controlled. To conduct such measurements, special-purpose tools have/can be developed, as discussed in Section 3.5.

Tools and techniques to support modeling and simulation, as a source of evaluative data (included in the outline of Section 3.3), constitute a large, separate area of the literature. Because simulation should be coupled with formal experimentation techniques, we briefly characterize it accordingly in Section 3.8.

To enable the formal analysis of HCI performance by comparing it against some theoretical models, the supportive tools are very special-purpose. They depend on whatever model(s) is(are) used for comparison. Indeed, those models are a kind of tool. In addition, the analysis must have a very clearly specified procedure, or algorithm, to guide the analyst through the formal analysis.

Finally, a great variety of "tests" are available as potential sources of evaluative data. Such tests can involve hybrid combinations of the other data sources. Probably most important is the set of supportive tools and techniques that have been developed in the area of experimentation. They are outlined in Section 3.7. However, other tests that are less formal in nature can also be used. For example, they might only involve visual or verbal testing of users by experts, with the results being subjective assessments of (i.e., opinions on) observed performance. Such alternatives will be illustrated, among others, in later chapters.

3.5. Measurement Devices

Evaluation that involves the physical measurement of quantitative values requires support from special devices. Included are the intermediary measurement tools and techniques mentioned earlier. As pointed out in Section 2.6, the need for evaluation in general arises both during and after HCI design. However, evaluation based on measurement is more restrictive in its applicability. It requires either

- An existing, concrete object that can be measured, either in its real, operational form or in a prototype/surrogate version, or
- A substantial, valid model of the object that can be measured through computer-based (programmed) simulation of its structure, behavior, and performance.

Each of the options is described further below. It is inadequate for purposes of objective measurement to have just a plan or general specification for the object's design. Further, we must distinguish what is to be measured (1) *about a computer* as the object and (2) *with a computer*, about itself or about the other objects (e.g., users) of interest, or about models of objects (using simulation). As was mentioned in Chapter 1, we are not particularly interested in evaluating the computer's internal performance as such. Unless it has user-noticeable negative effects on interface performance, we leave such evaluations to hardware engineers and operating system designers.

3.5.1. Measuring Real Objects

Our primary evaluation interest is directed at the performance of the human–computer relationship and any major module that contributes to it. To evaluate real HCI objects in a manner that is as objective as possible and based on measurements, two major alternatives are available. Both can be attributed to the logical or physical, intermediary module included in Fig. 3.2.

- *Internal*: using software-based tools, integrated into the existing modules of an interface architecture, running under an operating system with a real-time clock, to measure and count various processes, activities, time delays, frequencies of utilization, etc.
- *External*: using a separate measurement tool, designed as an intermediary hardware/software device that can be inserted (preferably unobtrusively) between the user-visible interface and the application; it can intercept all externally evident transactions and measure and count definable activities, delays, usages, etc.

The internal measurement alternative is very prominent in software environments. We can learn from the techniques developed for computer systems performance evaluation (Kant, 1992). Introduction of any special code for measurement should adhere to well-known software engineering principles, including modularity, removability, replaceability, and others. On the other hand, the external measurement approach implies availability of an independent measurement system. It can either be implemented on a separate piece of hardware (e.g., Rosenthal *et al.*, 1976), or it can be introjected as a separate module within a modular interface (e.g., a UIMS). As a result, useful data about the services rendered by a computer to a user can be collected (e.g., Abrams and Treu, 1977).

It is also possible to design a software tool that incorporates the

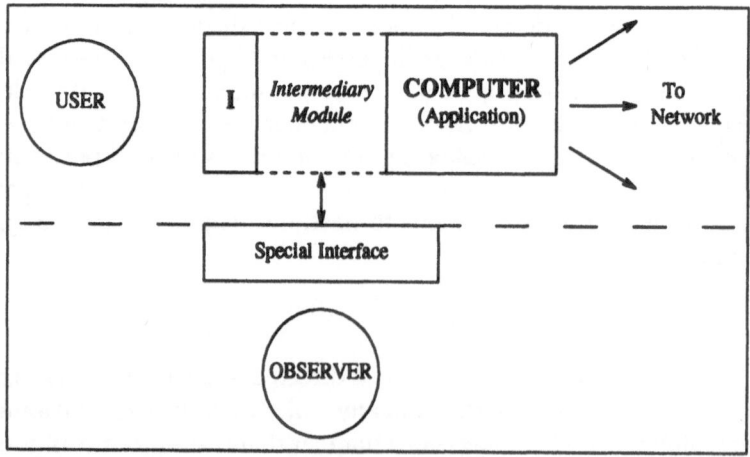

FIGURE 3.2. Special intermediary tools.

"networking" of (1) a target user, (2) the application software of interest residing in a target computer, and (3) a third party, the observer. Either with direct personal intervention or with software-controlled stimuli, the observer can conduct real-time observation and measurement of a user's interaction with the application software (Treu, 1972). This "transparent stimulation" alternative is implied by the lower part of Fig. 3.2.

3.5.2. Measuring Simulated Objects

In addition to measuring real, existing objects in HCI, representative models can be "measured" as well. The computer again serves as the measurement tool. But now, the model is not merely a general description of an object, it must be translated into a formal simulation model. To enable its measurement and evaluation, it has to be implemented in a programmed form for execution on a computer. To do this all in a credible way, the tools and techniques developed in the area of modeling and simulation are necessary. Included must be model validation and verification. A large literature is available. Among useful resources are the books by Gordon (1978), Fishman (1978), Lewis and Smith (1979), and Law and Kelton (1991). We return to simulation in Section 3.8.

3.6. Experimentation

HCI evaluation can involve a number of different methods and techniques, depending on its purpose. However, if formal testing is to be carried out in the context of HCI experiments, efforts have to be made to ensure that appropriate experimental design procedures are employed.

Definition 3.1. **Experimental design**: a plan for the organization and conduct of an experiment, followed by the statistical analysis of its results.

As Winer (1971) said: "Without adequate experimental design, potentially fruitful hypotheses cannot be tested with any acceptable degree of precision." On the other hand, it is necessary to develop such hypotheses. Without them, or without clearly specified testing goals, even a beautifully designed experiment may be in vain. A carefully planned, experimentally based evaluation becomes more time-consuming and expensive. But the results are likely to be more objective and, hence, more credible.

Figure 3.3 gives an overview of the major phases involved in experimental design and the subsequent statistical analysis of experimental data. Although the technical "design" part is represented as only one phase, we also use the term to encompass all four phases of experimental study. A

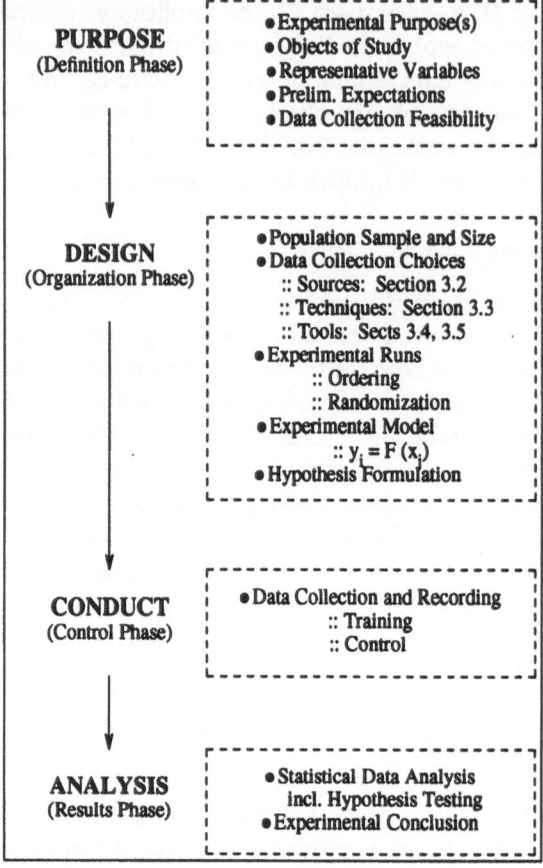

FIGURE 3.3. Overview of experimental design phases.

very sizable literature exists on this specialty. The interested reader is encouraged to locate appropriate libraries (especially in natural science, behavioral science, and engineering departments) to obtain help. In addition, illustrative studies found in the HCI literature can be used as general models. Chapter 8 will identify selected methodological attributes for a number of such studies. This chapter only provides high-level guidance, by outlining the major topics and the alternatives that apply. It is not feasible in this book to present a detailed description of all aspects of experimental design methodology.

Among the classic resources that remain valuable are the books by Fisher (1951), who described the basic statistical principles relevant to experimental design, and by Cochran and Cox (1957), who presented a detailed collection of experimental designs. Other useful references include the books by Hicks (1964), Winer (1971), Myers (1972), Kirk (1982), Damon and Harvey (1987), and Mead (1988). The chapter on experiment design in the book by Kant (1992) is also helpful.

With regard to Fig. 3.3, the following sections contain capsule descriptions of the major phases involved in an experimental study.

3.6.1. Purpose and Parameters

As is true of any evaluation (to be discussed in Chapter 8), an experimental study should start out with definition of its purpose(s). What is to be determined or learned through the study? Which HCI constituents or units (e.g., users, computers, interactive devices, software tools, user–computer transactions) are to be the objects of experimental focus? Answers will impact on the *population* of experimental units (e.g., users) from which a representative *sample* will have to be drawn.

Further, which specific *variables* are to represent the HCI units to be studied? For example, if we want to assess some aspect of the user's performance (e.g., task completion rate) with respect to how it might be affected by different levels of computer performance, then those parameters and their projected relationships must be established (or hypothesized). The factors called *dependent variables* or *response variables*, such as in user performance above, must be distinguished from the factors called *independent variables* that represent selected characteristics of the computer (in above example). Variations in the former are to be studied as "dependent on" changes in the latter. The latter (i.e., the independent variables) are controlled at different values or levels, using *treatments*. Combinations of treatments must be decided to represent the different factor levels (or values, or options) for which the experiment is to be run. There can be one or more factor(s) serving as the independent variables being manipulated. Experimental results are then to determine whether, how, and how much the different treatments or treatment combinations will affect the values of the dependent variables. Within this general cause-and-effect model, the experimenter obviously must have some preliminary notions on what results might be expected or might be hypothesized. More on hypotheses later.

Notice that in the above example we could reverse the situation by experimenting instead with how a computer's assessed performance (now interpreted in terms of dependent variables) may be subject to the capabilities and limitations (independent variables) reflected by users or user types. Thus, the focus and objectives behind an experimental effort have to be well defined. Also, during the preliminary formulation of what is to be studied relative to what else, it must be recognized that the collection of necessary experimental data must be feasible. The sources of data (Section 3.2) to be used for both types of variables (dependent and independent) must be available and/or controllable, and suitable techniques and tools for collection or measurement of the data (Sections 3.3 through 3.5) must be identified and understood. It must be possible to apply the different levels of treatment (independent variables) in reliable ways. All variables that are not factors to be studied in the experiment must be properly controlled or kept constant. At least their effects must be minimized through randomization (see below).

3.6.2. *Experimental Design*

Following the definitional phase of establishing purpose and parameters, the experimenter is faced with actually designing the experiment. A number of interrelated questions must be addressed and answered. For example, if the objects to be studied involve the need to select a representative sample, then techniques for *sampling*, including determination of *sample size*, must be utilized. Further, because the experimental objects are to be represented by variables, choices must be made with regard to the data collection/measurement options that are most appropriate and effective. But such questions only identify (1) the types of data that are to represent the experimental objects and (2) the number of such objects (in sample) to be considered. Also decided must be (3) the quantity of data to be collected (including how many repetitive runs) and (4) the organizational pattern or *ordering* that should envelop the data collection procedure and also the subsequent data analysis.

The quantity of data depends on the sample size to be included in the experiment, such as the number of users selected to serve as experimental subjects or the number of transactions to be measured per user. Selection of sample size, in turn, is dependent on (Hicks, 1964):

- The size of differences in the data values that are to be detected in the experiment
- The size of variation that is present in the experimental data
- The size of risks to be tolerated (with regard to possibly reaching erroneous conclusions) in the experimental results

The various resource books give guidance (or refer the reader to tables) on how to determine sample sizes under different conditions.

The different kinds of orderings of experiments impact the number of runs required, the sequence of conducting those runs, as well as the analysis of the resulting data. Many chapters in the literature on experimental design are dedicated to describing such orderings. Throughout, there is concern about *randomization* among the blocks of any ordering. It must be used to ensure that any variables that cannot be controlled will have their effects averaged out.

Among the most prominent orderings, which are often reflected by chapter titles and/or by terms in subject indexes of the resource books, are:

- *Single-factor experiments*: only one factor is studied with respect to its effect on the measured (dependent) variable
- *Latin square experiments*: each level (treatment) of each factor is combined just once with each level of two other factors
- *Greco-Latin square experiments*: using four factors in an arrangement that combines each level of each factor only once with each level of the other three factors
- *Factorial experiments*: all levels of each factor are combined with all levels of every other factor
- *2^n factorial experiments*: involving factorial design with n factors, each of them at just two levels
- *3^n factorial experiments*: as above, except with n factors each at three levels

A number of other orderings can be added to the above list. Furthermore, many variations exist, depending on (1) special restrictions or conditions applied, (2) exactly how many factors are involved, (3) whether they are within-subjects or between-subjects factors, (4) how the ordering is randomized, (5) whether repetitions in measurement are required, and others. A prospective experimenter must wade through the options, select the one(s) most likely to be conducive to his/her experimental purpose(s), and then, if possible, find any published examples illustrating their use. Such examples can provide useful guidance and even support step-by-step emulation. The books already cited include meaningful examples. Other publications listed in the Bibliography include descriptions of specific experimental designs that were employed. Such studies are referenced in later chapters, especially in Chapter 8.

In any case, an experimenter should, however, not merely accept someone else's experimental design on faith and at face value. It is most important that such a design be studied and understood in the context of the total, relevant methodology and then be related and adapted to local needs, conditions, and constraints. Even though "standard" experimental designs exist, it is rare to find them to be perfect fits, especially for experiments involving the behavioral sciences (Winer, 1971). Hence, it is up to the skill and ingenuity of the experimenter to modify any standard design into a design that is indeed appropriate.

Based on successful completion of the definitional and design phases (Fig. 3.3), it should then be possible for the experimenter to articulate (1) the underlying model that represents the planned experiment and (2) the hypothesis or hypotheses that is/are stipulated as being tested. The model should be describable or expressible in the following generic, functional form:

$$\text{dependent variable} = F(\text{independent variable(s)})$$

where F is a function. Such an expression must be supplemented with specification of any experimental conditions and restrictions, including the randomization method to be applied to the design.

Also included in the experimental design phase must be the formulation of any hypotheses to be tested. This is yet another important topic to be studied and understood by the experimenter. A *statistical hypothesis* is a statement about a statistical population that one wishes to either (1) support or accept or (2) refute or reject, based on the experimental data. Then, a *statistical test* is a set of rules and sequence of steps that can be used to reach a decision about a hypothesis (e.g., see Winer, 1971). Thus, this topic is set up *before* the conduct of the experiment (next subsection), but then must be concluded *after* it is finished (as mentioned in Section 3.7).

3.6.3. Experimental Conduct

In this phase of an experimental study, all of the preparatory work must be brought to fruition in a very careful, well-controlled manner. This is somewhat analogous to the implementation phase in HCI design: it also must adhere strictly to the specifications that resulted during preparation for design. Among the key considerations during the conduct of experiments are:

- *Control of context or environment*: to ensure that conditions are conducive to conducting the experiment, including controlling such factors as temperature, lighting, noise, disruptions, etc.
- *Control of all factors not being studied*: to the extent feasible, making sure that the dependent variables to be measured are indeed dependent on (or a function of) only the independent variables (treatments) that are being deliberately changed and applied
- *Control of experimental sequence*: to make sure that treatments are being carried out in the time-based sequence required by the experimental design (ordering), in relation to the groupings of experimental objects involved
- *Control of data/values accuracy and precision*: to ensure that both the treatment levels (or options selected) as well as the measurement

results are accurate and precise, within acceptable margins or thresholds

In addition, the experimenter must prepare or set up the objects of experimental interest in a manner that ensures stability, reliability, and consistency during experimental conduct. This means, for example, loading the computer with only the essential software and instituting any limits on other users working on the computer at the same time. The latter may be needed to establish a particular work load under which a multiuser system is to be measured. With regard to users who are to serve as experimental subjects, the experimenter has to provide suitable instruction or tutoring, possibly supplemented with effective visual aids. The users have to be trained to a level that satisfies the experimental assumptions about the abilities of the user population from which a sample is drawn.

3.7. Statistical Analysis

Statistics can be defined as the methods and means for obtaining and analyzing quantitative data. The evaluative data that are somehow collected or measured from selected sources (objects) are statistics. They are subject to analysis. But, depending on the kind of analysis to be applied, the statistics differ (e.g., Leabo, 1972; Damon and Harvey, 1987):

Definition 3.2. **Descriptive statistics**: producing and presenting an informative description of the data collected, to include the sources and various meaningful summary measures, such as averages and standard deviations; data analysis without the use of probability theory.

Definition 3.3. **Inductive statistics**: making estimates, predictions, and generalizations, based on sample observations; using the scientific method and probability theory to reach general decisions (conclusions) from only partial information (sample data).

The distinctions in definition above have implications for the evaluation methods considered in this book. Both types of statistics are meaningful and potentially useful. They can serve different evaluation purposes and objectives. Accordingly, different kinds of evaluation studies are called for. This will be elaborated in Chapter 8. For now, we are only interested in outlining the relevant tools and techniques and in identifying selected resources in the literature.

Leabo (1972) has presented a helpful overview. For descriptive statistics, the tools are basically categorized into:

- *Empirical frequency distributions*, with distinctions between discrete and continuous distributions
- *Measures of central position*, including the arithmetic mean, median, and mode
- *Measures of dispersion*, including the range, standard deviation from the mean, and variance

Above-indicated descriptive measures also become involved in inductive statistics. But now they provide inputs to assumptions made about the population of objects to be measured or tested. For example, it becomes important to know that the mean of the sample is adequately close to the (assumed) mean of the population to be represented by the sample. Furthermore, they become inherent constituents of the analysis techniques that are employed *in conjunction with* the experimental design orderings selected. In other words, these techniques are intimately tied into the blocking patterns and treatment orders mentioned in Section 3.6.2. A number of different analysis techniques can be found in the experimental design books included in this book's bibliography, e.g., Hicks (1964), Cooper (1969), Winer (1971), and Damon and Harvey (1987). Included among the many different techniques are:

- *Analysis of variance*, enabling tests of significance between or among treatment means; one-way and multiway classifications of the data must be distinguished (e.g., Damon and Harvey, 1987); the test of significance is based on accepting or rejecting the *null hypothesis*, i.e., that there is no difference.
- *Regression analysis*, based on making multiple observations on each experimental object, studying the dependence of one variable on another.
- *Correlation analysis*, to determine to what extent two variables vary together (i.e., are correlated); unlike regression, no emphasis is made here on the one variable being dependent or not on the other.
- *Analysis of covariance*, combining the techniques of analysis of variance and regression in certain ways.

So, as is implied above, single-factor and multifactor experiments must be distinguished both in terms of their orderings (previous section) and in the types of analysis applicable. A number of books specialize in a particular kind of analysis. Examples are Bishop *et al.* (1975), Reynolds (1977), and Pedhazur (1982). Others specialize in analyzing a particular kind of datum, e.g., behavioral (e.g., Kirk, 1982; Monk, 1986).

In order to utilize any of the above-outlined statistical analysis techniques and resources, the experimenter must understand a number of special concepts and techniques and know how to apply them. They include:

- *Statistical estimation* of population parameters based on the sample data drawn; these involve mostly the needs to make point estimates (e.g., the mean) and interval estimates (interval that includes a parameter of interest).
- *Hypothesis testing*, including specific steps from setting it up to drawing a conclusion at some specified level of significance, based on a test that is selected as appropriate.

In any hypothesis testing based on sample statistics and probability, it must be expected that the conclusion may be in error with some probability. The choices are: Type I error—when the hypothesis is actually true but is rejected based on the sample observations, and Type II error—when the hypothesis is accepted while it is actually false. Thus, the test consists of specific rule(s) for accepting or rejecting a stated hypothesis, with a stated level of confidence on how likely it is that the conclusion is correct. Each of a number of important test statistics (e.g., t, F, χ^2) has its own particular decision rules for testing hypotheses. One has to study those rules and then access and utilize corresponding tables.

Unfortunately, much of the coverage in the area of experimental design and statistical analysis is heavily laden with statistical jargon. (That is of course also true of the terminology in other areas of specialty.) But, with the help of good resources, including recent efforts to deemphasize the relevant mathematical theory and focus mainly on principles for practical application (e.g., Mead, 1988), it is possible to take good advantage of the methodology. It does require substantial effort, however, to do so correctly and with confidence.

Finally, the results of experimentation should be presented meaningfully for consumption by those intended to use them. They should not be encumbered by statistical terminology that is difficult for the layperson to appreciate. User-oriented software tools for the analysis and presentation of experimental data can be helpful.

A considerable variety of software packages for statistical analysis is available. The HCI evaluator would be wise to acquire or gain access to an appropriate and proven package, rather than waste time in writing new software for this purpose. According to the premise advanced by Mead (1988), the analysis of experimental data should not be so difficult any more because of the availability nowadays of supportive, computer-based tools and techniques.

3.8. Simulation Experiments

In Sections 3.6 and 3.7, the underlying assumption was that experimental design is oriented to some real, existing objects to be measured. Such objects, when viewed as a sample of a larger population, can be interpreted as "modeling" that population in the sense of representing it. But that is not modeling in the sense developed in the area of modeling and simulation. The latter requires models that may represent either real or imagined systems, but the models do not in themselves have concrete, physical existence. As mentioned in Section 3.5, they are implemented via computer programs that are executed, thereby simulating the behavior and performance of the objects being modeled.

Thus, the experiment becomes tantamount to the execution of a computer-based simulation model. It also requires experimental design. But now, instead of having concrete factors and alternatives specified in advance, as "given," we must make many more assumptions about the structure and parameters of the model under consideration. The experimental objectives, therefore, tend to be more broad and variable. With regard to specific performance measures, we may want to determine which of potentially many parameters are most influential. Results may not be as precise and reliable as with other (nonsimulation) experiments. This is especially true because they are extremely contingent on careful validation of the original model and then the verification of its implementation by computer program. Nevertheless, simulation results can be very useful, particularly in making performance assessments during HCI design, but also, in selected ways, during HCI evaluation studies.

To carry out a simulation experiment, appropriate experimental design is also necessary. The input factors, or independent variables, must be distinguished as being either controllable (or changeable) or uncontrollable, depending on what is possible in the real system. Then, an experiment becomes essentially based on determining how the selected, controllable factors, as they are changed from one computer run to the next (providing for different treatment values or levels), affect the specified performance measures, i.e., the dependent variables, while all other factors are controlled or kept constant. It is, in general, not feasible to run all possible combinations of factors in a simulation experiment. That approach is too costly in terms of both computer resources required for making so many runs and also computer and human resources needed for analyzing the massive performance data that can result. Therefore, it is important to use experimental design in planning for the runs that are definitely essential and that are likely to be most efficient and effective in producing useful conclusions.

Law and Kelton (1991) have given a good introduction to this material, with emphasis on 2^k factorial designs for use in early stages of simulation-based experiments. Other helpful resources include Box *et al.* (1978), Box and Draper (1987), and, for simulation of computer performance, Kant (1992). More advanced analysis goals require techniques such as "meta-modeling" and "response surface methods." As is true for regular experiments, the organization of the design, in terms of input variables and performance outputs (responses), has determining influence on the kind of statistical analysis that is most appropriate for application to the simulation results.

Exercises

3.1. Critique the outline of data collection sources found in Section 3.2. Are any sources missing? Are any redundant sources included? Explain.

3.2. Critique the data collection and measurement techniques outlined in Section 3.3. Notice that these are also interpreted as "means" toward evaluation; they are not yet treated as "evaluation methods." Do you consider some of them as involving more than "getting data collected or measured," i.e., do some also imply the evaluation of the collected data? Explain.

3.3. Figure 3.1 characterizes the effects that data collection techniques might have on users. Would you make any reassignments in that figure? Why are "observations" located in two different boxes? Can you do both obtrusive and unobtrusive forms of testing? How? (Note: do not misread *stimulation* for *simulation*.)

3.4. Read Kant (1992) to determine the kinds of measurement techniques and tools that can be implemented within a computer system. Summarize the results, with emphasis on the techniques that can support HCI measurement studies.

3.5. In one of the books cited in the text (or some other source), read about population *sampling* techniques, including determination of sample size under specific conditions. Write a definitive report on the topic.

3.6. Repeat Exercise 3.5 for the topic *hypothesis formulation and testing*.

3.7. Repeat Exercise 3.5 for the topic *experimental design organization*, or block ordering. Restrict your attention to one of the major orderings outlined in Section 3.6.2. (Note: Your instructor may assign which one you should consider.)

3.8. Repeat Exercise 3.5 for the topic *descriptive statistics*, as defined in Section 3.7.

3.9. Repeat Exercise 3.5 for the topic *statistical analysis techniques* that are associated with different experimental designs. As in Exercise 3.7 (and dependent on your instructor's preferences), you may restrict your attention to a selected type of analysis.

3.10. Tools and techniques that support HCI design essentially involve the *means* for representing and accepting design information (including models of desirable interface appearance and behavior) and transforming that information into the design product. Can an analogous statement be made about tools and techniques that support HCI evaluation? (Hint: Is the input to the evaluation study only information about the results of the design? Or is more than that required?)

3.11. Assume that you have an interface designed and implemented. You want to conduct an experiment that will determine how well the interface might serve an existing group of 100 users. In order to arrive at statistically significant results, discuss each of the following: (a) how to select a representative sample from the target user population, to serve as experimental subjects; (b) the kinds of data (or factors) that should be measured; (c) how the experimental user–computer sessions must be organized and controlled; (d) alternative techniques that are available to analyze the resulting measured data. (Note: This question is only intended to motivate the student to become familiar with the relevant experimental framework. To conduct a real and reliable experiment, much more extensive consideration has to be given to the points outlined.)

3.12. In HCI design, there is the concept of having a powerful and versatile software "workbench" available to provide all the tools and techniques that a designer might need. Is it realistic to consider an evaluation workbench that would serve analogous purposes for evaluation? If so, describe it. If not, why not?

3.13. Consider how an experiment that involves both computers as well as humans as experimental subjects (i.e., as objects of evaluation) must differ from an experiment involving only computers. Outline and justify the differences.

3.14. Read appropriate sections in the book by Law and Kelton (1991) and in any other resources to determine how and why the evaluative data resulting from simulation experiments differ from the data resulting from experiments involving computers and humans. Discuss the results of your search.

3.15. With reference to Fig. 3.2, suppose you are the expert observer sitting at a powerful, special interface, located in a room separate from that of the user. [Note: Chapanis's (1975) experimental research setup generally relates to the situation suggested.] You have real-time access to what the user is doing in interaction with some computer-based application, say, "information storage and retrieval." Your support staff can implement the intermediary software for whatever types of manipulations or interventions you want to invoke within the interface experienced by the user. That is, you can request (by pushing some function button) any one of a number of different stimuli to be presented to the user. The purpose of such stimulation would be to determine how the user might react to them. What kinds of stimuli would you want to be able to issue? Outline them and, for each one, identify the kinds of responses (including symptoms of emotion) you might expect from the user.

INTERFACE STRUCTURES

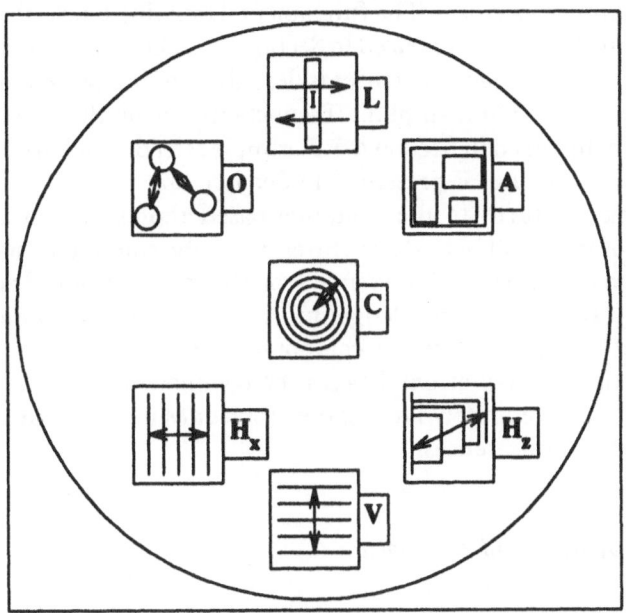

4.1. Overview

Design features in HCI are based on choice of interaction technique and style, the relevant user-observable models, and the supportive software models and modules (Treu, 1994, Chapters 6–8). A number of those features are dependent on various kinds of structural representations. In this chapter, we want to formalize structure as a feature that really should impact both HCI design and HCI evaluation. Hence, it should ideally be included in the coverage of design methodology. However, in view of the fact that measurement of HCI is critically dependent on structure, and because it was not feasible to duplicate the chapter in the two volumes, the choice was made to include it in this book.

A methodological basis is developed in this chapter for bridging, or undergirding, the interaction gap between the user and computer entities of the HCI dichotomy. This is done using "interface structures." These are patterns that can be identified and justified as providing meaningful organizational support within the interaction framework enveloping *both* user and computer (Treu, 1992).

Section 4.2 presents a definition and motivation for this approach. Primary emphasis is on developing the sets of patterns representing user and computer, respectively. The fundamental building blocks for "objects" are distinguished and symbolized in Section 4.3. Then, in Section 4.4, each of a basic set of interface structures is described, as it represents cognition and memory in the human mind. Distinctions among the representation systems are discussed in Section 4.5. A sample selection of hybrid versions of the basic structures is presented in Section 4.6.

Section 4.7 turns to the computer-based representation and interpretation of basic and hybrid structures. From the computer's standpoint, justification for structures is dependent on the various physical and logical patterns reflected by knowledge/information communicated to, and stored and manipulated in, the computer system.

Most of this chapter emphasizes the commonalities in structure between user and computer. The chapter concludes in a brief discussion of their structural differences.

4.2. *Motivation and Approach*

Gaines and Shaw (1986) have advocated the creation of "foundations for engineering the human–computer interface." With respect to the user and computer subsystems in HCI, they said: "It is necessary to have models of both subsystems that can be used together in a way that accounts naturally for their interaction, for the reflection of the user model needed in the computer and for the reflection of the computer that is the user's model."

Models are available that are reasonably pragmatic and conducive to being used for interface engineering, without requiring the engineer to be knowledgeable in all of the theoretical details of user psychology. Enough supportive evidence exists. One fundamental aspect relevant to both the user model and the computer model in HCI is that of *structure*. The concept of structure is extremely prevalent in computer design, organization, and functioning. Examples are data structures, file structures, structured programs, system architectures, telecommunication protocols, and network structures. Without these, computers and computer networks would not exist. But structure is also crucial to the user's mind and how it deals with representations of knowledge.

Definition 4.1. **Interface structure**: a conceptual, logical, or physical pattern that is used in representing objects and that is conducive to both the user and the computer; the organizational and/or relational pattern among parts or elements of the interface.

The baseline model for determining interface structures relevant to HCI is indicated in Fig. 4.1 (Treu, 1989). Consistent with Gaines and Shaw's (1986) suggestion quoted above, special models of the user and computer subsystems can be formulated and then used together in underpinning their interaction. Results of reviewing the different forms of representing knowledge, as they pertain to each of the two communicating entities of Fig. 4.1, are described in the following sections. In each case, the representations are "stripped down" to their structural skeletons. That is, the application-specific meanings and interpretive processes are removed, revealing the fundamental patterns that are of interest.

This extraction is purposeful. It is like separating the basic tree structure, as a data structure, from the many potentially relevant applications (e.g., family trees, sort trees) and focusing only on the pattern and generic operations inherent to the tree, not the interpretation of its constituent parts or the processes that carry out that interpretation. To create fundamental design constructs useful to the interface designer, who may not have expertise in each of the HCI disciplines, it is best to concentrate on the basics. Complication and confusion related to applications-specific details and terminology should be avoided, if possible. Rumelhart and Norman (1988) said, with regard to the difficulties in using unnecessarily powerful representations (e.g., predicate calculus) to model

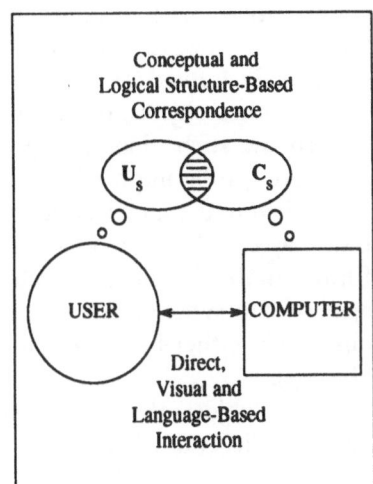

FIGURE 4.1. User–computer relationship based on knowledge structures. [Reprinted from Treu (1989) with kind permission from World Scientific Publishing Co.]

human thought: "After all, a model of human representation should find easy what people find easy, difficult what people find difficult." Analogously, the designer's model of the structured user interface should, first and foremost, accommodate the design elements that are easily understood. After learning those, the basic model can be extended, if necessary, to deal with increasingly difficult cases.

The basic structures portrayed in this chapter are indeed easy to understand. However, they can become elements of significantly more complex and varied forms of representation of knowledge. Combinations and extensions of the structures can enable representation at whatever level of complexity desired.

We are specifically interested in the membership of the set intersection indicated by Fig. 4.1, that is,

$$U_s \cap C_s$$

As Definition 4.1 points out, the resulting structures should be amenable to the human mind as well as conducive to supportive computer processing. These structures are defined and justified in this chapter. In Chapter 10, the human–computer structural mappings are discussed. Then, in Chapter 12, a formal definition and an illustrative specification of interface structure are presented, along with potential benefits of this structure-based, user–computer representation model.

4.3. Structural Symbols

To represent any kinds of knowledge units or information entities, whether they exist in conceptual, logical, or physical forms, the basic building block we can use is the general-purpose *object* of representation. It was already defined (Definition 1.1); it can be associated with other objects, contain other objects, or be contained by them.

To use such objects as pieces of knowledge/information on which structure can be imposed, or for which structure can be composed, it is convenient to use a variety of structural symbols. A reasonable starting set is displayed by Fig. 4.2. That set is likely to be changed or expanded in the future. In the definitions developed below, it becomes apparent that some symbols are synonymous or contain one another. For example, an area object may either be used as a node object or contain one or more node object(s).

Also, objects that are contained within a pattern may be associated either explicitly or implicitly. In some cases, the association is indicated via

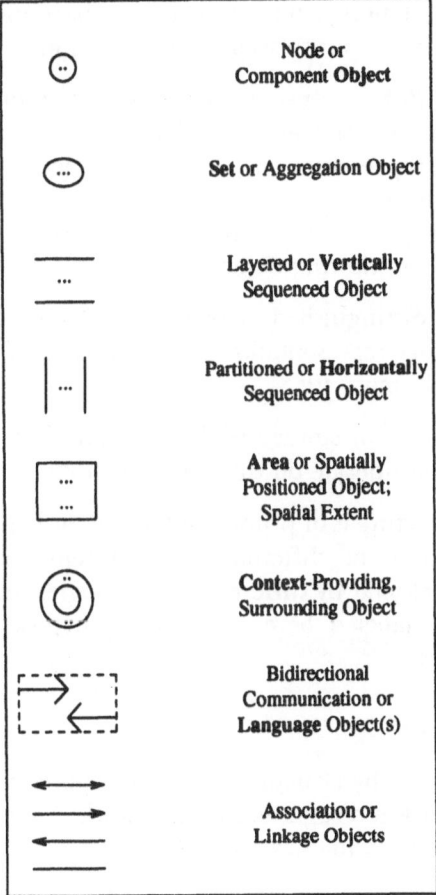

FIGURE 4.2. Symbols used for different objects.

explicit links or group membership; in others, it is implied by virtue of relative placement or contiguity.

4.4. Human-Evidenced Structures

Much evidence exists about structures applicable to human memory and thought. It not only comes from personal experience and introspection-based examples of how people are dependent on structure in their daily lives; it is also confirmed by the pertinent literature in psychology and cognitive science. We know that several significant categories of knowledge representation systems exist (Rumelhart and Norman, 1988). Most important for our purposes are the following:

1. *Propositionally based* representations, involving concepts, ideas, symbols, words, etc., as objects
2. *Analogical* representations, involving objects with dimensions, sizes, shapes, etc.
3. *Procedural* representations, involving steps, sequences, lists, instructions, etc., constituting objects.

These are further distinguished in Section 4.5. Here we emphasize their commonalities. Every representation system consists of at least two parts (Rumelhart and Norman, 1988):

- Data structures for storage of data in some format
- Processes that operate on the data structures

The element of structure is of primary interest to us here. It is remarkably pervasive throughout the different kinds of representation. Although structures are enveloped by different terminologies, depending on who first discovered and labeled them and for what purpose, they show significant commonalities.

4.4.1. Object-Oriented Structures

First, we look at the structures that are especially conducive to the ways human memory and cognition seem to work. A very important, basic interface structure is defined as follows:

Definition 4.2. **O-structure**: an object-oriented pattern of nodes that are explicitly associated; an association network or graph consisting of a set of node objects interconnected in some pattern using association links.

The two constituents of the O-structure are the first- and last-listed symbols in Fig. 4.2. The association links can in themselves be viewed as objects. They represent explicitly identified relations. These differ from objects associated implicitly, e.g., by means of relative positioning or set membership. The links may be singly or doubly directed (with arrowheads) or undirected, depending on the particular application involved in the representation. The O-structure is symbolized, along with indicative keywords, in the diagram of Fig. 4.3.

What justification exists for the claim that it is basic to the functioning of the human mind? The mind is certainly associative in nature (e.g., Hebb, 1949; Hunt, 1962) and employs conceptual plans and organiza-

FIGURE 4.3. O-structure. [This figure and Figs. 4.4–4.19 are reprinted (some in altered form) from Treu (1992) with kind permission from Academic Press.]

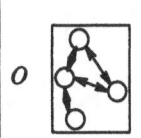

O

Knowledge Objects; Concepts;
Information Entities;
Association Links; Arcs;
Linked Objects, Nodes;
Networks; Graphs; Paths; Scripts;
Spatial Location, Distance

tional techniques for effective functioning (e.g., Miller *et al.*, 1960; Cofer, 1967). We form association links between/among objects all the time. Memory exercises show that the links are stored somehow and utilized later for remembering. Association criteria include having two or more objects (1) share the same time frame, with respect to when they occurred, were created, or observed, (2) share the same physical location or proximity, (3) pertain to the same subject material or other information category, based on some logical or physical features, and (4) belong to some other definable relationship, including relations from mathematics (especially logic). Using such criteria, our mental associations form pairwise linked objects, e.g., two papers published in the same journal, or two couples who were married on the same day; or associations in networks or graphs, e.g., a network of professional colleagues, or a map of airline routes among major cities; and in special subgraphs such as paths, e.g., a succession of cities in which a person has lived.

Networks of associations contributed to the development of various named structures such as semantic networks (Quillian, 1968). Concepts are represented by nodes and the relations, or associations, among them are handled by means of labeled, directed arcs. To avoid confusion, the types and tokens of the represented concepts must be distinguished. Using the notion of distance between two concepts, closeness can be represented by having them joined by means of an association link and assigning a weight to the link as a measure of closeness.

4.4.2. Set-Oriented Structures

The human mind also associates objects in groups or sets. Examples are files containing programs in the same language, books about a particular subject, or words all starting with the same letter.

Definition 4.3. **S-structure**: an unordered collection or grouping of objects that are associated according to a feature or characteristic that they have in common; objects represented by sets of features.

According to this definition, we can group objects into sets as well as represent objects by means of sets (of features). The latter implies that, if we have:

- Object A represented by Features 1, 3, and 4, and
- Object B represented by Features 2, 3, and 5,

we can compare the two sets, using Boolean operations, to determine what the objects have in common (Feature 3) and how they differ. The S-structure symbol and its indicative keywords are shown in Fig. 4.4. Compared with other interface structures defined in this section, the S-structure is more likely to be used for conceptual and logical representations of objects, rather than in physical patterns. It is especially relevant to conceptualization and formulation of queries for information retrieval purposes. The required Boolean combinations of search terms (i.e., the features of objects being sought) correspond directly to the Venn diagram symbol used for this structure.

4.4.3. Vertically Layered Structures

A very prominent inclination of the human mind is to structure or arrange objects vertically:

Definition 4.4. **V-structure**: a vertical organization, sequencing, or layering of objects that are either similar or different in some aspects.

If the objects, or object layers, are similar, emphasis tends to be on association related to vertical ordering; if they are different, their association is more likely related to object representation ranging from the abstract or high level to the concrete or low level. The V-structure symbol and keywords are displayed in Fig. 4.5.

Within our natural 3-D environment, a sense of direction matters. In particular, the mind relates significantly to the up-and-down orientation. An alphabetized list of words, arranged in a strict column (or menu), is

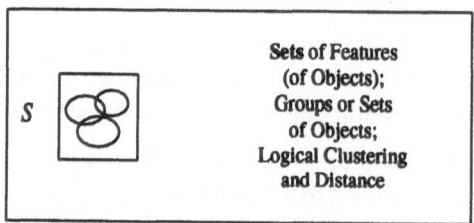

FIGURE 4.4. S-structure.

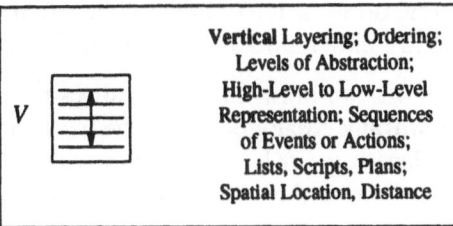

FIGURE 4.5. V-structure.

more easily understood and searched than if the same list were horizontally displayed. It is also convenient to work with top-down and bottom-up approaches to design. In computer programming (and graphics representation), the top levels imply greater generality or abstraction (the total picture) while the lower levels connote more specificity or detail (the picture parts). In other cases, the level is primarily associated with spatial location of physical objects, such as the second drawer from the top in a filing cabinet, or the fourth floor in an office building.

In the category of *propositionally based* representations, objects can simply be structured into lists. List structures and related operations resemble human memory and association in many ways (Newell and Simon, 1961). They are structures for arranging elementary information processes involving symbols and symbol tokens, with associative relationships among the symbol types (Simon and Newell, 1964).

The representation systems mentioned thus far attempt to represent all knowledge in a single, uniform format. That is not adequate for many types of knowledge. One version of the V-structure is to distinguish high-level from low-level representations. Higher levels of structure are needed to enable the representation of the more complex relationships among the lower-level objects. As a result, structures like frames (Minsky, 1975), schemata (Rumelhart and Ortony, 1977), and scripts and plans (Schank and Abelson, 1977) were developed. Although some of these are related to the V-structure, they are more appropriately discussed in the context of hybrid patterns, in Section 4.6.

4.4.4. Horizontally Layered Structures

With reference to a Cartesian coordinate system, the V-structure consists of layers or boundary planes that are parallel to each other and perpendicular to the y-axis. We can reorient that structure so that the layers relate likewise to either the x-axis or the z-axis.

Definition 4.5. **H-structures**: a horizontal organization or succession of layered objects that are either similar or different in some aspects.

Figure 4.6 indicates the two horizontal alternatives to which the human mind relates most naturally. Analogous to the V-structure, our minds work well with horizontal layerings, or left-to-right (or vice versa) patterns (the H_x-structure, oriented along the x-axis) and near-to-distant or front-to-rear partitions (the H_z-structure, oriented along the z-axis). For an English-like language, the left-to-right ordering of words is compelling. Horizontal patterns also persist in dealing with our physical environment. We remember and search spatially through a row of houses along a street, a row of offices along a floor, a row of filing cabinets in an office. These are relevant to either the x-axis or z-axis (perspective depth) orientation.

Further, any knowledge objects pertaining to sequences of events or actions can be represented not only using the V-structure but also the H-structures. Events and actions can be modeled in sequences oriented in any direction.

4.4.5. Spatial, Area-Spanning Structures

Arrangements of objects need not be restricted to successive layers or nodes oriented along the x-, y-, or z-axes. Objects can, in general, be arranged in any pattern.

Definition 4.6. **A-structure**: any spatially positioned pattern of objects each of which occupies a two-dimensional area.

The symbol and keywords for the A-structure are listed in Fig. 4.7. This pattern is motivated in part by the *analogical* representation category and in part by the HCI surface that enables visual representation of knowledge objects, including physical and imaged objects. Because "windows" are so prevalent in the physical and logical organization of the spatial display (e.g., Bly and Rosenberg, 1986), the window object is used here to portray any object (of whatever shape) that requires spatial extent, location, and distance, both within an object and between/among objects.

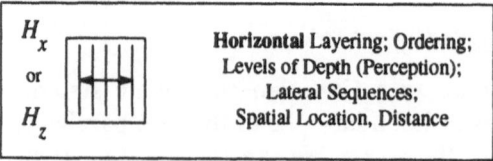

H_x
or
H_z

Horizontal Layering; Ordering;
Levels of Depth (Perception);
Lateral Sequences;
Spatial Location, Distance

FIGURE 4.6. H-structures.

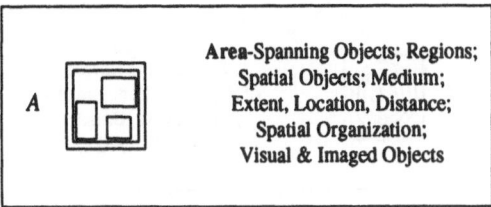

FIGURE 4.7. A-structure.

Thus, the reader should interpret the windowlike boxes (in Fig. 4.7) to stand for any object, or the rectangular "extent" (used in computer graphics) that surrounds it, regardless of its shape.

A reasonable extension of the two-dimensional A-structure is a pattern of three-dimensional objects each of which occupies volume and can be enclosed in a rectangular 3-D *box*. We could call this pattern a B-structure, but do not separately define it here.

4.4.6. Context-Providing Structures

Another useful structure also consists of layers, but they are arranged in a "concentric" pattern.

Definition 4.7. **C-structure**: an arrangement in which a central object is enveloped by successive layers of context or surroundings, spaced at physically or logically increasing distances.

These layers are not necessarily circular or concentric. They may be very irregular in shape, and the spacings between layers are variable (Treu *et al.*, 1989). This kind of structure also seems natural to the human mind. It is symbolic of what we can visualize about our physical environment (our home, in a neighborhood, in a city, in a county, etc.) as well as our social support system (one's family, other relatives, friends, neighbors, etc.). Figure 4.8 symbolizes this structure.

4.4.7. Language-Oriented Structures

One more basic structure is crucial in representing knowledge objects. It is involved in organized, language-based communication:

Definition 4.8. **L-structure**: the bidirectional pattern inherent to two-way communication between two entities using the objects that constitute a language.

The structure is summarized by Fig. 4.9. It has been an implicit ingredient to many studies of human-to-human communication, e.g., in

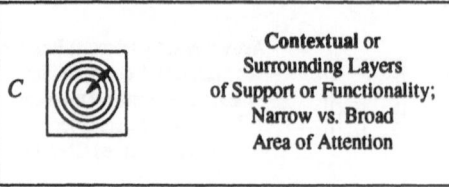

FIGURE 4.8. C-structure.

problem-solving (Chapanis, 1975). At a high level, it involves an alternating sequence of messages, or inputs and outputs. Using telecommunications terminology (Tanenbaum, 1988), the preferred model for human interaction with another human is "half-duplex." That is, one person talks, finishes talking, and somehow signals that the other person now can do likewise. In effect, only one channel is used, but it is redirected whenever one party finishes. If it were "full-duplex" communication instead, the ability to talk in both directions at the same time is available, including interrupting each other. This simultaneous, two-channel model has obvious problems when used between people.

At a lower level of representation, each such message must be expressed according to some language model, e.g., a natural language grammar. The latter can be formulated in a tree structure which, when traversed, results in generation of word sequences. Each arrow of the basic L-structure, therefore, becomes a structured composite, as is illustrated later.

4.5. Representation Distinctions

Unlike the *propositionally based* representations, the *analogical* representation systems deal more with mental images, or visual imagery. The structure and orientation of images, and the mental ability to transform them, are very important considerations. Kosslyn and Schwartz (1978)

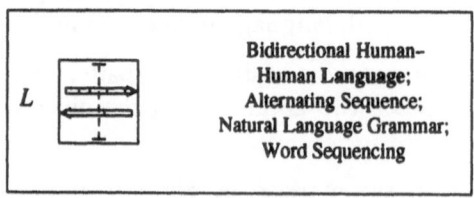

FIGURE 4.9. L-structure.

showed that the imagery is performed in a spatial medium such that (1) distance between parts of a representation corresponds to distance between those same parts in the imagined object and (2) a limit to the spatial extent of an image applies, that is, an image may be too large to enable its total representation at one time. In any case, each of the interface structures defined in Section 4.4 is potentially subject to visual imagery and, hence, to exhibiting the above-indicated characteristics.

The spatial structure of an image's "surface" representation also may have, according to Kosslyn (1980), a deeper, underlying representation that is somehow propositionally based. Further, the surface image can be interpreted or processed by the mind to arrive at more abstract-level versions of the image. It seems similar to visual processing in general. Most important, for purposes of this chapter, is the implied result that imaged objects are the analogues of physical objects. Therefore, given that structure is certainly significant to physical objects, it follows that it must also be essential to the representation of imaged or imagined objects.

Both the propositionally based and the analogical representation systems are of the *declarative* variety, emphasizing the representation of knowledge itself. The *procedural* category, on the other hand, pertains to how to do things, that is, knowledge about performing actions and knowledge about mental strategies for performing those actions on the representational structures of the mind (Rumelhart and Norman, 1988). In other words, this category relates to how to represent procedures or procedural sequences. Two major classes exist: one in which the procedural knowledge is accessible to inspection and one in which it is not, i.e., it is hidden away and only the resulting procedural output becomes available.

Procedural representation is of course well known in computer science, because computer programs are themselves procedural. Further, those programs, in turn, process data represented in data structures. Both the programs and the data upon which they operate exhibit structure while representing knowledge. The type of structure used is dependent on the application (knowledge) as well as on the computer-based implementation that is chosen.

Among the notable examples of procedural representation are the well-known production systems (Waterman and Hayes-Roth, 1978). They function based on schemata that have access to a common data structure. They are mentioned again in the next section.

A fourth category of knowledge representation, namely the *distributed* or *superpositional* system, is concerned literally with how knowledge is physically stored in memory. Although this is not really of interest in this chapter, it is noteworthy that associative memory structures and connectivity networks are very prominent in this type of system.

4.6. Hybrid Combinations

In the four layered structures defined, the layers themselves and the boundaries between them can be viewed as objects of representation. Alternatively, any layer can be used to "contain" or encapsulate other objects, delimiting their (physical, logical, or conceptual) location relative to objects in adjacent layers. This distinction leads naturally to the composition of two or more structures into hybrid structures. The binary operator "+" is used as follows:

$$A + B \rightarrow B \text{ "is superimposed on" } A$$

Thus, if we wish to impose a vertical layering (V-structure) on an association network (O-structure), we denote it by O + V. Alternatively, if we start out with a vertical layering (with each layer containing various objects) and we wish to impose an association network on selected objects, then V + O symbolizes the resulting hybrid. Note that a subscript, e.g., in $(O + V)_1$, merely distinguishes a particular version of the indicated type of hybrid structure.

Many hybrid structures can be formed in conjunction with the V-structure. Vertical levels have a natural mapping into hierarchical patterns or trees. This is indicated by the first-listed symbol, $(O + V)_1$, in Fig. 4.10. Levels take on the meanings attributed to the node levels (e.g., level for the parents, or level for the children, in a family tree). In addition, a vertical layering enables the encapsulation, at a given level, of the objects contained, even if not explicitly linked. It provides the shared context for those objects, i.e., commonalities between a particular object and all other objects at that level.

A path of object-oriented associations can be superimposed on each of the vertical or horizontal layerings. For example, if one drives along a city street to discover available fast food restaurants, a horizontal association trail (with restaurant nodes in physical order along the street) is developed. The width/depth of a layer is delimited by some meaningful criterion, such as approximate length of a city block. Then, depending on density/sparseness of restaurants on that street, the number of layers (or street blocks) involved in the path may vary. In other words, not every layer is necessarily of interest.

Schema-like knowledge structures can also be interpreted as hybrids. A simple example is a frame (Minsky, 1975). It can be used with the second-listed and also the last-listed symbols in Fig. 4.10. A frame stores the properties or attributes of objects in slots. Another example is the script (Schank and Abelson, 1977). It is a specialization of a frame in

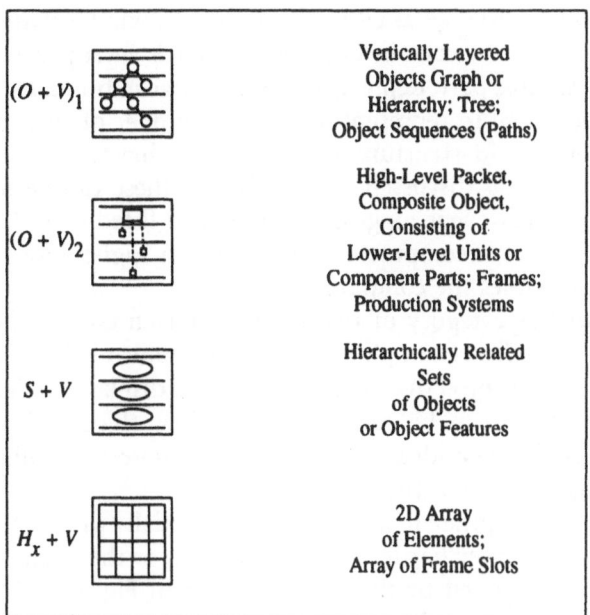

Vertically Layered
Objects Graph or
Hierarchy; Tree;
Object Sequences (Paths)

$(O + V)_1$

High-Level Packet,
Composite Object,
Consisting of
Lower-Level Units or
Component Parts; Frames;
Production Systems

$(O + V)_2$

Hierarchically Related
Sets
of Objects
or Object Features

$S + V$

2D Array
of Elements;
Array of Frame Slots

$H_x + V$

FIGURE 4.10. Example V-based hybrid structures.

providing a frequently occurring sequence of events. A script is not actually stored in memory in a sequence; instead, the represented sequence may be derived from a structure like an association graph. It can be viewed as a specialized path through a network. A more general and more abstract version of a script, oriented to satisfying specific motivations and goals, is called a plan. Terms like *frames* and *scripts* have been called "structured objects" (Jackson, 1986).

The systematic composition of structured units of knowledge applies to such hybrids. Among the "most salient psychological aspects of knowledge" mentioned by Rumelhart and Norman (1988), besides the association networks, is the fact that lower-level details representing a concept or other object can be packaged into a functional unit, resulting in a compositive knowledge object. Such representation obviously implies internal structure, not only structure in relation to other objects. The internal structure is dependent on one or more of the patterns listed in Figs. 4.3 through 4.11.

Accordingly, schemata were developed (Rumelhart and Ortony, 1977) to represent generalized concepts, including the underlying objects, events, actions, and sequences thereof. Among their features, schemata can represent knowledge at all levels of abstraction. They are packets of information that can contain one another. Each such packet contains a fixed and a variable part. Representing knowledge in human memory then becomes equivalent to representing a great number of such packets.

Another hybrid structure involves sets. Objects can also be categorized into sets, as discussed previously, and these can be related hierarchically. This pattern is suggested by the third-listed hybrid in Fig. 4.10. For example, a set of computers is hierarchically higher-level than the set of memory modules the computers contain.

One further category of hybrids is based on conjunction with the A-structure. The first example in Fig. 4.11 is motivated by spatial extent, location, and interobject distances pertaining to displayed objects of whatever shape. They can be rectangular window objects displayed on a computer screen. The idea is then to superimpose a specific pattern of objects using the O-structure.

It is also appropriate to position objects spatially within the layers of a C-structure. The layer borders may be implicit, or they may be explicitly indicated, as suggested by the second hybrid in Fig. 4.11. This kind of pattern becomes especially useful in attempts to provide the user with visible layers of contextual support surrounding the main task at hand. This model has been used with regard to interface design that promotes a network-oriented perspective (Treu, 1994, Chapter 12).

The third hybrid in Fig. 4.11 relates to the designer's choice of interaction techniques and styles. The inherent full duplex communication channel between user and computer requires that the visible interface area

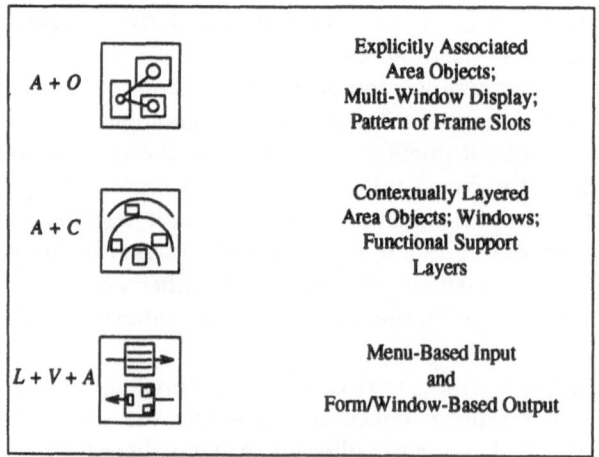

FIGURE 4.11. Example A-based hybrid structures.

be laid out in a manner accommodating both (1) the structure of the input technique (e.g., menu-based) and (2) the structure of the output technique (e.g., some pattern of objects displayed in a window). In addition, those structures have to be suitably combined and positioned, to enable them to coexist in the available screen area.

The hybrid patterns illustrated in Figs. 4.10 and 4.11 can be interpreted in many ways. For example, a vertical layering superimposed on the horizontal (x-axis) layering gives a 2-D array effect ($H_x + V$) such as the array of windows on one side of a high-rise office building. This is the last-listed hybrid in Fig. 4.10. Alternatively, if the leftmost object in such a row represents a book, and if each of the other columns stands for some feature portraying the book's contents, then a collection of books can be organized according to the array pattern. In fact, a book's row representation identifies a set of features and a feature column represents a set of books.

In addition, many other hybrids are potentially important to the ways humans represent knowledge. Our minds must contend with many different patterns. For example, if the two horizontal layers are superimposed ($H_x + H_z$), the resulting spatial layout supports recall of object location on a horizontal plane, e.g., one's car in a parking lot.

A top-view, contextual layering can be easily superimposed on a hierarchical structure, or centralized network ($O + C$). For example, the central site of a hierarchical organization is contained in the innermost layer, with successive layers accommodating the lower-level sites, e.g., branch offices. Furthermore, the vertical layering can be mapped into the concentric layering, resulting in the equivalence of $(O + V)_1$ and $(O + C)$.

4.7. Computer-Based Structures

The original impetus for structures in computer-based representations came from interest in efficient computer processing, not from structures important to the user's mind. Although the mental models of computer designers surely played influential roles, the cognitive characteristics of users were not regarded as design criteria, until fairly recently. This section gives an overview of the computer-based structures, especially those affecting the user at the interface. Instead of categorizing them according to the knowledge representation systems, the structures are now organized based on elements of an HCI model. However, by means of the mnemonic, single-letter labels associated with the structures defined in previous sections (Figs. 4.3 through 4.9) and their hybrid versions (e.g., Figs. 4.10 and 4.11), patterns that are similar in the computer-based context are identified.

4.7.1. Interaction Language

The heavy emphasis on command language design in the 1970s was almost entirely restricted to languages that were very serial in nature, consisting of sequences $(L + H_x)$ of alphanumeric character strings and sentences. They represented a very thin thread between the powerful human mind and the execution of programs in the computer's task domain.

Early versions contained little high-level structure, other than the alternating, bidirectional input–output sequences (Abrams and Treu, 1977), as implied by Fig. 4.12. Also, it involved the natural, left-to-right ordering of command components $(L + O)$. Otherwise, the inputs and outputs tended to be ad hoc in organization and cryptic in content (Treu, 1975a). One exception was the special-purpose interaction language, such as for retrieving sets of objects (S), e.g., bibliographic citations, responsive to some specified set of subject terms. The S-structure is repeated in Fig. 4.13, but from the computer's standpoint. The input commands of such query languages are structured according to the syntax of Boolean logic, although even that can result in nonuniform implementations (Treu, 1982).

Then, various forms of syntactic structure were imposed on interaction languages in general. One approach was to utilize BNF grammar representation, well known in the programming languages area, and extend it for application to interaction language. A number of studies (e.g., Reisner, 1981; Bournique and Treu, 1985; Chi, 1985) presented formal specifications of (graphical) interaction language using BNF-like notation. Ordered sequences of command components resulted, with each component dependent on permissible values identified by the grammar at some hierarchical level $((O + V)_1)$ of detail.

Lindquist (1985) also related interaction language to programming language-like structure, but in a different way. He expressed the dialog in terms of a high-level program. The structure of the dialog is then similar

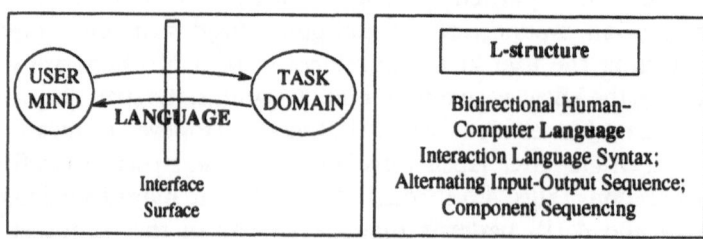

FIGURE 4.12. Serial interaction language.

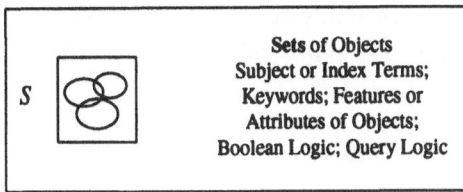

Sets of Objects
Subject or Index Terms;
Keywords; Features or
Attributes of Objects;
Boolean Logic; Query Logic

FIGURE 4.13. Sets represented in the computer.

to that of a program, or procedure (V or V + O), and hence is subject to the same kind of analysis, in terms of characteristics such as program structure and size.

But, while BNF and program structure are important to designers and programmers, they are not necessarily conducive to ordinary users who are not computer specialists. Foley (1979) presented a hierarchical model with the following vertical layering (V): conceptual model, semantic design, syntactic design, lexical design. The V-structure is confirmed by Fig. 4.14. Moran's (1981) multilevel model is analogous. It separates out those levels that specify syntax and physical (key press) conventions of the dialog from the higher-level conceptual component, involving task-oriented functionality and semantics as they relate to the user's mind. Interaction language itself can be implemented through two or more layers (e.g., L + V or L + H_x), and with different structural modes within each layer (e.g., L + V + A).

Interaction language sequencing is also extendible to time-based, user-oriented partitions of an interactive session. For example, Card and colleagues' keystroke model (1980, 1983) involves user accomplishment of a task with a specified method. It assumes that the top-level (V) structure of a unit task consists of the user's acquisition and then execution of a task method, with the task execution measured in time intervals for each of key-stroking, pointing, homing, drawing, mental preparation, and system

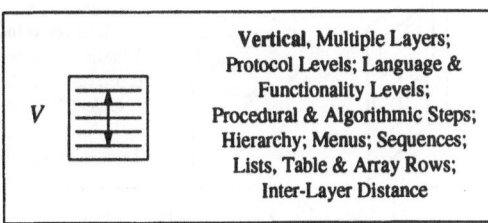

Vertical, Multiple Layers;
Protocol Levels; Language &
Functionality Levels;
Procedural & Algorithmic Steps;
Hierarchy; Menus; Sequences;
Lists, Table & Array Rows;
Inter-Layer Distance

FIGURE 4.14. Vertical patterns in the computer.

response. A user can certainly relate to such a logical sequence of time components (V, H_x, or H_z) representing an interactive session [L + (V or H_x or H_z)].

4.7.2. Visual Interface Surface

The structures in interaction language outlined thus far are largely dependent on the serial nature of traditional, written language. They can be enhanced through composite structures or templates, such as menus (L + V) (e.g., Somberg, 1987) and forms (L + A + O) for user inputs (e.g., Jeffries and Rosenberg, 1987). Also, user-oriented graphical languages (Treu, 1977), visual languages (Chang *et al.*, 1986), and pictorial systems (Chang, 1989) have gained increasing attention. Consequently, interaction language has become much wider in bandwidth and richer in expressiveness, and the language-based definition of the interface must be extended to include the directly observable and usable interface surface and the associated parallelism. That surface is depicted in Fig. 4.15. It can be organized into overlapping or tiled window areas (A). Interaction language can then be implemented via two or more windows (L + A). So, the A-structure certainly applies. The type of windowing that is preferable is dependent on the nature of the task and how much window manipulation it requires of the user (Bly and Rosenberg, 1986). Even "pretty windows" have been advocated (Gait, 1985) based on dimensioning each window such that its width and height form the *golden ratio* of Euclid.

Some studies have determined how best to organize the information spatially on the screen, with the menu arrangements (A + V + H_x) most conducive to human memory and use (Somberg, 1987). This means that not only the A-structure but also the V- and H_x-structures are relevant. The latter symbol and keywords are indicated in Fig. 4.16.

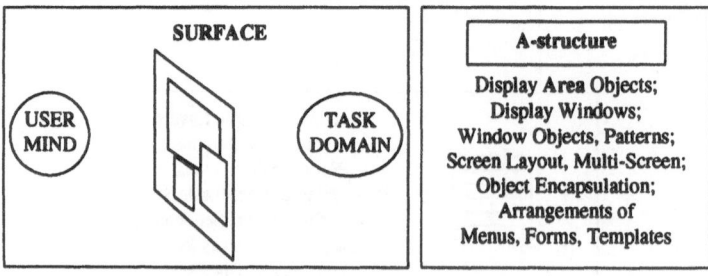

FIGURE 4.15. Visible interface area.

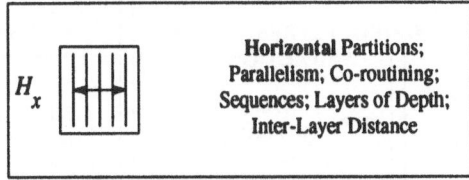

FIGURE 4.16. Lateral, horizontal partitions.

Woods's (1984) concept of "visual momentum" involves the user's ability to extract and integrate information across display areas. The key in increasing such momentum and in gaining greater parallelism in presentation is "to provide the viewer with data about the location of one view with respect to another or, more generally, with data about the relationships across display screens." One powerful technique for doing this is spatial organization (A and A + O), which "translates the normative user internal model into a perceptual map."

With respect to layout of the visible interface surface, K. L. Norman *et al.* (1986) observed that "the user has a structure with elements and relationships that map to the elements and relationships at the interface level." Depending on which "cognitive layout" of multiwindow and multiscreen (A + O) interfaces is adopted, continuity of (visual or mental) movement in the interaction can either be greatly facilitated or frustrated.

4.7.3. Task-Oriented Objects

Whatever screen organization is used, it must somehow correspond to the task space implemented in software and hardware behind the interface plane. However, knowledge objects portrayed for the user at the interface may have little resemblance to what is implemented behind the scene or what the user visualizes them to be. Analogous to the optics of a lens system, the task object a user sees is only a virtual image (Fig. 4.17) as opposed to the real thing (Treu, 1971).

Where the real object is defined and how it is structured in relation to other objects and transformed into one or more user-visible task objects, are important issues. They are dependent on "interface depth" and multispace object definitions (Chapter 10). From the standpoint of both the task organization and what the user sees at the interface, the O-structure is very important. A technically knowledgeable user may want to visualize data objects that are structured into records, stored in sectors, spinning around on platters of rotating disks, or to conceptualize linked lists as they support a line-oriented editor being used to write a report. But non-computer

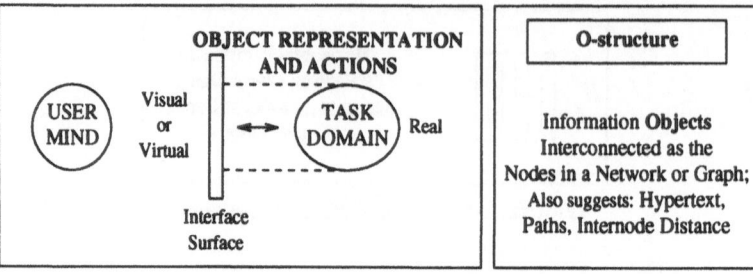

FIGURE 4.17. Behind the visible surface.

specialists need simplified object representations that are conducive to what the user knows and can remember, at least until the user can learn more and gain a deeper understanding of the computer-based application.

The currently prevalent object-oriented designs (e.g., OOPSLA, 1992) are responsive to this need. They can establish a simple connection between the object seen and the object defined in software. The term "object" is used again in its generic sense, consistent with Definition 1.1. Object-oriented patterns (e.g., $O + V$) apply to such areas as programming languages (e.g., Smalltalk, Goldberg and Robson, 1983) and command languages (e.g., Snodgrass, 1983). They also apply to other specialties in computer science, e.g., simulation and databases. The previously discussed layouts of window objects ($A + O$) are also in this category. Instead of being substantive objects directly associated with the task, they are facilitative objects (or widgets) that encapsulate or delimit the substantive objects.

Object orientation is very much advocated in HCI design (Treu, 1994). Many objects can be represented by easily recognizable, visual means at the interface surface. They can take on pictorial, iconic, symbolic, graphical, diagrammatic, and other forms. The design of language based on visual or nonvisual objects is relevant. According to Chang's dichotomy (1987), one type of visual language is for information processing, dealing with objects that have inherent visual representation or logical interpretation. The language itself may not be visual. The second type, called visual programming language, involves objects that are not inherently visual, while the language itself is visual in nature. Either type of language has some kind of composite structure (e.g., $L + O$). Efforts to structure the virtual task representation at the interface surface into more meaningful correspondence to what happens (at some level) in the task space have resulted in affecting interaction language itself.

4.7.4. Task Environment

The task that the user invokes and directs across the visible interface surface does not exist in a vacuum. In a state-of-the-art system or network, numerous other tasks, activities, events, etc., are in progress. It should be possible to reflect these in what is presented or available to a particular user (Fig. 4.18). A model for multilevel context (C) is applicable (Treu *et al.*, 1989).

The criteria for separating contextual layers are logical in nature. The layers themselves can correspond to software modules designed to instantiate them. The lowest/central level of context $(C + V)$ is "inherent" to the interaction language and its supportive interaction techniques. The previously discussed, bidirectional characteristics of language apply within that layer $(C + L)$. The other contextual levels can be assigned task-supportive, task-enhancing, and task-peripheral functions, respectively. This kind of task-surrounding interface structure is implied by Fig. 4.18 (Treu *et al.*, 1989).

Context can be thought of as structured concentrically (C), vertically $(C + V)$, or horizontally $[C + (H_x \text{ or } H_z)]$, depending on whether the most basic task objects and actions are viewed in the central core, at the bottom, or in one extreme layer of the model. Also, the $(A + C)$ composite of Fig. 4.11 applies.

4.7.5. Task-Specific Interface Depth

Interface depth is based on several different criteria or dimensions (Figs. 4.16 and 4.19). It can be dependent on how detailed the user's understanding must be of the task software and data structures, corresponding to programming language levels (V) ranging from very high to very low (machine code). It also can be based on task-oriented levels of functionality and, beyond those, the functionalities of the system and

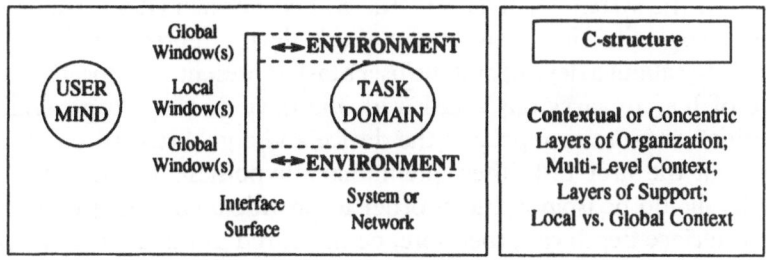

FIGURE 4.18. Surrounding the task.

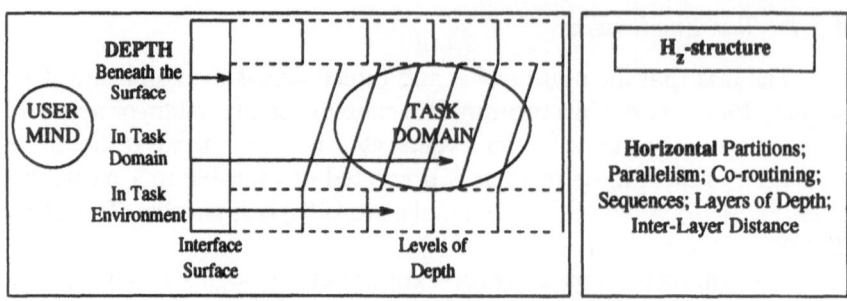

FIGURE 4.19. Interface depth dimensions.

network environment. In a hypertext (O) application based on an inherent hierarchy, for example, the user's ability to move from high-level nodes to low-level details $((O + V)_1)$, and vice versa, is indicative of one kind of depth. Such level-oriented depth is contingent, in part, on the user's ability to handle increasingly detailed, technical specifications of objects and, in part, on the display surface's capacity to present those objects in parallel $(A, A + O, \text{ or } A + C)$ and in a comprehensible and nonoverwhelming manner. It is not feasible to display or reveal everything, literally and functionally, on the visible screen.

Within such limitations, another kind of interface depth involves the illusion that the user is directly manipulating objects on the interface screen as if they were real (Shneiderman, 1982, 1983; Hutchins *et al.*, 1986). Such feeling of closeness to (or control over) the task may be desirable, especially for the novice user. But as that user learns and becomes more sophisticated, he/she is likely to reach more deeply into the system repertoire of software tools and techniques. This implies the existence of some structural patterns that represent a dimension of lateral distance or depth $(H_z \text{ or } (O + H_z))$ into the interface.

The notion of depth makes it reasonable to analyze how the pattern of virtual objects differs from the pattern of logical objects created and stored in the system. It relates to Kieras and Polson's (1985) analysis of "user complexity" in terms of the user's device representation (user's knowledge about a device) and the user's task representation (user's knowledge of how to carry out a task with the device). Using a generalized transition network to represent the device and a goal structure graph to represent the user task, their preliminary hypothesis was that the two graphs should be isomorphic in order to provide a good mapping.

Interface depth can, therefore, be measured as the degree of correspondence between two patterns. For example, an isomorphic mapping can be assigned a baseline depth value and then be compared against values resulting from other mappings. Such relative evaluations are discussed in Part III.

The above-suggested examples of interface depth are tied to software-based definitions of task objects. However, the software "space" is only one component in the multispace model defined in the next chapter. From the user's perspective, a kind of multispace partition (H_z) represents another form of interface depth, with the visible layer or partition closest to the user and the other layers somewhere behind that plane along the z-axis, away from the viewer.

4.8. User and Computer Differences

The commonalities in structuring knowledge representation, between the human mind and the computer, have been emphasized throughout this chapter. They are also evident in comparing the respective sets of keywords listed in the figures for each of the interface structures. Some of the sets are (nearly) identical.

But what about their differences? Some structures exist on each side of the HCI dichotomy that are not suitable for the other side. That is, they are not members of the intersection depicted by Fig. 4.1. For example, the computer implementation of a hash table, with an associated hashing function, is not very conducive to the novice (non-computer specialist) mind. While the user may learn to understand how it works, he/she does not find it easy to participate in storage and recall of an object located in hashed memory space, or in moving from one such object to another. The transitions (using hashing) are complex and seemingly indefinite. Another pattern too involved for ordinary users is the one evoked by recursion. An object that is processed recursively somehow seems convoluted or tends to lose the kind of predictable identity that is comforting to the mind. A more obvious example is the arbitrary positioning on the display screen of either tiled or overlapped windows. When a logical pattern is applicable, an illogical arrangement ("nonpattern") is not suitable. It deprives the user of the helpful spatial reference for associating one window with another, or for linking the high-level contents of one window with the detailed support data in another.

Likewise, the computer is very "uncomfortable" with certain characteristics of the human mind. This relates especially to patterns of mental movement within or across structures, rather than the number and complexity of structural types (which the computer can handle well). The user likes to skip in seemingly erratic manner from one point to another, without following the computer-accepted rules for tireless completion of what is started and for doing so according to a prescribed algorithm. System designers must of course constrain the user from flitting around in unpredictable ways and causing problems for the system. Ironically, while the user may be troubled by computer-generated randomness (e.g, in hashing), the computer has difficult coping with the kind of "randomness" displayed by the user.

Exercises

4.1. With specific relevance to HCI, give two examples of the use of each of the seven basic interface structures (Definitions 4.2 through 4.8), other than those mentioned in the text.

4.2. Can the elements of an O-structure be represented also by means of the S-structure? Explain.

4.3. Why might it be useful to also define a volume- or box-oriented B-structure, as an extension of the A-structure? Or is the latter adequate to represent any 3-D pattern of objects that can be displayed via a 2-D medium in HCI?

4.4. What problems can arise when an L-structure is implemented in full-duplex (rather than half-duplex) form for human–human communication? Are the same problems retained in human–computer interaction? Explain.

4.5. Give an example pertaining to HCI of each of the hybrid structures depicted by Figs. 4.10 and 4.11, other than those mentioned in the text.

4.6. Construct and describe four hybrid structures, other than those in Figs. 4.10 and 4.11. Base each one on two or more of the other patterns (basic or hybrid) defined in the text.

4.7. Compare the descriptions of each of the basic, human-evidenced structures (Section 4.4) with corresponding versions presented for the computer side (Section 4.6). In each case, discuss whether the structure seems primarily motivated or justified by (a) knowledge representation by the human mind, (b) computer peculiarities for representing information, or (c) both.

4.8. Answer Exercise 4.7 for the seven example hybrid structures listed in Figs. 4.10 and 4.11.

4.9. Prepare a critique of the fundamental interface structures defined in this chapter. Base your critique on either (a) specific structure(s) that you feel is(are) missing but necessary, and/or structure(s) you consider redundant or unnecessary, or (b) specific kinds of patterns of knowledge that cannot be represented using the structures defined.

4.10. Find definitions for "data structure" (the ordinary variety) and "abstract data structure" (or "abstract data type") from a book in computer science. Distinguish whether a physical pattern or a logical pattern (based on programmed procedure, not physical location) in data storage is involved. Using selected interface structures and example representations of objects in HCI, give an illustration of each type. (Note: As discussed in Chapter 10, this topic implies, among other things, that the structure implemented in a computer may not be apparent to the user at the visual interface.)

4.11. Do you agree that a user (if a novice) tends to have problems conceptualizing and understanding (a) hashing and (b) recursion? If yes, discuss the specific reasons. If no, why not? Suggest any other examples of patterns in computer-based implementations that are too complex for users who are not computer specialists?

4.12. If every type of knowledge representation includes (a) the data, structured in some pattern, and (b) a process to interpret and use the data, then are interface structures (as defined in this chapter) mostly meaningful for (a) or (b)? What about their combination? Explain. (Note: Remember that the purpose of interface structures is to present, or represent, objects in HCI in a manner conducive to both computer and user.)

4.13. Consider whether interface structures are really as important as claimed in this chapter. Are different users (or users' minds) different in their needs for structure or in their abilities to take advantage of structure? Does your answer imply that users should be given differing amounts of structural support? (Note: Some people have great difficulties in orienting themselves to the direction in which they are traveling. Does that mean that directional supports like compasses, maps, and street signs are not important to them?)

4.14. Are interface structures more important to HCI design or to HCI evaluation (as implied in Section 4.1)? Why?

BASIC MEASURES
OF PERFORMANCE

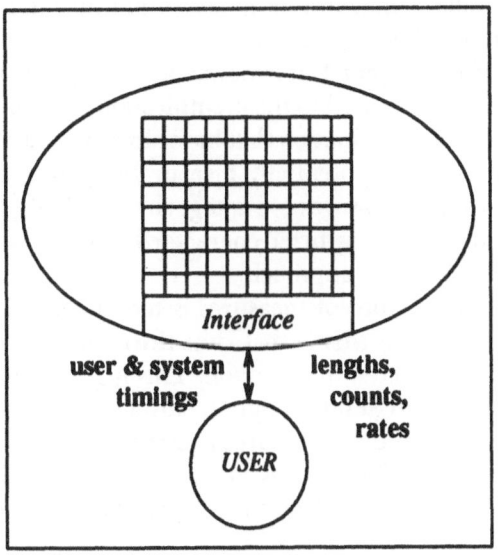

5.1. Overview

Not only is it desirable to include as much objectivity as possible in HCI design; it also should be very evident in HCI evaluation. Both are advocated as part of "interface engineering," in analogy to what is done in other engineering fields and as extensions of software engineering. A variety of structural underpinnings were developed for design (Treu, 1994), including schematics for design decisions. Such decisions are ultimately based on designer judgments, which are inherently subjective in nature. Nevertheless, the more systematic the decision-making and the more objective the factors feeding into a decision, the more reliable and credible the decision is likely to be.

Those causal factors include various performance assessments (Fig. 2.1). As is clear from the factors groupings for each of the user, the application of interest, and the target computer, and as is confirmed by the

general HCI design method (referred to in Chapter 2), results of performance measurement can/should play important roles both during a design
as well as in the follow-up evaluation of that design.

To enable measurement and subsequent evaluation of HCI performance, it is essential to have suitable measures. Terms such as "measurement" and "measure" are formally defined in Chapter 6. In the meantime,
the reader is assumed to be familiar with their commonly accepted
meanings. Measures, or metrics or formulas, are necessarily dependent on
structure, especially if they are designed to produce quantitative results
based on physical or logical measurements. The topic of interface structures was covered in Chapter 4. It is viewed as prerequisite to this material.

This chapter is dedicated to the identification and characterization of
basic measures for HCI evaluation that have already existed for some time.
First, in Section 5.2, the potentially measurable patterns are discussed.
Then, the well-known measures are categorized and tabulated in Section
5.3. They are followed by a brief characterization, in Section 5.4, of a
composite, figure-of-merit approach.

Finally, the importance of measures is reemphasized in Section 5.5.
They constitute a kind of theme that runs through the different types of
evaluation methods covered in this book. This is true even though different purposes, plans, and designs might be involved in those methods. The
multipurpose roles played by measures prompt various ways of extending
the basic measures described in this chapter toward rendering them more
appropriate and useful. They lead to the special tailoring of measures, as
considered in Chapter 7.

5.2. Measurable Patterns

Without structural patterns and paradigms, such as those presented
in Chapter 4, quantitative measurement really is not possible. This is true
whether we are trying to measure something about (1) the user entity, (2)
the computer entity, or (3) their interaction. Each of these cases is considered below. Their collective analysis is also discussed. Relevant patterns are
indicated (in parentheses) using the mnemonic labels of interface structures defined in Chapter 4.

5.2.1. About the User

With regard to the computer user, it is necessary to measure any
representative characteristics in either *direct* or *indirect* ways. The direct

approach can involve the measurement of various physiological indicators, such as blood pressure, heart rate, and eye movements. This topic is addressed further in consideration of user stress in Chapter 9. The patterns that are sought for that purpose are any distinctive fluctuations, or peak values, that are measurable during a user's reactions to continuous sequences of stimuli generated by computer behavior.

The indirect approach to measuring things about the user is the focus here. Given access to (1) observable or collectible evidence of user behavior in HCI and (2) a reasonably concrete representation of the user's mental model and/or the conceptual model used by the designer on behalf of the user, the evaluator can count, deduce, or infer a number of quantitative results. Included are:

1. Identification and grouping of recorded user choices of individual objects, among alternative objects available, such as in utilization of
   - Subsets of commands (S)
   - Subsets of widgets (S)
   - Subsets of hardware devices (S)
   - Subsets of software tools (S)
2. Identification of recorded patterns of usage in object subsequences or object layouts, such as
   - Repeated command (sub)sequences (L and O)
   - Repeated combinations of widgets and devices (O and A)
3. Determination of user expenditures of time for interactive activities such as
   - Selecting and entering specific commands (L and O)
   - Completing selected (sub)tasks (L and O)

In addition to the above, we can collect many types of data based on user opinions, via questionnaires or interviews, or on observations of users by experts. Such data are more subjective in nature. Nevertheless, they can be analyzed in terms of numeric values (e.g., counts, frequency distributions) and provide useful inputs to both the design and evaluation phases of HCI.

5.2.2. About the Computer Interface

As stated in Chapter 3, we are not interested in measuring computer hardware/software performance *unless* it has noticeable effects on the user at the interface. With regard to visible interface hardware, the measurable patterns are based on dimensions and distances between/among component parts (O and A). Hardware and software performance are especially evident through user-observable timings that can be measured (L and O). These include how quickly the system reacts to user input and with how much and what form of output.

As far as software itself is concerned, measurable patterns are also necessary to obtain quantitative results. This is confirmed by past efforts at measuring the psychological complexity of software (Curtis *et al.*, 1979) and also software usability (Lindquist, 1985), using both the Halstead (1977) and the McCabe (1976) metrics. They were based on various structural patterns reflected by computer programs.

Formal analysis of algorithms, and of the interface software implementing them, also would not work without underlying structure. In analyzing the complexity of an algorithm, using the well-known "big O" conventions, it is significant that an algorithm have an inherent and describable structure. For execution on a sequential machine, it consists of a finite sequence of steps, which usually subsumes subsequences involving iteration or looping (O and V). Success in this analysis does not depend on considering all of the miscellaneous details (e.g., how many steps in a loop, what types of statements involved, and the speed of the processor). It is adequate to determine in rough terms whether execution time for the programmed algorithm will require "on the order of" linear, quadratic, logarithmic, exponential, etc., time, as a function of one or more key variables.

How does such analysis relate to our interest in HCI? The time-based efficiency of an algorithm and the space-based efficiency of the data storage are actually rather narrow in scope. They nevertheless serve useful purposes, and HCI can capitalize on them. The composite HCI software is of course more complex than a single algorithm. In fact, it may be thought of as encompassing a number of complex algorithms executing simultaneously. As a result, the designer and evaluator should be familiar with analysis of algorithms. Such knowledge can serve to prevent and/or detect undesirable and unnecessary inefficiencies in interface performance.

5.2.3. *About User–Computer Interaction*

Beyond being able to measure patterns applicable to the user and the computer individually, a number of measurable patterns are inherent to their interaction. Illustrative examples are outlined below. As before, the most relevant structures are identified. Others can be added.

1. *Orderings* and *groupings* in interaction language, as evident on the visible interface surface, and as supported by parsing and positioning techniques:

- Syntax-based sequencing of command components (L and O)
- Sequencing of alternating inputs and outputs (L and O)
- Parallel displays of widgets, windows, and menus (A and O)
- Grouping of information objects (S and V)
- Positioning of interactive devices (O)
- Positioning and spatial location of information objects (O, V, H, and C)

2. *Correspondences* or *mappings* between/among the three major modules of the interface system:
   - Language levels or types (V and O)
   - User-perceived versus system-implemented language (V and O)
   - Object-oriented task definitions and actions, as implemented by the system, as displayed at the interface surface, and as conceptualized by the user (O)

3. Conceptual, logical, and physical *distances* or *depths*:
   - Levels of language (interaction and programming) (L and V)
   - Layers of software (systems and applications) (L and V)
   - Nodal (task) paths from application start to finish (O)
   - Window-to-window paths and directions (O, A, V, H, and C)
   - Levels of task-oriented functionality (V)
   - Levels of task-specific detail (V)
   - Levels of context (from task-inherent to task-peripheral) (A, V, H, and C)

As is apparent, the objects of measurement may be either physical or logical in nature. Examples of each category can be cited. A group of objects can be associated logically in a set (S) and then be physically displayed in a menu (A and V). A physical sequence of language components (L and O) can be counted and measured with respect to time (for entry or output). Also, physical distances among objects on a screen (e.g., widgets) can be measured (A and O). On the other hand, logical distances among various types of layers or levels of depth (V, H, C) must be based on clear and meaningful layer definitions. A transition from one layer to the next, or from one node in a graph to the next, has implications for the amount of effort necessary, either on the part of the interface system (through supportive processing) and/or on the part of the user (through required mental work). Similarly, measurement of the indicated correspondences or mappings can be based on selected pattern analysis techniques. "Closeness-of-fit" formulas, e.g., relating what the user visualizes and expects to what the interface actually produces (Chapter 10), can suggest the extent or degree to which one pattern (e.g., a graph of task objects) matches or mismatches the other. A mismatch is likely to make things more difficult for the user.

Cumulative Analysis. Emphasis thus far has been on measuring (or collecting data about) a single user in a single interactive session with a selected computer. Results of doing so, for a sample set of users over a number of different interactive sessions, possibly involving more than one computer for comparison purposes, lend themselves to a variety of collective analyses. Well-known statistical analysis techniques are available either for descriptive purposes or in conjunction with experimental design techniques, as outlined in Chapter 3. A number of patterns are representative of the higher-level or more collectively oriented forms of analysis. They include the sets of objects (S) being measured as well as the sequences of actions (V and O) those objects exhibit while being measured (V and O), e.g., via protocols that are recorded and analyzed.

5.3. Well-Known Measures

A number of basic measures pertaining to HCI have been known for years. Much work was done in the 1960s on the importance of "response time" to users of time-sharing systems (e.g., Carbonell *et al.*, 1968; Miller, 1968; Sackman, 1968, 1970). Those and other fundamental measures can generally be categorized as follows (Abrams and Treu, 1977):

1. Time-based measures
2. Measures of length or volume
3. Multiplicities and frequencies
4. Rate-based measures
5. Ratios and other measures

Each category is considered below. Representative measures are listed in Tables 5.1 through 5.3. Consistent with the discussion in Section 5.2, each measure can be distinguished with regard to whether it reflects one or more of the following:

- User action
- System (re-)action
- User-system interaction

Some of the measures have been used a lot. Others have been relatively ignored.

5.3.1. Time-Based Measures

Dynamic interaction between a user entity and a computer entity is by its very nature subject to many measurements that involve time. For example, measurement of the time to complete well-defined tasks has been modeled for years and extended again recently (MacKenzie and Buxton, 1992) to tasks that are two-dimensional. Such measures are especially relevant because humans and computers have different strengths and weaknesses when it comes to their time-based performances of various tasks.

Table 5.1 presents a listing of such measures. The first entry, system delay, represents a version of the commonly labeled response time. It is defined as the elapsed time between a user's last keystroke (or the equivalent action) and the system's first substantive reaction, e.g., first meaningful character displayed. Notice that it can be distinguished from acknowledgment delay, which is used for the time elapsed until the system acknowledges receipt of a user's input. This could simply be a nonsubstantive signal such as a line feed or its equivalent. The user is thereby reassured that the system has received the input and is working on it.

Corresponding to the two measures of system delay are the times taken to transmit the system response and acknowledgment, respectively. These are numbered M3 and M4 in the table. For a particular application, these measures can be indicative of how verbose, or how involved or complex, the system is in its output. This length of time carries implications for how much the user must read, assimilate, understand, etc., in carrying out selected tasks. There may be justification for why the system takes so long to output its responses; on the other hand, it may suggest that the system is sluggish or maybe inefficiently structured with regard to how or what it outputs to the user.

All of the timings used in Table 5.1 can be obtained by having the hardware capability to time-tag every character and symbol that is transmitted over the channel between user (terminal or workstation) and the target system. Consistent with Chapter 4, a sequential pattern is clearly inherent to the measurement of such objects. Several alternative structures can apply, and they are relevant at different levels of detail, depending on the granularity of objects measured (e.g., character-level, word-level, command-level).

Once such data are collected and recorded, they can be analyzed. Each of the resulting timings, t_i, used in the table is an interval representing the time required from the start of a delay or transmission period to its finish. For example, M1 is based on the time interval from the user input of carriage return, or equivalent, to first substantive character, or equivalent,

TABLE 5.1
Time-Based Measures[a]

I.D.	Name	Formula	Explanation	Interpretation
M1	System delay	$\Sigma t_i/n$	Where $1 \leq i \leq n$; providing the average of n timings	Implies length of time the user must wait in idle state
M2	Acknowledgment delay	"	As above, but for n acknowledgments	The user wants quick feedback that system has received input
M3	System transmit	"	" for n system responses	May indicate system verbosity and how much the user must digest
M4	Acknowledgment transmit	"	" for n ack's	Instead of brief signal, system may be too wordy in ack'ing
M5	User delay	"	" for n user commands, answers, or other actions of a certain type	May correlate to user effort required (reading, thinking, etc.) before next input to system
M6	User transmit	"	As above, for n user inputs of certain type	Reflects amount of interactive manipulation (typing, etc.) required
M7	Task completion	$\Sigma t_j/n$	$1 \leq j \leq n$, for a subsequence of task-specific transactions	User + system time required, on average, to do a selected type of task
M8	Selected subsession	"	With the j subscripts restricted to some subset of transactions	Duration of any part of a session, straddling tasks
M9	Intermodal transfer	"	Time spent in transitioning between modes (software modules)	May represent mental mapping to different model/ structure
M10	Total session	$(T_F - T_S)$	Difference between (real time) at finish and start of session	Represents total effort by user in interaction with computer

[a]This table and Tables 5.2 and 5.3 are reprinted (in revised form) from Abrams and Treu (1977) with kind permission from ACM Press.

output to the user. This measure is also called "lag" and has recently been analyzed with respect to its effects on user performance (MacKenzie and Ware, 1993).

Measures M1 through M9 are all expressed as averages over n occurrences of the same type. The data could of course also be analyzed in terms of other meaningful statistics, including standard deviations, variances, percentiles, worst and best case patterns, and others. Only M10 is expressed as a simple difference between two time points along the real time line. But, that can also be averaged across n sessions carried out by the user for specified purposes.

The first four measures in the table represent system behavior. The next two do likewise for the user. M5 is a measure that enables analysis of how difficult or complex the user finds the next action to be taken. Thus, for example, if the user typically (on average) takes a long time to enter a certain command, it may suggest something about the syntax and semantics it requires. Perhaps a particular command is unduly complicated, cryptic, or confusing. Such a conclusion is especially likely when the same user exhibits considerably smaller delays prior to utilizing other commands, either for similar or different purposes. M5 can, therefore, be associated with the amount of mental work required in specific user actions (Treu, 1975a). The term "think time" has often been used as a label for this measure. Thinking here includes conceptualizing, remembering, structuring, etc., a command as required by the system.

User transmit time, M6, may also be partly contingent on the complexity and length of a user input, as required by the system. If the interactive language is long-winded and complicated, the user has to spend more time entering it correctly. Indeed, such language is much more likely to cause user errors. Further, M6 also reflects pure skills in typing and in other interactive manipulation (e.g., with a mouse), which the user may or may not have acquired. Note that M5 and M6 can be defined either to be mutually exclusive (as suggested in the table) or, more realistically, to overlap (i.e., the user continues to think while typing).

The remaining time-based measures are oriented to the summation of times spent by both user and system in conjunction. That is, they either measure the entire duration of a user session with a system, using M10, or they subdivide the session on some basis. To do so, we introduce a "transaction" as consisting of everything that the user and the computer do to process one interactive action. This means that its measurement involves the sum of the user delay (M5), user transmit (M6), system delay (M1, and subsuming M2), and system transmit (M3, subsuming M4) times for a particular user input. A separate transaction time measure could be added to the table.

If it is possible to delimit tasks, in terms of the starting and ending points of any task-specific sequence of transactions, such time intervals can be separated out and analyzed. Then, it becomes possible to conclude that, on average, the target user completes a particular type of task on the target computer in the specified amount of time.

But the user may do a number of other things during the course of a session, besides attending to clearly defined tasks. For example, he/she may double-check on some file's existence in the directory, or read e-mail that has just arrived. For such and any other purposes, it may be useful to have the ability to measure the time expended for any subset of transactions in a session. These transactions may or may not be contiguous, and they may straddle boundaries between task sequences. M8 is included to represent such measurement. Finally, there is a special category of transactions representing the user's need to transition from one mode, or partition, to another. While such intermodal transfers are realistically important to separate one partition, and the corresponding software environment, from another, it can also be interpreted as imposing a special mental transformation on the user. That is, the user's structured mental model must be transformed or reoriented to accommodate a potentially very different framework. Such transformation relates to the topic of interface structures discussed in Chapter 4, especially the structure-based session signature (discussed in Chapter 12). The point is not to question whether such transitions should take place, but rather how frequently they must happen and how they are designed in order to facilitate them. Measure M9 can be utilized as one piece of evidence on whether intermodal transitions are easy or difficult for users to handle.

5.3.2. Measures of Length and Volume

We have progressed from a purely serial form of human–computer communication to increasingly parallel forms. This pattern is indicated by the range of interaction techniques used in HCI (Treu, 1994). But, whether serial or parallel in nature, we can measure or count the number of elements flowing in either direction across the interface. The basic elements may range from fundamental character codes (including control characters for signaling something) to units of text (words, sentences, paragraphs, etc.) to various types of information composites, such as menus, tables, diagrams, graphic objects, and pictures. Hence, the unit of length or volume of information communicated depends on the interaction technique employed.

For Table 5.2, we use "components," c_i, to represent whatever unit of information is being counted. Measures M11 through M13 capture several

TABLE 5.2
Lengths and Multiplicities

I.D.	Name	Formula	Explanation	Interpretation
	Length or volume			
M11	System response	$\Sigma c_i/n$	$1 \le i \le n$; providing the average number of components	Implies system verbosity or expressiveness in language
M12	Acknowledgment	"	As above, but for ack's	Closely related to M4
M13	User input	"	As for M11, except for user	Related to M6
M14	Task length	$\Sigma c_j/n$	No. of transactions, each = user input + system response	Interactive volume required to complete a task
M15	Subsession length	"	Some subset of transactions; work between/across tasks	Interactive volume required
M16	Session length	"	Total transactions in entire user–computer session	Total interactive volume
	Multiplicity			
M17	Command usage	Σc_j	Number of times a particular command is used in a session	Suggests importance to user; may need special design work
M18	Task	"	Number of times the same task is performed in a session	As above
M19	Mode	"	Number of times a specific mode is selected in a session	As above
M20	Mode switches	"	Number of times the user switches to a different mode	Implies (dis)continuity and mental transitions
M21	System errors	"	Number of errors tallied	Implies system reliability
M22	User errors	"	Errors committed by user	Implies user knowledge, skill, training, etc.

quantities involving either the system or the user individually. They are reasonably self-explanatory, and can be correlated with the corresponding time-based measures. However, there may be disparities between the volume of information communicated and the time that it takes to do so. If so, there may be reason to suspect some inefficiency. For example, a relatively short and straightforward output might take the system longer than one would expect. Likewise, if the user takes too long on the input side, for a reasonably short action, among the sources of this problem are undue complexity in command syntax, cumbersome or confusing interface structure, inadequate user preparedness, and others.

Measures M14 through M16 can be used to represent the amount or volume of work required, in terms of numbers of transactions, to carry out (1) a certain type of task, (2) some other subset of work, not necessarily tied to a well-defined task, and (3) the entire session. Each one is expressed as an average, over n tasks, n subsessions, or n sessions. In each case, the object of measurement (i.e., the task, subsession, session) must be properly defined and delimited. A transaction is understood to be the total length or volume of a user input and the corresponding system response.

Measures M17 through M22 can be used to count the objects selected or the events occurring in an interactive session. It is of course necessary to be able to identify the objects being counted. This should preferably be possible by searching (under software control) a database containing a detailed recording of everything that transpires in a session, for occurrences of clearly defined patterns. The patterns may be command strings or menu entries (for M17), task delimiters (for M18), invocations of mode switches by type (for M19 and M20). Also, errors that can be committed by system (M21) and user (M22) must be identifiable and recognizable, at least for well-known classes of errors. For example, diagnostic messages produced by the system can be searched.

Results of using M17 through M22 all have something to say about the importance (to the user) of the objects being counted and the potential need to attend to improving the design of the objects in question. Improvements may also be indicated in training the user, e.g., to make different or more advantageous selections (of commands, tasks, modes) and to commit fewer errors. It should be noted that, if the above types of interactive objects, or components, cannot be recognized and counted automatically, it is essential to introject human judgment to identify and delimit them. That should not be necessary for most of the measures defined thus far, except that some types of errors may be difficult to determine or it may be difficult to decide whether the system (because of poor design) or the user caused them.

5.3.3. Rate-Based Measures

Some of the measures in the previous tables gain added significance if they are converted to rates. That is, they can be expressed in terms of how many of the objects occur per unit of time. Three examples are listed in Table 5.3. A number of others could be added.

Interaction rates reflect how truly dynamic and intense the user–system interaction is, particularly with regard to relatively brief interchanges such as in editing. This rate may have a bearing on the mental energy expended by the user on a continuing basis. It is unlike the interactive pattern that is either sporadic or that provides long wait times for users to do other things (or to become frustrated about inadequate responsiveness).

TABLE 5.3
Rates and Other Measures

I.D.	Name	Formula	Explanation	Interpretation
	Rates			
M23	Interaction	Σc_i/time	Where c_i = transaction; time is in total # of units, e.g., hours	Indicates how interactive or conversational the session is
M24	Task completion	"	As above, except c_i = task	Relates M18 with M10
M25	Error	"	As above, except for # errors	Relates M21 or M22 to M10
	Ratios			
M26	Relative system delay	M1/M1′	Where M1′ is system delay on a different system/load	Indicates potential improvement under different conditions
M27	Relative user delay	M5/M5′	Where M5′ is user delay for a different user group	Indicates what can be done with better training, experience
M28	Relative task length	M14/M14′	Where M14′ is average length of a task on different system	Suggests that one or the other task sequence is more efficient
M29	Command usage	Σc_j/total #	Where c_j = specific command; total # is sum of all commands	Compares the popularity/importance of a particular command
M30	User idleness	M1/M10	Proportion of total session spent waiting for system response	Suggests time wasted, although user may do other things

The other two rates listed, M24 and M25, can help explain a user's productivity, or lack thereof, over a period of time (e.g., a session). The rate of completing tasks, especially if they are well-defined, says a lot about a user's skill as well as about the system design in support of that user. The error rate, whether for system or user, likewise reflects the level of performance of the entity committing the errors. Further, if M25 is low, M24 is likely to be higher.

Many relative measures are possible. They can be expressed as ratios, as illustrated by M26 through M30. A relative system delay or response time can be helpful in assessing how the target system is performing in comparison with (1) some other system, (2) the same system under different load conditions, or (3) some optimal value of response time. The latter might be determined for a specific kind of task as ideally suited to achieving productive user interaction with a system. It can, therefore, serve as a threshold value in evaluating this aspect of the interface.

Likewise, one can compare user delays for two different user groups (M27) and task lengths for two different ways of getting a task done (M28). Many other ratios are possible. For example, task completion rates (M24) can be compared on different systems or under different or ideal conditions. This can give a better sense of how realistic a certain level of productivity is, when compared with others that are known to be respectable or even the best possible.

The user's frequency of selection of certain commands, when compared with all other commands that are called upon (M29), implies something about its importance to the task at hand or about the user favoring it, or both. It can at least give impetus to studying the reasons for frequent selection in order to determine how it might be rendered even more useful or appealing. On the other hand, if a frequently used command is also associated with numerous errors (M25), perhaps it should be modified or replaced.

Finally, when it comes to concern about user efficiency, the user idleness ratio (M30) can be a meaningful indicator. But it must not be misinterpreted. The user may be taking advantage of long system delays in thinking about how to handle the next task or in doing other things. Nevertheless, M30 is a potentially useful quantitative indicator.

5.4. Figure-of-Merit

Given the many measures described in the preceding section, it is possible to select the most meaningful subset and use it in a composite, higher-level formula. This can be a function that relates and balances components depending on their importance and interaction with each other. Multiplicative and additive factors may be involved.

For example, the following, simple formula might be a useful figure-of-merit. It is a kind of weighted sum:

$$M_T = (\Sigma M_i \times x_i \times w_i) \div \Sigma w_i \qquad (5.1)$$

where the M_i are the individual measures. The w_i are weights assigned to the measures, respectively, by some knowledgeable person, to indicate relative importance. The x_i merely serve to normalize (or compare) the values resulting from each measure to a selected threshold. They have different units of measurement. Hence, when applied to the measure values, the resultant value of M_T is the sum of terms having the same dimensionality. An illustration of the use of this kind of composite measure is given in Chapter 8.

It should be reiterated that Tables 5.1 through 5.3 are not exhaustive; a number of other measures and reformulations of those that are listed can be added. Thus, the HCI evaluator, who wants to conduct a measures-based assessment of all or part of the interface, has a fairly long shopping list of measures from which to choose. Others will be discussed in Chapter 7. The choices should depend on the evaluation purpose, objects, objectives, and aspects, as defined in Chapter 6. After a selection is made, it must be incorporated in the rest of the evaluation methodology, as presented in Chapter 8.

5.5. Roles of Measures

By now it should be very apparent to the reader that measures are viewed as very significant elements of the HCI evaluation methodology being presented. Whether or not they are treated as such in the HCI literature, the characteristics and uses of measures are, in a sense, at the core of evaluation studies. They play determining roles in almost every kind of evaluation carried out, as will be amplified in Chapter 8.

This view is confirmed through the terminology formalized in the next chapter. Then, it is accentuated further by the design and construction of more advanced performance measures tailored for special purposes. Finally, the general evaluation method recommended in Chapter 8 is explicitly labeled as "measures-based." That label does not preclude utilization of the method with relatively limited attention to measures and formal measurement. Nevertheless, it acknowledges how HCI evaluation involves some kind of measurement, even if it only means counting opinions (sums, averages, distributions) or determining that a particular feature or problem exists (binary decision function) or that it performs through some response variable in a manner exceeding a minimally acceptable value (threshold comparison).

Exercises

5.1. Prepare a critique of the measurable patterns outlined in Section 5.2. Are there any patterns you would add to the list? Are any patterns ambiguous or would you delete some of them? Why?

5.2. With regard to various measurable patterns, the distinction is drawn between measurement in terms of either physical or logical units. For each of those two categories, make a list of the units of measurement that are clearly defined and that could be applied to (a subset of) the measurable patterns outlined in Section 5.2.

5.3. It is one thing to measure in terms of physical and logical units that are well defined; it is another matter to talk about measuring differences or mismatches between patterns of interest in HCI. Such patterns potentially include 1-D, 2-D, and 3-D orderings (e.g., sequences), arrangements, and images. In each of those three spaces, what general techniques are available for expressing the similarity and differences between one pattern and another? Assume Cartesian coordinate systems.

5.4. For each of Tables 5.1 through 5.3, (a) what measures (of the same type) could be added as important, and (b) which ones are not very meaningful and should be deleted? Give your reasons for each case.

5.5. Discuss technique(s) that could be used for delimiting (i.e., specifying start and end) of each of (a) tasks (Measure M7), (b) subsessions (Measure M8), and (c) modes (Measure M9). (Note: these should, in turn, support corresponding measures involving lengths, multiplicities, rates, etc.)

5.6. Counting user errors (M22) and calculation of error rates (M25) are frequently used in HCI evaluations (as confirmed by examples in Chapter 8). Consider the antithesis of making errors, namely *not* making errors. This would give a much more positive portrait of what the user is doing. Does such a measure exist? If so, what is it? If not, can you think of a measure that might work?

5.7. How can command usage (M29) be usefully employed in a follow-up to evaluation? Give several examples.

5.8. What are the advantages and disadvantages of using a single figure-of-merit (such as described in Section 5.4) to determine whether an interface, or some part thereof, is good, bad, or something else?

5.9. With regard to Definitions 3.2 and 3.3, consider evaluation studies that range from wanting purely descriptive results (e.g., determining that a specified performance value exceeds a given threshold) to requiring formal experimentation, including experimental design and hypothesis testing. Outline the types of measures that can be useful along that spectrum. Which measures can be shared by different kinds of studies? Which ones are not shareable, e.g., because they are very special-purpose or unique?

5.10. Can you identify any kinds of evaluative results that are substantive and meaningful, but which are not (or cannot be) based on use of some types of "measures"? Explain.

MEASUREMENT AND EVALUATION

HCI evaluation and various types of measurement should go hand in hand. Accordingly, Chapter 6 of this three-chapter section presents the definitions of major evaluative terms, including the important evaluative aspects. The latter are used in Chapter 7 to characterize, construct, and illustrate not only the existing measures (Chapter 5) but also new, tailored measures of evaluation. Then, Chapter 8 ties together the previously developed methodological terms, including structures and measures. It describes and distinguishes evaluation approaches and methods and illustrates them with reference to studies reported in the literature. This leads to presentation of a general, measures-based evaluation method, followed by selected examples and a profile of its use.

EVALUATION TERMS AND ASPECTS

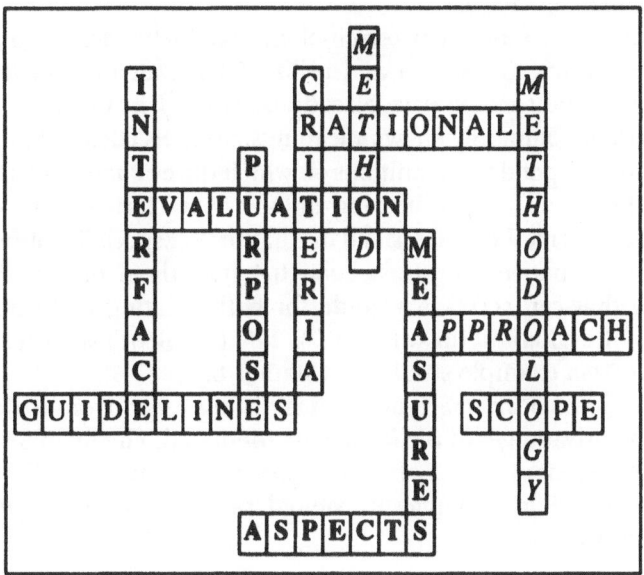

6.1. Overview

As suggested in Chapter 2, measurement and evaluation of interface designs may be required and invoked in several ways and places:

1. As an integral part of *design* methodology (Treu, 1994), or
2. As a follow-up to that design methodology, or
3. In independent efforts to assess performance of an existing design.

The first two ways imply that the designer must be sensitive to the need to carefully justify the design factors and principles used as well as the design decisions made, leading to design features. In other words, the designer should work *in anticipation* of undergoing evaluation at some point, during or after design. Each of the above-listed options should stimulate the designer to formulate specific criteria for determining whether or not the design goals are met. Notice that, therefore, the designer (who may not also be the evaluator) should preferably be cognizant of evaluation terminology and methodology.

In the third, above-listed option, that is, in evaluating some existing interface, the design principles may no longer be known or articulated. Hence, the evaluation must be based more on generally preferred or accepted levels of performance, as stipulated by the evaluator or someone else (e.g., management).

In any case, evaluation terminology should be clearly understood prior to attempts to develop and utilize HCI evaluation methodology. Various important terms have already been used in previous chapters, based on their commonly known meanings. Sections 6.2 and 6.3 present a series of interdependent definitions on which the evaluation methodology is built. They will have a bearing on the characteristics of evaluation approaches and methods described in Chapter 8. Especially influential are the major evaluative aspects. Section 6.4 uses them in constructing a hierarchy that can serve as a guide for both creating and categorizing measures of evaluation (in Chapter 7). The prevalent use of measures is highlighted via example studies in Chapter 8.

In Section 6.5, *relative* evaluation is distinguished from evaluating *in the absolute*. Advantages of the former are identified. Finally, in Section 6.6, some observations are made about the extensive terminology developed in this chapter. While that may be viewed as excessive, it is nevertheless deemed useful.

6.2. Definitions

The "object" of design in HCI (Definition 1.1) now becomes the "object" of evaluation, or else the containing or a contained object in that evaluation. Evaluation in general is "finding the value or amount of something, or the process of evaluating something." For our purposes, we tailor the term as follows:

Definition 6.1. **Interface evaluation**: an assessment of an interface object's performance or appearance; the process of carrying out such an assessment; the result of such an assessment.

Analogous to the definition of interface design (Treu, 1994), interface evaluation can connote each of (1) what is to be evaluated about a design, (2) how to do that evaluation, and (3) the evaluation results.

It becomes evident later in this chapter and in Chapter 7 that both qualitative and quantitative considerations may enter into an HCI evaluation. Both are subject to measurement, although in different ways. The "engineering" of an interface encompasses both design and evaluation. Therefore, it requires the means for determining as *objectively* as possible how well the interface was designed. Accordingly, we should couple evaluation with measurement:

Definition 6.2. **Interface measurement**: finding the extent, size, capacity, rate, and other quantitatively expressible attributes of an interface object and its performance.

Some data collection techniques and tools are specifically designed for such measurement, as discussed in Chapter 3. But there also exist other techniques, such as questionnaires and interviews, which enable the collection of opinions and other data from various human data sources, including users. Data of that kind can be analyzed and can produce quantitative values, as if they had been "measured" in the some way. The use of such data, along with the more objective performance data, was implied by Fig. 2.1.

In evaluating an interface, using measurement and other methods, it is important to be guided by an established purpose of the evaluation:

Definition 6.3. **Evaluation purpose**: the reason and motivation behind conducting an evaluation.

In interface design, the design purpose may be fairly innocuous, such as "to provide computer access for a particular group of people to a selected application," or it could be more demanding, such as "to provide a *better* interface than the one currently in place." In either case, the designer must determine (1) which design principles (goals) are to be pursued and (2) the details (techniques, tools, etc.) for satisfying the principles. Notice that the order is:

Design Purpose → Principles → Detailed Design (Factors, etc.)

By analogy, evaluation purpose gives relatively broad guidelines on how to proceed with evaluation. But, purely because of the nature of "evaluation," which immediately suggests that something or someone will be analyzed in a judgmental, critical manner, the evaluation purpose tends to be more definitive (for an evaluation) than is the design purpose (for a design).

A simple statement of purpose could be "to determine whether and how well a specified design principle was achieved in a design." But there may be other factors underlining the stated purpose. If the results of evaluation suggest that the interface is "ineffective," is it to be modified or replaced? If the users are found to be less than productive, are they to be better trained or replaced? Is the evaluation to be tantamount to an acceptance test for the system under consideration? The seriousness of the consequences of evaluation may give reason to impose greater expectations on the evaluation methodology.

6.2.1. Objectives and Scope

Just as design purpose and principles specify general goals that must be refined to more concrete levels, the evaluation purpose must lead to more specific aims. We use the term "objective" to become more exacting:

Definition 6.4. **Evaluation objective**: a specific aim or focus in an evaluation, as it relates to one or more objects to be considered either individually or in combination.

Several major evaluation objectives were outlined in Chapter 1, with reference to Table 1.1. They focused on the major modules in HCI as the evaluation objects. Further refinement of such objectives, guided by the evaluation purpose, leads to identification of the particular factors and features (i.e., variables) that represent the evaluation objects and that can be studied, measured, and evaluated.

The purpose and objective(s) imply just how much of the entire user–computer system is to be evaluated. An interface system is not necessarily evaluated in its totality. Maybe only the visible interface surface, maybe only the application software as accessed by the user, or maybe only the user him/herself is to be the object of evaluation. This means, in general, that the evaluator must know exactly what is to be considered variable in the HCI situation and what is to be maintained as constant or unchanging, providing the context within which the evaluation objects are to vary.

Definition 6.5. **Evaluation scope**: the target area, space, or extent of an object within which the evaluation activity is to operate or to which it is to be applied; the object(s) to be evaluated within the context of a set of interrelated objects.

As before, the generic Definition 1.1 of "object" is assumed. Let us illustrate the definition with an example. One of the most popular objects of HCI evaluation, in earlier years, was the text editing and word processing (WP) application (e.g., Roberts and Moran, 1983). Such studies typically focus(ed) on assessing selected performance characteristics of the software, while determining its inherent functionality and/or how well (especially how quickly) the user can take advantage of that functionality. Thus, the scope was limited to a specific piece of software, and the basic objective (Definition 6.4) was to analyze its features with regard to impacts on the user. Other examples of evaluation objective + scope will be evident among the studies outlined in Chapter 8.

Evaluation methodology should ideally provide support for any combination of evaluation purpose, objectives, and scope. That is a tall order. It means that the methodology should be adaptable to be either *comprehensive*, able to address all (or most) major evaluative considerations in an HCI situation, or *selective*, by focusing only on certain parts and aspects, to the exclusion of others.

The purpose, objectives, and scope, in turn, have influence on what must be measured. This is indicated in Fig. 6.1 by the three respective arrows pointing to the "evaluative aspects" box. Before defining the latter, we need to consider one more useful term: evaluation type.

6.2.2. Type of Evaluation

The type of evaluation can be viewed as a special conjunction, a refinement, or an elaboration of the evaluation purpose (Definition 6.3) and/or evaluation objective (Definition 6.4), within the relevant evaluation scope (Definition 6.5).

Definition 6.6. **Type of evaluation**: the nature of the evaluation study, in terms of its strategy or intent relative to its high-level purpose and objective(s).

Several major types can be identified. This can be done by means of the kind of question that the evaluation is intended to answer, or the manner in which it is to be answered. Major options are:

- *Descriptive*, i.e., how good or bad is it?
- *Diagnostic*, i.e., what is wrong (or right) with it?
- *Explanatory* (or Expository), i.e., why does it perform the way it does?
- *Prescriptive* (or Predictive), i.e., how could it be improved (or degraded)?

In each case, the "it" refers either to the "object(s)" being evaluated, within the evaluation scope, *or* to the impact of one object upon another. Also, for each named type, the question can be extended by the following qualifier: . . . compared with expected or desired performance (or impact). This qualifier can be accommodated by means of relative/comparative evaluation, as discussed in Section 6.5.

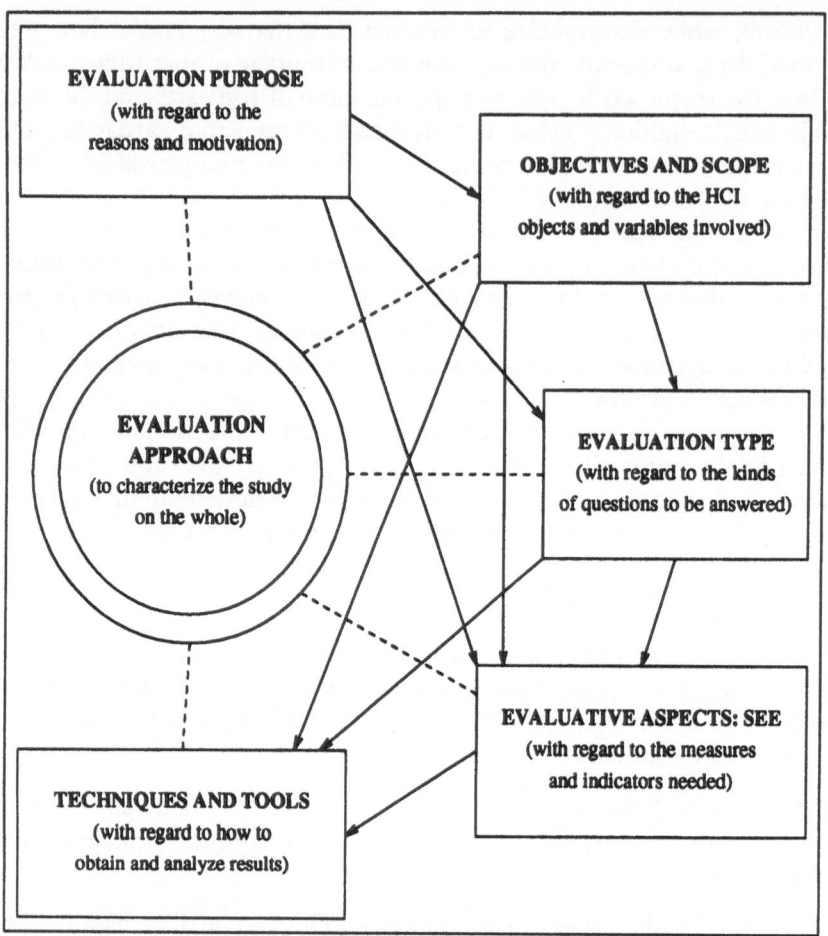

FIGURE 6.1. Methodological terms and interactions.

Other types could be added, by combining, replacing, or renaming some of the above. Common practices and preferences among HCI investigators may dictate other terminology (see also Section 6.6). However, we are purposely defining the types according to what they are intended to accomplish, not the means or methods to be used for accomplishing it. The means and methods can include analysis, experimentation, and others, designed for the collection and analysis of required data, as was discussed in Chapter 3. they must be determined as part of the overall evaluation method (Definition 6.15), as will be clarified in Chapter 8.

Consider some examples of evaluation type. Suppose that the evaluation purpose is to study the productivity of a group of computer users. The high-level objectives indicated might be to assess (1) the performance of users, individually and in comparison with each other, while keeping computer performance variables constant, and also (2) the implications of existing computer features on the performance of users. These two objectives are among those listed in Table 1.1. Notice that "purpose" and "objectives" may become merged or even identical, depending on who is defining them and how systematically the evaluation is carried out. So, what type of evaluation seems to be called for? As long as the purpose implies that something is wrong (e.g., "they are not productive enough"), the *diagnostic* version seems reasonable. If the purpose is instead to determine simply how well the users are doing, without prejudgment on anything being wrong, the *descriptive* type would seem more appropriate.

If the purpose, furthermore, requires evidence on why the users are performing in certain ways, or better/worse than they performed before, then the *explanatory* type might be most revealing. It could conceivably also be based on or become a variation of the diagnostic type (above) or of the prescriptive type (below). The *prescriptive* type is specifically intended to serve any attempts to compare and change interface objects or features, for whatever reasons, or to determine and explain their interactions and effects. By being able to illustrate that selected changes in factors (representing user, computer, or application) or in interaction features (e.g., interaction techniques, styles, widgets) do/will produce demonstrable changes in performance (response variables), management and designers obtain evidence to support more informed decision-making on HCI design and acquisition. We should reiterate here that the above examples can be restated, by focusing on the performance of other HCI modules, instead of the user module.

Type of evaluation also plays a role in influencing the evaluative aspects and measures to become involved, as suggested in Fig. 6.1. The evaluative aspects are defined next.

6.2.3. Evaluative Aspects

Even if evaluation purpose, objectives, and scope are clearly specified, and if the appropriate type of evaluation is identified, the evaluator must determine "on what basis" or "with respect to what" the evaluation is to be carried out. This means that it must be decided which evaluative "aspect(s)" is(are) to be emphasized in the evaluation.

Definition 6.7. **Evaluative aspect**: one viewpoint in an evaluation; a direction or orientation adopted in an evaluation with regard to the type of evaluative evidence sought; one category of considerations addressed in an evaluation.

This definition sounds vacuous until it is elaborated and illustrated. In essence, the use of evaluative aspects is to get some handle on how the "goodness" or "badness" of an interface design is to be assessed. That is, relative to what considerations is the interface to be evaluated? Considerations can be categorized into three major groups, and various combinations or interactions among them. Those three aspects are defined next.

Definition 6.8. **Synergism**: a united action between different agents; harmonious cooperation with each other.

This term is related to the word *symbiosis* (Licklider, 1960), meaning "the association or living together of two unlike organisms for the benefit of each other." However, synergism tends to diminish the biological implications of the latter. The reader may also consider "synergy" as an appropriate alternative.

Synergism reflects those characteristics and features both of the user (or user's mind) and of the computer interface that contribute to enhance or constrain the user's ability to carry out a selected task in conjunction with the system. In other words, it encompasses the performance factors reflected by the major HCI objects, with the understanding that interest is restricted to evidence of *harmonious conjunction* of user and interface.

But achieving a synergistic relationship is not the only consideration in evaluating an interface. For example, does the interface support the user in getting a lot of work done?

Definition 6.9. **Efficiency**: producing an effect without unnecessary expenditures of time, energy, and other resources; the level or amount of such expenditures.

This evaluative aspect invokes *quantitative* considerations involving time, volume, capacity, frequency, speed, configuration, and cost, as reflected by the entire interface system or part thereof. The user, the application, the interface, or some combination of all three may be determined to be efficient or inefficient in various ways.

In addition to questions about synergism and efficiency, an evaluation may also have to answer questions about the "goodness" of the product of interaction.

Definition 6.10. **Effectiveness**: producing a desirable effect or result; achieving quality in the interaction product; the level or gradation of the quality achieved.

In this book, this aspect is taken to reflect those *qualitative* considerations (exclusive of synergistic quality) that represent how well the system (or part thereof) is functioning, especially in terms of the product that results. HCI performance can be assessed through one or more of the above three evaluative aspects. This is elaborated in Section 6.4.

6.2.4. Measures and Evaluation Criteria

In order to enable HCI measurement (Definition 6.2), in accordance with the three major evaluative aspects (Definitions 6.8, 6.9, and 6.10), we need appropriate measures.

Definition 6.11. **Measure of evaluation**: a formula or metric that relates to one or more evaluative aspects; a formula that, if evaluated using appropriate data values for its variables, contributes to the evaluation of an object.

Chapter 5 already described a number of well-known measures and also discussed the importance and prevalence of measures in HCI evaluation. Chapter 7 will model the construction and use of tailored measures and indicators of performance. The word "measure" tends to be reserved for the cases in which data are obtained from physical measurement. The word "indicator" is more generic. It can be used not only to encompass measures, in the above sense, but also for the numeric data resulting from collecting and analyzing opinions. Hence, the two terms are at times merged, especially when both meanings are relevant in a multiaspect evaluation.

Like the specific criteria needed to help the designer in making the necessary design decisions (Treu, 1994), we need criteria for making judgments on whether an interface is performing well or not.

Definition 6.12. **Evaluation criterion**: a rule or standard for making a judgment on the performance, appearance, and impact of an object; a decision-making rule and priority for assessing whether and how well an object satisfies its design goals (principles); a statistical test to make such a decision.

A general format is indicated in Fig. 6.2. Criteria form the basis for evaluative decision-making, with the assumption that appropriate measurement results are made available to which the criteria can be applied. The results are thereby interpreted, as discussed in Chapter 8. Some important questions must be answered before criteria can be formulated properly. Examples are: Is the interface to be compared against another

GIVEN each of the following:			COMPARE and SPECIFY:
Evaluation Purpose(s) and SEE Aspect(s) of Interest	The Most Appropriate Measures and other Indicators of Performance $\{M_i\}$	Corresponding Individual Weightings, Composite Rankings, Thresholds for Comparison	(Relative) Performance Conclusions

FIGURE 6.2. Format of an evaluation criterion.

one, or is it to be evaluated autonomously on its own merits? This relates to the issue of relative versus absolute evaluation (Section 6.5). Is the evaluation to be selective, with only certain variables to be manipulated, measured, and controlled? This will determine the variability of the evaluation objects within the scope of evaluation (Section 6.5). The evaluation criteria must of course be selected as appropriate to the objects and the variables (or measures) representing those objects.

6.3. Approach and Method

The terms defined in previous sections can delineate "what" is to be evaluated, "why," and "with regard to what." Now, we consider terms that mainly deal with "how" to do so. Collectively, the definitions presented thus far can be used as building blocks for formulating an evaluation methodology:

Definition 6.13. **Evaluation methodology**: the science of method for evaluating something; the system of approaches, methods, and means used in evaluating objects.

The composite methodological package for evaluating HCI must be built on suitable evaluation approaches and methods, in order to enable the evaluator to achieve the purpose and objectives of an evaluation in a systematic manner.

Definition 6.14. **Evaluation approach**: the general characteristics of conducting an evaluation, based on its intended purpose, objectives, scope, type of evaluation, evaluative aspects, and any supportive techniques and tools.

EVALUATION TERMS AND ASPECTS

That definition is quite a mouthful. It is reflected directly by the diagram of Fig. 6.1, in which all five boxes in the semicircular formation point (via dashed lines) to the "approach." An approach is, therefore, a set of descriptors characterizing an evaluation; it is not interpreted to be some kind of high-level procedure.

In HCI design, we talk about top-down, bottom-up, and other approaches. In HCI evaluation, such terms are not as directly meaningful, although top-down refinement of what is to be evaluated is certainly relevant. Example labels for an evaluation approach include:

- *Comprehensive evaluation*, relating it to the evaluation scope (Definition 6.5)
- *Comparative evaluation*, relating it to the evaluative decision-making logic employed (Definition 6.12 and Section 6.5)
- Some *named approach*, e.g., SEE (Section 6.4) or *BE³ST* (Section 8.9), which emphasize a special characteristic, such as a combination of evaluative aspects involved
- *Experimental approach*, relating it generally to a specific means or method for evaluation (Chapter 3)

The above examples show how a heterogeneous assortment of labels can be attributed to an approach. This pattern is confirmed by Fig. 6.1 and will be discussed further in Chapter 8.

Because an "approach" is still a rather general term, we need a more exact evaluation method that is procedural in nature and that can, therefore, be followed by the evaluator.

Definition 6.15. **Evaluation method**: a specific plan or a procedure according to which a design (product) can be evaluated.

A method can encompass all of the terms (in the semicircle) of Fig. 6.1, but it takes them into a step-by-step sequence for consideration by the evaluator. It ties together the various pieces of a methodology, including specific, detailed techniques on how to measure, collect, analyze, etc., the data required to reach evaluative conclusions, relative to the evaluation purpose, objectives, scope, and aspects of interest. Supportive tools and techniques, including experimental design and statistical analysis, were characterized in Chapter 3. They will also be apparent in the overall evaluation method portrayed in Chapter 8. Notice that the term "technique" is considered as more special-purpose and technical than the term "method." Whenever possible and reasonable (in this text), a technique is used as supportive of one or more steps in the more general procedure called method. But there are times when they are interchanged, as will be seen in Chapter 8.

Finally, it is not only important that the *designer* record the design rationales surrounding the interface features selected in HCI design (Treu, 1994); it is also desirable that the *evaluator* record the rationales behind reaching evaluative conclusions. To some extent these are reflected by the evaluation criteria employed. However, the criteria, priorities, and other factors used are not necessarily revealed by evaluators among their evaluation results. They should be.

Definition 6.16. **Evaluation rationale**: an explanation of the evaluation method, aspect(s), measure(s), criteria, etc., that were employed in the evaluation of an interface object or of selected feature(s) of that object.

Requiring such recordings will tend to enhance the communication of decision-making, both in design and in evaluation, and thereby will also contribute to advancing the state-of-the-art of HCI.

Finally, we add one more definition with general implications. In a sense, it can have something to say about any of the other methodological terms we have defined. To assist the HCI evaluator, there are many published evaluation "guidelines," analogous to those in design.

Definition 6.17. **Evaluation guideline**: any instruction set forth, as a guide, on how to carry out an evaluation.

An evaluation guideline can be formatted in a variety of ways. It can in fact subsume the various other terms (purpose, objectives, aspects, etc.).

Guidelines can have a useful place, if they represent sound experience and practice, and recommendations by/from expert evaluators. However, they must not be viewed as substitutes for thorough analysis and determination of the particular evaluation approach, method, etc., to be utilized in a given study. Guidelines, if used, must be carefully integrated to ensure that they are consistent with the entire methodology to be employed. It should be noted here that evaluation guidelines as defined above should, in general, be distinguished from design guidelines. The latter are used in the "comparison against guidelines," defined as a usability evaluation method, as discussed in Chapter 8.

6.4.   Interaspect Combinations

Synergism (Definition 6.8), efficiency (Definition 6.9), and effectiveness (Definition 6.10) as major aspects of evaluation (Definition 6.6) constitute the mnemonically labeled "SEE" approach to evaluation. They allow for various interesting interactions. For example, an interface system can be found to be efficient without being effective, and vice versa. Also, just because a system is efficient does not imply it is synergistic. In addition, it could conceivably be synergistic without being either efficient or effective, though that is unlikely.

Measures, or formulas into which measured data can be substituted for evaluative processing, are available in each of the three SEE aspect categories. That was already implied, in part, in Chapter 5, and it will be demonstrated further in Chapter 7. Such categorization is useful. It has also been employed in performance evaluation methodology specifically designed for computer systems. For example, Kant (1992) organized the measures for that purpose into the following groups: responsiveness, usage level, missionability, dependability, and productivity. All of these can be interpreted as subcategories of the efficiency category.

Interactions among SEE measures can be considered. A variety of aspect combinations and corresponding measures will be described and illustrated in Chapter 7. The SEE hierarchy is displayed in Fig. 6.3. It is used, in Chapter 7, to guide the selection of existing measures and the construction of suitably tailored, new performance measures. Then, the resulting measures can become part of the overall evaluation methodology, as discussed in Chapter 8.

Besides their usefulness in constructing measures, evaluative aspects can be expected, for good reason, to show relationships to design princi-

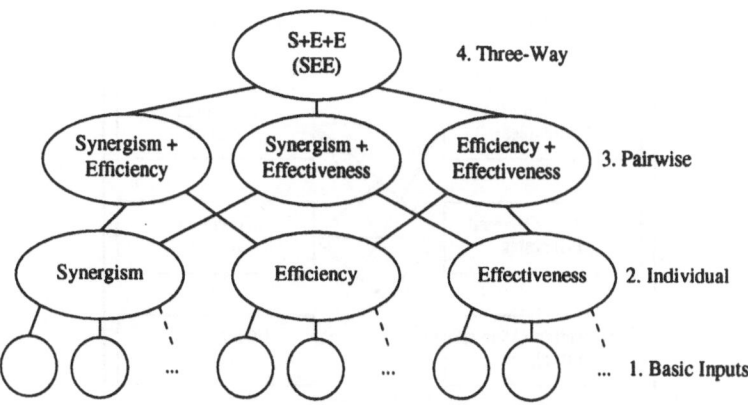

FIGURE 6.3. Hierarchy of evaluative aspects.

ples. It would be helpful to have a distinctive, preferably one-to-one mapping apply, e.g., between the user-oriented principles and synergism. But that is obviously too simplistic. Although "synergistic" as well as "efficient" and "effective" could be added to a table of broad design principles, each category of principles (like the user-oriented principles of Table 2.1) may call upon every evaluative aspect, as suggested by Fig. 6.4. Conversely, each evaluative aspect may relate to multiple sets of design principles. In general, any user-oriented design principle (selected from Table 2.1 or other sources) may require evaluation in one, two, or all three of the evaluative aspects.

Thus, the evaluative aspects represent a meaningful taxonomy of evaluative considerations, transcending the design principles oriented to the different HCI objects. Although one could try to tailor measures of evaluation to each of the design principles individually (Table 2.1), it is preferable to use a high-level composite model, like the SEE hierarchy, to make the evaluation task more manageable, comprehensive, and cohesive.

6.5. Absolute versus Relative Evaluation

Important to note is that HCI evaluation *in the absolute*, that is, without the ability to compare against comparable, measured values (for other systems) or HCI standards, is a difficult undertaking. It is analogous to

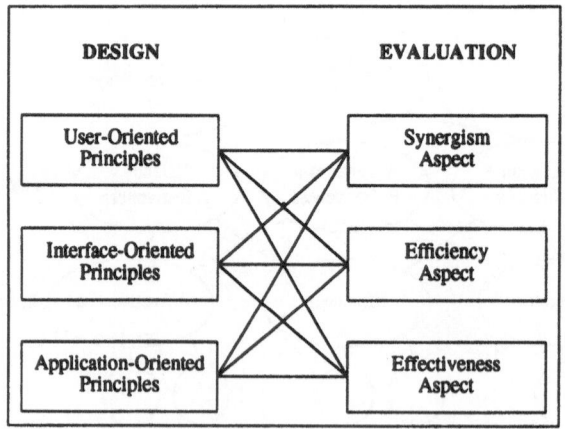

FIGURE 6.4. Design principles and evaluative aspects.

evaluating a teacher in a highly specialized subject field, without having any other such teacher to relate to or to use as a reference point. One may be able to come up with generic judgments, even supportive data, but it is difficult to assess how good they are without having a basepoint for comparison.

Whenever possible, it is desirable to carry out *relative* or *comparative* evaluation, in which specific performance measures and other indicators for selected features can be compared against similar data representing the same or other HCI objects. Such objects may actually be in existence, e.g., a system installed by a competitor. Alternatively, the object used for comparison can be an idealized performance composite. For example, if the management/design team has accumulated knowledge, from whatever sources, about desirable or minimally acceptable thresholds, and if they are able to prioritize among the measures and other indicators, then the results can be used meaningfully for relative evaluation purposes. This possibility is confirmed in Chapters 7 and 8.

Further, a comparison may simply involve determination of how changes in some factors (independent variables) that represent an object will cause changes in the response (dependent) variables representing another object. The question is, then, whether the change in response is significant enough to reach the conclusion that one treatment (e.g., a value, level, option in the interface) is better than another. Such comparative evaluation obviously relates to the experimental design method described in Chapter 3.

If relative evaluation is feasible, that fact can be reflected in the measures utilized and, subsequently, in the criteria employed to decide how well an interface object is doing or can do, relative to some other one, or to a variation of it. For example, in the above-cited study by Roberts and Moran (1983), relative evaluation was carried out on nine different text editors. Empirical measures used were task completion time, error-making and correcting time, and task learning time. Resulting values were then compared. Such time-based and other measures are defined in Chapters 5 and 7. Chapter 8 will further emphasize the importance of being able to compare evaluative results via different methods.

6.6. Matters of Semantics

It is recognized that the terminology developed in this chapter may seem excessive. At times, it may appear as though one term could adequately serve the purposes of two or more of the definitions given. In the literature, terms like *evaluation purpose*, *objective*, and *goal* are frequently interchanged; so are *approach*, *method*, and also *type*. Thus, the reader may feel that we are overdoing the definition business, by splitting semantic hairs.

Perhaps that is true. But the intention behind presenting the various definitions is primarily to articulate and clarify distinctions that are indeed considered meaningful and useful to evaluation methodology, *regardless of how they are labeled*. So, while the terminology chosen is not always consistent with its usage in the literature, the distinctions in meaning are important. They will hopefully serve to better delineate the constituents of HCI evaluation methodology on the whole.

Exercises

6.1. HCI design involves design "objects" and treats design goals as being equivalent to design principles. However, in this chapter, while analogously referring to evaluation "objects," we do not define an evaluation goal to be the equivalent of some kind of "evaluation principle." Instead, a broader kind of "evaluation purpose" and also "evaluation objective" are defined. Does this seem reasonable? Do you agree with the distinctions? Prepare a case for or against it. (Note: consider the fact that an evaluation is dependent on a design; on the other hand, is a design necessarily dependent on an evaluation?)

6.2. With reference to Exercise 6.1, is it possible to formulate some meaningful "evaluation principles"? If so, give examples, and consider whether these would relate to (a) how the evaluation should be conducted or (b) evaluative features of the design being evaluated? Are these two options accommodated by any other terms defined in this chapter? Explain.

6.3. Since "effectiveness" is assumed to be exclusive of synergistic quality, can a case also be made that "efficiency" should be exclusive of synergistic quantity? Present a well-reasoned position in either direction.

6.4. Consider Fig. 6.2. Is it possible and reasonable to interpret the test of a hypothesis in an experiment (mentioned in Chapter 3) as providing a criterion for evaluation? If so, how? Explain.

6.5. With reference to Fig. 6.4, give examples of how each of the (a) synergism, (b) efficiency, and (c) effectiveness aspects can relate to all three of the sets of U-, I-, and A-oriented design principles.

6.6. According to Fig. 2.1, the major HCI objects all can be represented, in part, by performance factors. What are the potential sources of such performance information? Is formal evaluation methodology required to obtain it? Or are other means available?

6.7. Compare "design scope" with "evaluation scope" (Definition 6.5). Are they mostly similar (or analogous), or are they different? Focus mainly on the difficulties in conducting selective design and evaluation, respectively, while keeping everything else (outside the authorized scope) constant.

6.8. Does the design side of HCI hold an analogy to the distinction between "absolute versus relative evaluation" (i.e., is there something like designing relative to something else or doing so in the absolute)? If so, what is it? If not, explain.

6.9. Consider the definitions of evaluation approach (Definition 6.14) and method (Definition 6.15). Does the distinction of treating the former as a set of methodological descriptors and the latter as a sequence (generally) of those same descriptors make sense? Can they both serve useful purposes? Make a case for or against this terminology.

TAILORED MEASURES OF PERFORMANCE

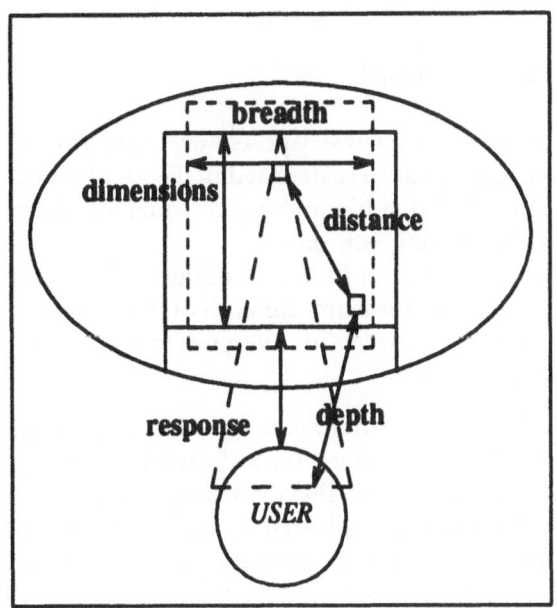

7.1. Overview

The repertoire of well-known measures described in Chapter 5 is useful. But it seems inadequate for serving other than relatively basic types of performance assessments. Hence, it is desirable to consider the construction of new and potentially more meaningful, multiaspect measures. This topic is motivated in two ways. First, in Section 7.2, we relate the basic measures to the nodes of the SEE aspects hierarchy presented in Chapter 6. Then, a proposed "interface acceptance test" is analyzed, in Section 7.3, using the terminology developed. It illustrates both what has already been done and the potential for extension to more complex types of tests.

In Section 7.4, the construction of new measures is outlined and exemplified. It shows how such measures can be specifically tailored to the purposes, objectives, and of course the objects of a particular evaluation study. It also confirms once again the importance of interface structures (Chapter 4) for providing the underlying patterns that are measurable.

The chapter concludes with consideration of other, more complex measures that are conceivable. The examples discussed remain rather abstract in definition and are subject to being formalized and validated. Chances are that such measures will be developed for application to HCI performance studies in the future.

7.2. SEE *Hierarchy Model*

The three major, evaluative aspects were defined in Chapter 6, and their various combinations were depicted in the SEE hierarchy of Fig. 6.3. We now want to utilize that hierarchy as a model for identifying existing measures and for creating new ones.

Relevant measures exist within each of the three SEE aspects. But, it is also possible to consider measures for each of the pairwise and three-way combinations of SEE aspects. With reference to Fig. 6.3, the levels can be interpreted to represent:

- *Level 1*: Basic, single-variable, or unidimensional quantities that are obtainable for each of the three SEE strata separately; these include the data values that are directly measured or otherwise collected.
- *Level 2*: Multivalue, multivariable, and multidimensional formulas or functions based on the quantities resulting from Level 1, again within each SEE category; these include basic summations, averages, products, etc., and also more complex formulas.
- *Level 3*: Pairwise combination, interrelation, or trade-off measures among the three SEE aspects; this is where lower-level measures from any subset of two evaluative aspects are combined.
- *Level 4*: Combination measures or formulas that provide summary information about all three SEE aspects collectively.

As already noted, we are especially interested in measures that are based on objective tests and physical measurements. They relate mostly to efficiency and, to a lesser extent, also to effectiveness, as evidenced by the well-known measures discussed in Chapter 5. For example, the measure of *system delay time* (M1) with regard to different types of user commands is based on the sequential (stimulus–response) structure of interaction language and belongs to the efficiency branch of the hierarchy. It is dependent on individual timings (Level 1), which are then averaged (Level 2). An analogous characterization applies to *task completion time* (M7) for a specified kind of task. It also belongs to the efficiency branch. It is partly dependent on the delay time measure but also reflects other factors, e.g., task complexity, language verbosity, and user think time (viewed in efficiency terms only).

The *number of errors* (M22) committed by the user *per unit time* (M25), on the other hand, may be a basic measure interpreted to be either in the efficiency branch (if one is concerned about the resulting delays in getting the task completed) or in the effectiveness branch (if at least some of the errors may be reflected in the task product and hence affect its quality). Again, the raw data collected at Level 1 are then combined in a formula at Level 2 of the SEE hierarchy.

For a different illustration of low-level effectiveness measures, consider the application of CAD&E. Suppose that the quality of a resulting design product is assessed largely by the *margin of safety* achieved, e.g., in temperature or pressure, for a particular system component. That is, let

H_d = the danger point (threshold) for a specified system component
H_a = the actual point achieved in the design analysis

The latter value clearly is a Level 1 data item. Depending on whether the difference between the two values is measured directly or calculated separately, it can be interpreted as either a Level 1 or Level 2 data item reflecting the quality of the design product:

$$Q_P = H_d - H_a$$

If this value is related to some minimally required or standard safety margin, the following "quality improvement factor" results, still at Level 2 of the effectiveness branch:

$$M_Q = (Q_P - Q_S)/Q_S$$

where we assume that all variables have positive values. The result could be positive or negative depending on how the measured value compares with the standard value. Notice that this example suggests that Level 2 can be split into different sublayers.

In some cases, however, the data may not result from objective measurements as such; they may instead be numeric indicators tallied from user responses via questionnaires, interviews, or even on-line stimulation and reaction (Treu, 1972). While such data are more subjective than may be desired for a particular evaluation, they do serve useful purposes and, especially in the synergism branch of the hierarchy, they may be the best data available. An exception to this involves the measurement of user stress, as discussed in Chapter 9.

To illustrate low-level measures in the synergism branch, suppose that each group of users is asked to rate whether a given interface (or interface feature) is preferable to another one. We assume that "preference" is defined to be based on some form of synergistic behavior experienced by the user. If a user prefers the interface/feature in question, possible ratings might range from 1 (somewhat preferred) to 5 (very much preferred). If the interfaces/features are deemed equivalent or if the alternative is preferable, ratings range from 0 (no difference) to -5. Each user thereby supplies the following:

$$p_i = \text{preference rating given by } i\text{th user}$$

which is a simple data item collected at Level 1. It, in turn, can be used in a Level 2 measure to encompass similar data from all users in the sample group:

$$M_P = \Sigma\ u_i/(n/100)$$

where each u_i is simply given the value 1 for all $p_i > 0$, and 0 for all $p_i \leq 0$. Measure M_P is the "percentage of n users preferring the interface/feature" being evaluated. If one wants to be more specific in gauging the strength of preference, the actual p_i data can be used in a collective formula (see Exercise 7.3).

7.2.1. Pairwise Combinations

The "quality improvement factor" discussed above motivates an illustration of how effectiveness and efficiency can be combined in a measure at Level 3. Indeed, such a measure may actually suggest a contrast or trade-off between the two aspects, rather than correlation and harmony. For example, measured data may show that an improvement in product quality, M_Q, can only be accomplished with greater expenditure of user time (M7) and, hence, cost (efficiency). As a result, there may be limits specified on how "good" the product *should* be, lest it become too expensive (in personnel costs, etc.). On the other hand, if it is determined through measurement and analysis that some other CAD&E interface system (or interface feature) enables the same users to achieve greater quality (M_Q) in less time (M7), then management and users have good reason for looking into the feasibility of switching to the other interface or interface feature.

In like manner, we can consider measures that combine either effectiveness or efficiency with synergism. Depending on how a user feels about the interface and its environment, both the quality and quantity of work are likely to be affected. A greater level of user satisfaction should lead to better and more work. Section 7.4 describes the construction of one such measure. However, the hypothesis does not necessarily hold. For example, a user who is happy with the performance of an attractive interface feature may thereby be distracted into doing things, including very creative things, which are not viewed as productive by management. Furthermore, user satisfaction may require more expensive hardware and software. Thus, there are intriguing trade-offs indicated for each pairing of evaluative aspects considered.

7.2.2. Three-Way Combination

The discussion above already implies that the measurement situation becomes increasingly complex as one moves to higher levels in the SEE hierarchy. After obtaining quantitative data about the three aspects individually, and then relating them in pairwise patterns at Level 3, the question is whether a composite portrait is possible, if it is deemed desirable.

This is not easy, especially for evaluators who feel that the quantitative orientation can be carried too far. That possibility is acknowledged here. However, if an evaluation team is able to select the most meaningful and high-priority measures, in a way that is not arbitrary and responds directly to the stipulations and guidelines set up by management, a composite result can be very useful in substantiating (explaining, comparing, contradicting, etc.) evaluative judgments rendered.

In general, for n measures and other indicators selected as meaningful, a vector quantity results:

$$V_M = (M_1, M_2, \ldots, M_n)$$

Each element (measure) is represented by a value. But this evaluative profile must somehow be made usable. Minimally one must be able to compare it against a similar profile obtained for another interface system. A measure analogous to the figure-of-merit of Section 5.4, or some variation thereof, can be applied.

As another and quite different approach, one can formulate a test that is simply based on a conjunction of selected, individual measures and relevant conditions. An example is analyzed next.

7.3. Acceptance Test Measure

Various low-level measures discussed in Chapter 5 have been used successfully by HCI evaluators for years. They continue to be useful. For example, such measures are quite adequate to accommodate the hypothetical interface acceptance test proposed by Shneiderman (1982) and endorsed by Draper and Norman (1985):

> . . .after 75 min of training, 40 typical users should be able to accomplish 80 percent of the benchmark tasks in 35 min with fewer than 12 errors.

It is instructive to analyze the requirements of this test with regard to the types of measures and SEE aspects defined earlier. In the order mentioned, let us consider the components:

- *Training time*
- Selected number of "typical" users
- *Percent completion of assigned work*
- Selected (number of) benchmark tasks
- *Task completion time*
- *Number of errors*

Notice that the "measures" are only those indicated in italics. Two of them involve simple measurements of time, consistent with Table 5.1. One of them can be interpreted as either an error count, according to Table 5.2, or an error rate, according to Table 5.3. Those three measures are clearly quantitative in nature and can be produced using objective means (e.g., under software control). This assumes that the type of error is unambiguous and hence requires no human judgment.

The third measure, namely the percent completion of the assigned task, could be determined either using objective or subjective means. That depends on how the percentage is arrived at. If it is based on counting the number of items produced (e.g., lines of programmed code), then a quantitative value can result. It would be consistent with the rates and ratios examples of Table 5.3. If that is not possible and evaluator judgment is required, then the result is really an estimate that is partly subjective.

Where do the four measures fit with regard to the SEE hierarchy? The two time-based measures belong to the efficiency branch; the errors count is most appropriate in reflecting the quality of the product, hence carrying effectiveness implications; the percent completion of assigned tasks also seems most concerned with efficiency, or "productivity." Notice that the test as it stands does not suggest that the synergism branch be incorporated somehow. It could be, as a variant of the test, as was indicated by Shneiderman (1982). For example, one can move to a higher node in the SEE hierarchy and take the user's level of satisfaction with the interface into account. This will be illustrated in the next section.

Several of the components in the acceptance test actually are oriented to methodological considerations, such as those presented in Chapter 8. For each measure, a specific threshold value is cited, thereby facilitating the evaluative decision-making. Someone must of course select and justify those thresholds.

In addition, the test implies that the evaluator must know how to (1) select the specified number (sample) of users, to be representative (as typical) of the target population of users, and (2) select an appropriate number (sample) of benchmark tasks, also to be representative of the tasks to be conducted in the target application domain. For both of these, the evaluator must have the selection criteria specified in accordance with knowledge of the users, the interface, and the application, on one hand, and knowledge of proper experimental design procedures (Chapter 3), on the other hand.

Most important to observe from the above-analyzed test is the fact that it is not very complicated. It utilizes only a small subset of the fairly basic measures that are known to us (Chapter 5). Of course, the more measures we add, the more difficult and demanding the evaluation task becomes. It can get even worse if we attempt to introduce more complex types of measures, as is done later in this chapter. Yet, with improved methodology and more documented experience in using it, the measures-based evaluation task should become easier.

7.4. Constructing New Measures

The measures discussed thus far are potentially useful, but they can be limiting in efforts to be really comprehensive as well as objective. We should be able to move toward answering far more interesting and complex questions about user–system interaction. Consider the relatively simple error rate, although recognizing that there exist many different types of errors. We need much more substantive analysis of the causes of errors. Maybe the errors occur because of fundamental design flaws, such as an inadequate mapping between the task objects as implemented behind the interface and those visible to the user. That would require a higher-level measure combining efficiency aspects with synergism considerations. Perhaps the error rate can be reduced and the quality of the task product improved by simplifying the measurable complexity of the interaction language. This suggests a multidimensional measure combining efficiency and effectiveness aspects.

Particularly useful measures could result on behalf of the inexperienced, learning users. Maybe the 20% of users who do not satisfy the acceptance test (previous section) simply do not have the background to handle what they might perceive, correctly or incorrectly, to be excessive complexity in the interface. There is a difference between real complexity and apparent complexity experienced at the interface. The same state-ment can be made about real and apparent simplicity. We need objective ways for dealing with these concepts. For example, if we can show that measurably reduced complexity (e.g., in terms of command components, task objects manipulated, etc.) enables a novice user to perform better (both in efficiency and effectiveness), over a period of time, the interface can be designed accordingly. This may mean that the user has to be led to believe that the system is (or appears to be) much simpler than it really is and than it will reveal itself to be, as he/she gains more experience and insight.

Other high-level measures could be oriented to gauge just how many levels of context (or help) should be provided to a learning user attempting to accomplish a certain task. With reference to the principles listed in Table 2.1, how can we determine whether an interface is truly "facilitative" and "unconstraining"? If improvements in performance (implying efficiency as well as effectiveness) could be measured in relation to giving the user more and more assistance on how to do things better or differently (implying synergism), results could be remarkable. Such multiaspect measures (in-volving all three SEE considerations) could be constructed in terms of

> the increase(s)/decrease(s) in selected performance measure(s) GIVEN a gradual/periodic change in the amount of context/help provided adaptively by the system.

This complementary or conditional format, giving credit to the respective contributions made by the user and the interface system, should become increasingly prominent in interface evaluation.

With such motivation in mind, let us try to formulate measures, or mathematical expressions, so that their values will be representative of selected SEE aspects. Assuming that all important methodological consid-erations for evaluation (as outlined in the next chapter) are well under-stood, the following procedure can be used:

1. Purpose: express the overall purpose of the particular measure to be constructed, i.e., what it is intended to measure. The purpose may be to determine whether a characteristic inherent to a spe-cified design goal (e.g., from Table 2.1) has been satisfied.
2. Category: relate the intended purpose to the appropriate level and branch of the hierarchy of SEE aspects (Fig. 6.3). That will give focus as well as guidance on whether other pertinent measures already exist or may be constructible.
3. Structure(s): identify the pertinent interface part(s) and any rele-vant interface structure(s) (Chapter 4) that may supply the base(s) on which the measure can be built.

4. Formula: construct the formula representing the measure.
5. Testing: as appropriate and possible, using validation and experimental design procedures.
6. Iteration: repeat the above steps as necessary.
7. Name: if result is successful, assign a descriptive name to the measure and include it in the categorized repertoire of measures from which the evaluator can select.

Application of descriptive statistical measures (e.g., mean, standard deviation, variance) is an important part of the measure design process. The evaluator must be knowledgeable in such statistics.

The above procedure is illustrated on a well-known measure as follows:

Example A

1. Purpose: to determine how quickly a system responds to user commands.
2. Category: since the purpose seems mostly oriented to a quantitative consideration, namely measurement of time intervals, the major SEE aspect involved is *efficiency*. It is a basic, unidimensional measure. It is not to be confused either with "responsiveness" (which can also involve synergism) or with time measurements implying quality, e.g., in real-time process control.
3. Structure: this measure must be hinged on the sequential order in interaction language (L-structure), specifically in terms of alternating stimulus–response "objects" (O-structure) between user and system.
4. Formula:

$$R_{ave} = \Sigma \, (t_{arr,i} - t_{dep,i})/n$$

where the differences between "time of departure of the last character in the command from the user to the system" and "time of arrival of the first meaningful character in the system's response" are summed and averaged over n responses. Thus, this is a Level 2 measure.
5. Test: to be applied under various conditions and for different types of applications and users.
6. Iteration: including identification of useful statistical measures applied to the results obtained.
7. Name: average response time, or average system delay time.

This is recognized to be Measure M1 in Table 5.1. Notice that the purpose of a measure may be to determine directly whether a design principle (e.g., P36) is met. In that case, it is closely linked to the evaluation purpose (Definition 6.3). However, in general, the purpose of a measure should not be viewed as synonymous with evaluation purpose or with evaluation objective. The former should be supportive of the latter two.

The measure of Example A reflects only what a single user experiences. Similar results for m users can be averaged, producing a somewhat higher-level but still Level 2 measure for a user group. We can do likewise for the other time-based measures cited in Section 5.3. Included are the multicomponent efficiency formulas, such as those that distinguish different time factors and compare response time and user think time with total elapsed time in completing an interactive session (or product).

Example low-level constructions similar to the above can also be outlined for the effectiveness and synergism branches of the SEE hierarchy. However, interface structures (as defined in Chapter 4) may not be applicable to them. In such cases, the "measures" must be based on other factors.

The assessment of quality in the "product" resulting from computer use should include, when possible, measurable or demonstrable characteristics that are inherent to (or at least representative of) the product. One example was cited in Section 7.2 relating to improvements in safety margins. Another example is the measurement of the "goodness" of an interactively generated simulation program, such as in terms of how accurate and valid it is in representing the modeled system. In that case, one can explicitly compare the data resulting from the simulation model with those of the simulated system, if the latter system exists. Note that we are talking here about the use of simulation as an application area, not as a method for evaluation.

At other times, quality is less tangible, based on the perceptions of persons who are knowledgeable and can render judgments. As a result, it may be desirable in such cases to tally human evaluators' *rankings of product quality* and to utilize these indicators as part of the evaluation process.

A similar characterization applies to the design of synergism measures. Regardless of user faults or limitations, one basic synergism indicator is a *user satisfaction rating*. On the other hand, if we argue on behalf of the interface system (or the HCI designer), we might observe that the error-prone user may not be following even simple instructions and therefore may deserve a low *user qualification rating*. Relating the latter rating to the satisfaction rating can reveal some interesting explanations of the degree of synergism attained between user and system.

Beyond such relatively fundamental distinctions, it is possible to deal with synergism in conjunction with efficiency and effectiveness at a higher level of the SEE hierarchy and in a more objective manner. This is illustrated by the following example.

Example B

1. Purpose: to determine how efficient the users of a target application are or can be, depending on how satisfied they are with the interface and its facilities.
2. Category: since this concerns efficiency, we must be able to obtain a quantitative input, such as the number of transactions, pages, reports, models, etc., that are produced per user per time period. However, this is also to be related to the synergism factor of user satisfaction. Consequently, the third level of the SEE hierarchy becomes relevant in combining *efficiency* with *synergism*.
3. Structure: the underlying structure is related primarily to the efficiency aspect. It involves order in the language (or product representation), as it is created and output, along the real time line and with identifiable boundaries or separations to enable counting. In addition, it can be viewed as a scenario or cluster of associated objects constituting the products. So, both L- and O-structures can apply. Structure related to the user satisfaction component may not be explicitly identifiable. More in-depth analysis could lead to determination that the user's (dis)satisfaction is based on the degree of correspondence (O-structure) between mental expectations and what the system actually provides.
4. Formula:

$$P_{comp,t} = (\Sigma\, U_{s,i}/m)/(\Sigma\, U_{u,j}/n)$$

which is a ratio between the average number of entities produced by the m users with satisfaction levels exceeding threshold t and the same kind of average for the n users with satisfaction level equal to or less than the threshold t.
5. Test as appropriate.
6. Iterate as necessary.
7. Name: comparative satisfaction-based productivity.

This productivity measure is designed to involve a combination of efficiency and synergism aspects, at Level 3 of Fig. 6.3. It could be extended to also reflect effectiveness, thereby converting it to a Level 4 measure. For example, if it is possible to assess levels of product quality (such as accuracy, reliability, attractiveness), the measure could utilize numbers of high-, medium-, and low-quality results produced by satisfied and unsatisfied users, respectively. This could mean factoring the comparative productivity formula into components, each representing a distinct product quality level with a suitable weighting (multiplier value) built in.

7.5. More Complex Measures

The illustrated measures of response time (Example A) and productivity (Example B) are relatively straightforward in their design. When trying to address the more subtle and complicated performance features, the task becomes much more difficult.

Indicative is the following discussion, in outline form, of "interface power" versus "ease of learning and use" (ELU) trade-off. Draper and Norman (1985) defined interface power to be the achievement of speed and convenience of use for the practiced user, analogous to program speed. ELU, especially for the novice user, is analogous to program space. Their argument was that if interface power is optimized, the level of skill required of users will be too high to make its use practical. On the other hand, if ELU is optimized, the interface may be "too laborious for a regular user to employ productively."

Let us give the above trade-off a related but different interpretation. Suppose we assume that the total available interface power (in terms of the usual speed, capacity, etc.) remains constant. But we subsume under the power definition the interface's ability to acquire knowledge about the user and to employ it in providing support, especially for the learning user. This view is portrayed in a general way by Fig. 7.1. For the novice user, most of the system power is dedicated to helping him/her during the learning process. After the user is more experienced, such help becomes largely unnecessary and hence may be minimal. As a result, most of the available interface power can now be expended to achieve genuine speed.

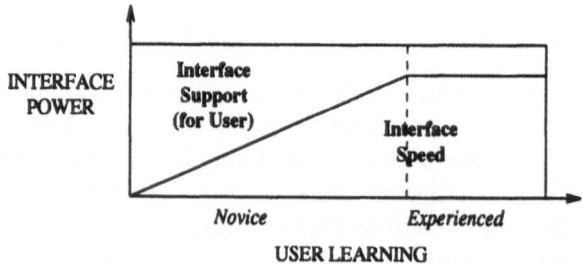

FIGURE 7.1. Interface power to support learning.

With this revised definition of interface power, we can hypothesize the design of measures that address only the learnability and usability support provided. These are mainly to benefit the learning user who does not as yet care about pure speed and efficiency. For a particular task to be carried out by such a user, a fundamental question concerns the level of complexity or simplicity of that task, as it is experienced by and as it affects that user. This leads to a distinction between the following two measures:

1. **Real complexity** (RC) of the task: Based on
   - Actual internal implementation
   - Software and algorithms used
   - Information storage, structure, location, distribution
   - Locality, distributedness, parallelism in execution
   - Input and output requirements
   - Confirmation (of the above) at the visible interface

2. **Apparent complexity** (AC) of the task: That part or subset of the RC that is actually revealed to and required of (or to be understood by) the user. Note that this could conceivably be greater than RC, if the interface is so poorly designed that it seems more complex than it really is. But we are ignoring that possibility in what follows.

Distinctions between what is perceived as real rather than apparent (or unreal or virtual) are drawn in Chapter 11, with regard to the extent to which a user becomes involved in (understanding, participating in) the interaction, depending on interaction style.

If we focus only on that component of interface power, which is the contribution by the interface to making the task-specific interaction "appear" (to the user) to be less complex than it really is, while at the same time encouraging the user to learn more, we can consider it to be some function F of variables RC and AC:

$$P_{support} = F(RC, AC)$$

For discussion purposes, this part of interface power may be viewed as simply the difference between RC and AC. However, that is undoubtedly an oversimplification, as implied below.

It seems possible to compose measure(s) of task complexity using combinations of the structural entities (Chapter 4) and SEE aspects. Following are some of the lower-level measures (or variables) on which both RC and AC may be dependent:

1. **Facultative correspondence** (FC): the mapping of task representation and actions, as implemented behind the interface, into the user-visible interface and user-expressible language constructs in a

manner conducive (or close) to the expectations of the user's mental model and to what the user wants to accomplish.
- Relevant Structural Pattern(s): L, O, A
- Relevant SEE Aspect(s): Synergism, Efficiency

2. **Depth penetration** or **distributedness probing** (DP): orderly transitioning between or among levels of detail, within an interaction state, from one such state to another, and through the surrounding (distributed) environmental regions.
   - Structural Pattern(s): L, V, C, H
   - SEE Aspect(s): Synergism, Effectiveness

3. **Supportive context** (SC): providing specific forms (or layers) of help to the user, for both task-specific and task-peripheral purposes.
   - Structural Pattern(s): C, A
   - SEE Aspect(s): Synergism, Efficiency, Effectiveness

4. **System adaptiveness** (SA): compensating for the user's current state of learning, knowledge, experience, interest, capability.
   - Structural Pattern(s): L, O, A, V, C, H
   - SEE Aspect(s): Synergism, Efficiency, Effectiveness

To deliver either the AC or RC type of interaction to the user in a task-specific manner, all four of the above-indicated measures are potentially applicable. That is,

$$RC = f(FC, DP, SC, SA)$$

and

$$AC = g(FC, DP, SC, SA)$$

The precise definitions of functions like f and g, as well as the measures on which they are dependent, are obviously subject to much research and experimentation. They are only indicated in hypothetical terms at this stage. It is hoped that the reader will get ideas on different possibilities and pursue them. Some relevant measures have been reported in the literature. For example, Kieras and Polson's (1985) mapping of device and task representations, Hutchins and colleagues' (1986) definitions of "semantic distance" and "articulatory distance" in interface language, and Woods's (1984) measure of "visual momentum," may play roles in the FC dimension of task complexity (either RC or AC).

The substance (although not form) of the four component measures is addressed in other chapters: FC in Chapter 10 and DP in Chapter 11 of this book; SC and SA, from design standpoints, in Chapters 12 and 13 of the companion book.

7.6. Other Prospects

It is interesting to peruse the literature while concentrating on the many different, desirable characteristics that have been attributed to or advocated for HCI. Some of them have come wrapped in so-called design guidelines, others within specified design principles or goals. A number of them are reflected among the user-oriented design principles listed in Table 2.1. But that list is far from complete. Further, those principles are not homogeneous as such, except in the sense that they all are to be oriented to representing and benefiting the user and his/her needs. In terms of their definitions and levels of applicability they are rather diverse.

The question about them to be asked in this chapter is whether each of those principles, as well as others not listed in Table 2.1, does or can correspond to measures, metrics, or statistical formulas that represent the intended, desirable characteristic in a meaningful manner. With regard to the evaluative aspects (SEE), we already observed that all three have the potential of being relevant to the user-oriented principles collectively. Individually, the principles may best relate to only one or two, rather than all three, of the evaluative aspects. Implied in this discussion is the need to analyze each principle toward providing HCI evaluators with the means for assessing whether the principle has been satisfied. In this case, the means is interpreted to be one or more suitable measure(s).

A subset of the principles in Table 2.1 has been operative relatively often, judging from the types of measures that have been utilized in various performance studies. This will be seen in the outline of evaluation studies presented in Chapter 8. Included have been: accuracy (P2), facilitation (P20), response time (P36), and usability (P44). The following partial portraits illustrate the types of measures employed:

- *Accuracy*: number of errors of different types that are committed (by user or system objects); such counts and rates were defined in Chapter 5.
- *Facilitation*: making things easier is often measured by various types of time-based measures, e.g., task completion time (Chapter 5) and how these may be improved by selected design features (independent variables, treatments); improved accuracy (above) can also pertain.
- *Response time*: this is a fundamental measure (Chapter 5) that focuses on the system's response in time, via the interface; it can also have a bearing on facilitation (above).
- *Usability*: depending on how this is defined, it can encompass the above-indicated measures plus a variety of others.

Usability, as pointed out in Chapter 8 and also in the companion book, has been addressed extensively. We give it a more narrow definition than many HCI investigators. The dictionary uses words like "fit, convenient, or available for use" to convey the meaning of "usable." "Fit" can relate to "adaptable" (P3) and/or "adaptive" (P4), and thereby also to being "compatible" (P9); it can also refer to being "suitable" (relating to P11 in Table 2.1). But, even if usability subsumes those several principles, it can be argued that quite a number of other principles are not yet covered.

Several of the principles listed in Table 2.1, namely P4, P13, and P20, are somehow incorporated among the more complex measures hypothesized in the previous section. A couple of the measures (FC and DP), however, contain elements that are not (explicitly) represented by principles in the table. For example, user cognitive "mobility" and "momentum," within the available network of interactive states and levels, are not listed. However, principles like P6, P14, P29, and others, in combination, can be used to justify such measures.

Many of the principles listed in Table 2.1 are rarely, if ever, considered in evaluation studies. Others were purposely excluded from the table, even though they are frequently mentioned. Three examples are:

- *User-centered*: this seems to be the equivalent of being user-oriented, which is a very general, although meaningful goal to strive for; nevertheless, it seems to require considerable refinement (into lower-level goals) before it becomes a realistically attainable principle.
- *User-friendly*: this is a catchword that is attractive especially for purposes of writing computer sales brochures; but, to enable its assessment within HCI performance studies, it must be precisely defined and delimited, or replaced by other principles; in that sense, it is similar to "user-centered."
- *Satisfactory*, or satisfying: this is certainly a very important goal; but it is also very broad and complex; nevertheless, a stab at defining, dissecting, and measuring it is made later, in Chapter 9; it is based on the hypothesis that if you can measure user stress, you should be able to deduce something about user satisfaction.

The above-indicated prospects for additional principles and corresponding measures are not close to exhausting the possibilities. Consider just the following additional examples extracted from the literature:

- *Natural*: as in the interaction between user and computer; this notion was suggested by Foley and Wallace (1974), among others; what does "natural" really mean, when relating a human information processor to a computer-based information processor? Does it imply a "conversational" style of interaction, the pros and cons of which were considered by Nickerson (1977)? What other principles might it be based on? Can it be measured in some way? It could conceivably require measures relating to all three SEE aspects.

- *Graceful*: also with regard to human interaction with the computer; the term was used by Hayes and Reddy (1983); what does it mean and imply? Is it also associated with "natural" interaction? Can it be represented in some identifiable or measurable way? By definition, it can be linked with Principles P5 and perhaps also P18 and others; any measures would probably relate to the synergism and/or effectiveness aspects only, unless gracefulness at times also requires efficient activity.

- *Sociable*: this was suggested in the context of user-oriented design by Taulbee *et al.* (1975); unlike most other principles discussed thus far, it reaches beyond the single-user model to the increasingly important networks of users that are, in a sense, superimposed on networks of computer resources; how should we address this multiuser situation, involving applications like electronic mail and conferencing, as well as various types of computer-supported cooperative work (CSCW)? One principle that is applicable, in part, is P29; but there is much more to be captured, through suitable measures, if truly meaningful evaluation is to take place.

- *Accountable*: not merely in the sense of accounting for use of resources and then having to pay for the resulting bills; instead, as also suggested by Taulbee *et al.* (1975), it should also encompass management responsibilities for providing "the features and capabilities" that permit the user's determination of explanations of problems (experienced or anticipated) with accessing, using, etc., the computer resources, this can include the notion of responsiveness from management, not necessarily in person but also via other means, including software-supported knowledge and communication; while one's initial reaction might be that the efficiency aspect would be most appropriate in guiding the design of suitable measures, the other two aspects might also be applicable.

The prospects of creating additional measures, appropriately tied to the above-indicated and other principles of design, are very intriguing. The reader is urged to consider this area as being potentially very fruitful. The fact that our choice of measures has been very limited, as confirmed by the studies reviewed in Chapter 8, should give additional motivation.

Exercises

7.1. Consider splitting Level 2 of the SEE hierarchy into sublayers. On what basis could they be distinguished? Define a descriptive model.

7.2. With regard to Exercise 7.1, does it also make sense to define sublayers for the other three levels of the SEE hierarchy? If so, how would you do it? If not, why not?

7.3. M_p in Section 7.3 gives a simplified "percentage of users preferring an interface" without taking the actual preference ratings, or strengths of preference into account. Construct a revised version of that measure that does incorporate the different numeric ratings.

7.4. Assuming that the acceptance test discussed in Section 7.3 only reflects efficiency and effectiveness considerations, how could one or more synergism considerations be added to it? Would that addition make the test better in some way? Explain.

7.5. Is it possible to express the acceptance test statement (Section 7.3) as some kind of a summary or figure-of-merit formula? If so, do so, If not, why not?

7.6. Are interface structures (Chapter 4) only applicable to efficiency types of measures? Or can they also be used for certain kinds of effectiveness and synergism assessments? Explain and illustrate.

7.7. Use the measure construction procedure outlined in Section 7.4 to create an efficiency-oriented measure of "comparative task completion rate," based on M10, M18, and M24.

7.8. Repeat Exercise 7.7 for an effectiveness-oriented measure, to determine how aesthetically appealing and correct (according to some documented specifications) the layout of the front page is (e.g., of a newspaper), resulting from a document processing system application. Make your own assumptions on layout specifications. Comment on the feasibility of producing such a measure.

7.9. Repeat Exercise 7.7 for a synergism-oriented measure, to determine the rate at which users of System A switch to a newly provided alternative System B, because they have discovered that its interface is better for meeting their needs.

7.10. Convert the comparative satisfaction-based productivity measure (Example B) in the text to a Level 4 measure that also incorporates some effectiveness consideration(s).

7.11. People talk about the "gap" or "gulf" between the human user and the computer at the interface. Which of the four hypothesized types of measures (FC, DP, SC, and SA) seems most appropriate for assessing how wide/narrow that gap is? Do you consider some subset of the four measures to be necessary for that assessment? Can you hypothesize other high-level measures that should be added to that set?

7.12. With respect to Exercise 7.11, read Hutchins *et al.* (1986) to determine their definitions of semantic and articulatory distances. Are these encompassed by the four hypothesized measures (FC, DP, SC, and SA)? Or do they suggest another type of measure? Explain.

7.13. Consider and compare the four major categories of measures characterized in this chapter and Chapter 5:

a. Well-known measures (Section 5.3)
b. Figure-of-merit and other composites (Sections 5.4 and 7.3)
c. Newly constructed measures (Sections 7.2 and 7.4)
d. Hypothesized, more complex measures (Sections 7.5 and 7.6)

Give a well-reasoned ranking of those categories, with regard to how realistic, useful, and credible they might be, both now and in the future, in any measurement-oriented evaluation of HCI.

7.14. Categorize all of the principles listed in Table 2.1 with regard to whether (a) the principles are frequently pursued, and suitable measures are easily available, (b) suitable measures are available, but the principles they represent seem to be rarely applied, (c) suitable measures are conceivable but likely to be difficult if not impossible to create and/or use.

7.15. Repeat Exercise 7.14 for the principles mentioned in Sections 7.5 and 7.6 but not included in Table 2.1.

7.16. Analyze the meaning of "graceful" HCI and attempt to design one or more measures for it.

7.17. Repeat Exercise 7.16 for "sociable" HCI.

EVALUATION APPROACHES AND METHODS

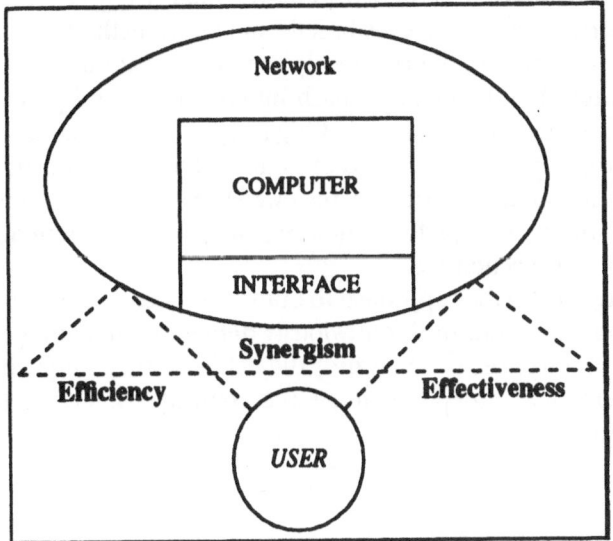

8.1. Overview

While characterizing the background of HCI evaluation in Chapter 1, summarizing HCI design methodology in Chapter 2, and describing other prerequisite knowledge areas in the chapters of Part II, we have built up a backdrop for the purpose of this chapter: to present the approaches and methods for evaluating the products of HCI design. Use of relevant terminology was scattered throughout earlier chapters and then pulled together and defined in Chapter 6.

Evaluating the efficiency of an algorithm (implemented by computer program) is normally comparatively easy, although even that can become rather difficult. However, evaluating all or part of a human–computer interface can be orders of magnitude more complex, depending on how it is done. Accordingly, and as suggested in a number of places in this book, the task of developing HCI evaluation methodology is quite a challenge. Indeed, its further development and refinement will remain a challenge for years to come, as will be evident to the reader after studying this chapter (and the rest of this book).

In Section 8.2, several distinctions pertaining to evaluation approach are pointed out. Methods that illustrate what is being done currently are described in Section 8.3. Then, the methods are distinguished, in Section 8.4, with regard to two major, alternative categories. Emphasis is on the fundamental importance of measures to any method for evaluation, especially methods that are designed to be reasonably objective.

In Section 8.5, a measures-based evaluation method is outlined and discussed. It draws on the previously presented materials and integrates the attributes of evaluation approach into one high-level procedure. Section 8.6 discusses how the data resulting from use of the evaluation method must be properly interpreted and presented. Then, a profile of evaluation studies is presented and critically reviewed in Section 8.7. It is followed by a figure-of-merit example for combining and presenting evaluative results. This is done in Section 8.8.

Finally, one further approach to evaluation is characterized in Section 8.9. It takes the results of the previously defined evaluation methods into account for purposes of analyzing the "effects" they might have on an organization that is dependent on the computer interface technology being evaluated.

8.2. Distinctions in Approach

In HCI evaluation, unlike design, the alternative high-level orientations are not characterized in terms of whether they are top-down, bottom-up, or adhere to some other such orientation. It makes more sense to portray an evaluation approach with regard to distinctions such as the following:

1. The *comprehensiveness or selectivity* of the evaluation; this relates to the evaluation scope (Definition 6.5) and to the extent to which the results are representative of the entire system or only part of it.
2. The *evaluative aspects* to be emphasized and pursued; these relate to the SEE model (Definitions 6.8 through 6.10) and the corresponding types of measures of evaluation (Definition 6.11) utilized.
3. The *objective and/or subjective nature* of evaluative data used; this relates to reliance on factual data (measured, monitored, or ob-

served) and/or opinions (judgments) from/about various data sources.

4. The *formal* or *informal* types of evaluation techniques and tools employed; this relates to how the evaluation is conducted; it indicates whether evaluative data are to be obtained and analyzed with adherence to strict procedural (experimental) rules, or through relatively unstructured discovery or probing (e.g., using heuristics), or in comparison with established guidelines or models, or in other ways, including hybrid combinations.

The first two distinctions delimit "how much" of the interface is to be evaluated and "with regard to what" that evaluation is to be carried out. The third distinction indicates whether the evaluator is expected to utilize data that are physically measurable (e.g., response time) and/or identifiable (e.g., error rate) or data that are subjective "indicators" of performance, such as those based on user, observer, and other expert opinions. The fourth distinction in approach suggests that, regardless of the choices made with respect to the other three distinctions, an approach is contingent on whether/how a study is formally organized and conducted. It thereby suggests specific methods and means to be utilized in obtaining the results and for analyzing them to reach evaluative conclusions.

The above-indicated distinctions and others can be used singly or in combination as attributes of the "approach" to evaluation. This was already portrayed by Fig. 6.1. Thus, for instance, one can consider using an approach that (1) is selective, (2) emphasizes specified evaluative aspect(s), (3) depends on subjective data, and (4) utilizes a formal experimental design for conducting the study.

One further term is noteworthy: a *structured* approach. It is part of the title of this book. An evaluation approach that is structured suggests any one or more of the following:

- The relevant material is *presented* in an organized and logical pattern.
- The methodology (including evaluation objects, purpose, objectives, methods, techniques, tools) that instantiates the approach is *defined* in a meaningful and logical pattern.
- One or more specific method(s) is(are) included in the methodology, to enable the evaluator to *carry out* the evaluation in a logical pattern.

The words "logical pattern" are common to all three attributes of a structured approach. But the pattern must also be coherent, meaningful, and usable.

Finally, we should recognize here, as was mentioned in Chapter 2 in reviewing the design phase, that any management-imposed constraints on an evaluation may have significant bearing on the thoroughness with which it is conducted and on the credibility of what comes out of the study. Further, the evaluator or the evaluation team must be appropriately qualified if the HCI evaluation is to be carried out successfully. Thus, either managers or evaluators can significantly detract from or enhance an evaluation, regardless of what approach is selected for use.

8.3. Methods in Use

Within an evaluation "approach," or in correspondence to it, one or more "methods" are required to carry out the evaluation as intended. That is, given some subset of the distinctions outlined in the previous section, the evaluator must select the method(s) that are suitable. Actually, as mentioned in Section 6.6, the two terms can easily become confused and at times may seem synonymous. The same is true of "method" and "technique." Indeed, we use these interchangeably in a number of places in this text. The reason is mainly to be consistent with word usage in published papers and books. The reader will observe this from the following discussion and from the literature that is cited. Most important is to learn to distinguish the meanings behind different terms, even though the terms may be used inconsistently.

A brief portrait of earlier evaluation methods and a discussion of the relative lack of attention to HCI evaluation were given in Chapter 1. HCI designers frequently did not want to conduct evaluations or were not required to do so. But, in more recent years, with the HCI field maturing, that attitude has changed substantially. Formal test procedures for user interfaces are being advocated (e.g., Draper and Norman, 1985). Largely motivated by decisions that have to be made in real-world environments, e.g., about what type of computer interface to acquire and/or to design, interest in evaluation has increased significantly.

8.3.1. Usability Evaluation Methods

Among the evaluation methods that have been defined and tested are those that specifically address the "usability" of interfaces. This emphasis is consistent with the sizable literature on usability that has been developed since the mid-1980s, starting with efforts by investigators like Spence (1985), Lindquist (1985), Gould and Lewis (1985), Bennett (1986), and

Whiteside *et al.* (1988). One categorization of applicable methods is the following (Jeffries *et al.*, 1991):

1. *Heuristic evaluation*: using HCI experts who, based on personal knowledge and experience, can carry out in-depth analyses of interface designs, to isolate those features that may cause problems in usability (e.g., Nielsen and Molich, 1990; Nielsen, 1992); it should include written heuristics to guide the evaluators.

2. *Comparison against guidelines*: using published design guidelines (e.g., Shneiderman, 1992; Brown, 1988), which indicate various features that should be exhibited by an interface, and determining how many of the guidelines are satisfied.

3. *Cognitive walk-throughs*: using the interface developers to "walk through" the interface in a model-specific, task-oriented manner (e.g., Lewis *et al.*, 1990; Wharton *et al.*, 1992); given an understanding of the target user's goals and knowledge, the evaluators compare these against the interface's behavior; discrepancies between what the interface actually does and what the user would expect are recorded.

4. *Usability testing*: using empirical tests (e.g., Karat *et al.*, 1992), appropriately controlled and reflecting real-world situations, to gather and analyze data pertaining to successes and failures in interface usability.

Actually, the above list of four methods is an oversimplification of the current state of usability evaluation. A number of different versions exist for several of the methods. On the other hand, some of the above may be categorized together. For example, the first three, according to Karat *et al.* (1992), all belong to "usability walk-through methods," or pluralistic walk-throughs, along with such methods as *think-aloud evaluations* and *scenario-based reviews*. Nielsen (1992) calls this entire category "usability inspection methods," also including methods like *claims analysis* (Carroll *et al.*, 1991). They all depend on the skills and judgments of some group of evaluators.

An alternative characterization of current usability evaluation methods is to distinguish (1) heuristic techniques, (2) user testing, either in laboratory-based, empirical setups or in operational situations, and (3) formal analyses with respect to some accepted interface specifications or model. Nielsen and Phillips (1993) utilized these distinctions in a recent comparison of the usability of two interfaces. They designed five different studies (three heuristic versions, one GOMS analysis, and one user testing) and then utilized four task-by-interface combinations. Data on mean time estimates provided the basis for comparison of the methods.

Different methods are being tested and their pros and cons are being presented and debated. Jeffries *et al.* (1991) point out that heuristic evaluation and usability testing have drawbacks, including: (1) HCI experts who can conduct them are scarce, (2) they are difficult to use until after design is finished, (3) technical and organizational gaps can occur between HCI experts and interface developers, and (4) empirical testing is expensive and time-consuming. The other two methods, using guidelines and cognitive walk-throughs, are intended to alleviate these problems.

After comparing the four alternatives, Jeffries *et al.* (1991) generally concluded: heuristic evaluation (as they actually carried it out) produced the best results, finding the most and the most serious problems; comparison against guidelines was best in finding recurring and general problems; the cognitive walk-through was "roughly comparable in performance to guidelines"; and usability testing was second only to heuristic testing, in finding serious problems, and it was very good in finding recurring and general problems. Usability testing generally ended up as rated second best.

What do other investigators say about the methods and, specifically, about the above-indicated results obtained by comparing the methods? Karat *et al.* (1992) pose probing questions about walk-through techniques, including: (1) Which is more effective: an individual evaluator or a team of evaluators? (2) Which are more effective in evaluating an interface: interface developers (and representative end users) or HCI specialists? (3) Should the evaluation be carried out with respect to prescribed tasks or allow for individually directed exploration? (4) Exactly what is the role of usability heuristics and guidelines for experienced interface developers who evaluate an interface?

Notice how these questions all deal with methodological considerations and factors pertaining to the use of evaluators who are called on to render judgments. Karat *et al.* (1992) deal with the questions extensively. Their conclusions, after comparing empirical testing with walk-throughs, are: empirical usability testing identified the largest number of problems in the interface, including a significant number of serious problems missed by the walk-through methods. Nielsen and Phillips (1993), in their study on estimating relative usability, found that empirical user testing was relatively more expensive but provided better performance estimates.

A further sampling of the current HCI evaluation literature includes: use of a cognitive *jog-through* (Rowley and Rhoades, 1992), a fast-paced version of the walk-through; the conclusion that design guidelines are extremely variable in content and dependency on them should be minimized (Tetzlaff and Schwartz, 1991); and usability problems and solutions can be identified by analyzing the detailed transcripts of user sessions to detect repeated patterns in user actions (Siachi and Hix, 1991). The latter can then lead to designer focus on the patterns that are important to users and that should be accommodated with improved features.

Interestingly, Nielsen and Landauer (1993) have reported on a mathematical model for the detection of usability problems "as a function of number of users tested or heuristic evaluators employed." The model (a Poisson process) is suggested as useful for deciding how much evaluation may be enough. In other words, given the expense of conducting evaluations, such a model could be used to determine the point of diminishing returns, at which one might as well not evaluate any further.

The methods in use that we have characterized thus far are almost exclusively oriented to the evaluation of "usability." That term has been variously defined. Sweeney *et al.* (1993) consider it to be "an emergent quality of an optimum design, which is reflected in the effective and satisfying use of" a human–computer interface. They proceed to present a framework for usability evaluation, in terms of the following dimensions: (1) approach to evaluation (defined as dependent on the source of evaluative data), (2) type of evaluation (diagnostic, summative, and certification), and (3) time of evaluation in the product's life cycle. The approaches that are distinguished are user-based, theory-based, and expert-based. This is a useful article, although its terminology is not always consistent with ours (Exercise 8.17).

8.3.2. Empirical and Other Methods

The goal of evaluating usability is unquestionably important. It must be remembered, however, that the purpose of this book (and its companion book) is to develop comprehensive methodology that can be oriented to any subset of the major HCI objects and features, based on any selection of design principles (goals) and evaluative aspects deemed significant. Thus, for example, usability is only one design principle (P44, Table 2.1), albeit a very significant and dominant one. Depending on how it is interpreted (e.g., see Guillemette, 1991), it can indeed represent the synthesis of several principles and evaluative aspects. This also is confirmed by Sweeney and colleagues' (1993) definition quoted earlier. Nevertheless, evaluating usability is not viewed in our methodology as the equivalent of total HCI evaluation.

Further, it is important for the reader to observe that the usability evaluation methods that are currently being used are largely oriented to the identification, classification, and rating of *problems* existing in the interface. Methods are compared with respect to which one succeeds in detecting more of the (more important) problems. Interfaces are, then, compared with regard to how many and what types of problems they are found to exhibit. From this standpoint, the methods can generally be categorized as representing the diagnostic type of evaluation (Section 6.2.2).

But what about the other types? They have also gained attention in the HCI community, as already implied by the empirical testing and formal analysis methods mentioned among usability studies. Many reported studies have been variously descriptive, explanatory, and predictive in nature, or some combination of these types (Section 6.2.2). The method involving formal comparison against some accepted, guideline model, such as Card and colleagues' (1983) GOMS model, has been employed by some investigators (e.g., Nielsen and Phillips, 1993; Gray *et al.*, 1992; John and Vera, 1992). The use of analytical models has thus far been shown to be effective for evaluating existing interface designs. However, according to Gugerty (1993), their effectiveness in predicting performance of new interfaces remains to be demonstrated.

Especially prevalent have been experimental studies that compared different interaction techniques and styles (i.e., design features) relative to selected performance variables used to represent sample users. A number of such studies are cited in the context of HCI design methodology (Treu, 1994, Chapter 6), while presenting the design features that are available for consideration by designers. Following are illustrative studies that involve *comparisons* of interaction techniques and/or styles. In each case, selected methodological details are indicated briefly, hopefully enough to give the reader some idea on what it is about and whether it should be pursued further.

- *Form-based versus language-based interaction* (Jeffries and Rosenberg, 1987): an experiment to examine whether a forms interface is more effective than a language-based interface, for either programmers or nonprogrammers, for a selection of 16 mail-filtering tasks (half of them logically simple, and half logically complex); employed a $2 \times 2 \times 8$ repeated measures analysis of variance; the measure was task completion time.
- *DMI versus command-driven interaction* (Svendson, 1991): this study included an experiment based on the Towers of Hanoi problem; it employed a 2×2 factorial design, with factors being (1) the two interface techniques/styles and (2) "saliency," distinguished as either (a) high—with visual feedback or (b) low—with no visual feedback; basic measures included the number of errors, number of trials, and most time per trial; a second experiment examined expressed user preferences for the two interfaces.

- *DMI versus command-line environments* (Morgan *et al.*, 1991): an experiment to compare a command line interface with a DMI interface (WIMP: Windows Icons Mice and Pull down menus); subjects were organized into groups, each experiencing both interfaces; a standard counterbalanced order within-subjects design was employed; basic measures included number of errors, number of commands, and time between commands; user preferences were also collected and analyzed.

- *DMI versus command-based interaction* (Eberts and Bittianda, 1993): to examine the mental models preferred by users; based on two experiments, including a three-factor (condition × subject × question type) repeated-measures analysis of variance, with question type repeated for subjects.

- *Icon versus text* and *DMI versus menus* (Benbasat and Todd, 1993): two experiments to examine the effects of different techniques on the performance of casual users; involved experimental design for testing the unconfounded effects of two factors, each at two levels: (1) *mode of interaction*, with DMI compared against menu-based, and (2) *representation of interface components*, using either icons or text to represent object and commands; the measures used were task completion time and number of errors committed.

Other studies involve *comparisons* of alternative characteristics of a particular interaction technique. Menu-based interaction has been especially popular, as has DMI. Examples:

- *Rule-based versus positionally constant arrangements of menu items* (Somberg, 1987): an experiment to examine the independent effects of menu item arrangement and positional constancy in menus; used two different formats (linear and quadrangular) and four different orderings (alphabetic, probability of selection, random, positional constancy), resulting in eight groups of four subjects each, with random assignment of subjects; then carried out four-way analysis of variance, based on the measured data on response time.

- *Pie-shaped versus linear menus* (Callahan *et al.*, 1988): an experiment to examine (1) whether pie menus decrease seek time and error rates for menu items and (2) whether pie menus are useful in certain menu applications (suited for circular format, diametrically opposed item sets, etc.) and, conversely, whether linear menus are useful for sets of linear items; employed a 2 × 3 randomized block design, leading to repeated measures analysis of variance; the measures used are indicated above.

- *Walking versus pull-down menus* (Walker *et al.*, 1991): three experiments to investigate the effects of different menus on item selection using a mouse; the experiments had different purposes as well as different designs; the latter were (1) five-factor, incomplete, mixed design, (2) three-factor, mixed design, and (3) factorial mixed design, respectively; measures included selection time, accuracy (percentage of trials resulting in wrong choice), and movement time.
- *Two aspects of DMI* (Ballas *et al.*, 1992): an experiment involving four different interfaces constructed to reflect combinations of two aspects: (direct or indirect) *engagement* and (low or high) *semantic distance*; the interfaces built represented one DMI, one command line, and two hybrid types of interaction; the goals were to evaluate (1) comparative performance benefits of the DMI interface for a pilot having to switch from automatic to manual mode and (2) the two aspects of DMI; subjects had to perform two tasks, involving sequences of required cockpit decisions; measures included user response time and "automation deficit," representing a comparison of user performance between first decision and seventh decision.

The last of the above studies obviously also belongs to the earlier category, comparing different interaction techniques/styles.

Icons and iconic interaction have also gained considerable attention with regard to their specific effects. Examples:

- *Effects of icon design* (Blankenberger and Hahn, 1991): experiments to examine the effects of "articulatory distance" (difference between picture and meaning) on performance in menu-selection tasks; used three different icon sets and one text set, with icons either positioned randomly or in fixed locations; subjects were assigned randomly to four groups, each completing 11 blocks; employed a three-factor (group × block × position) analysis of variance, with repetitions in block and position; the basic measures used in several experiments included user reaction time, reading time, arm movement time, recognition time, and percent errors.
- *Effects of icons and descriptors* (MacGregor, 1992): one experiment to examine the reasons for performance improvements resulting from icons in menus; used three different menu types (labels only, labels plus descriptors, labels plus icons) and six menu pages, from two different levels of a menu index; subjects were randomly assigned to the three menu types, and the design employed was split-plot factorial with menu type as between-subject factor and menu level as within-subject factor; basic measures were response time and number of errors.

Among other studies (listed in the Bibliography) that involve icons and menus are those of Lansdale *et al.* (1990) and Kacmar (1991).

Studies of the effects of specific interface characteristics on user performance have also involved the more graphic techniques. For example, the use of diagrammatic displays has been considered:

- *Effects of diagrammatic displays* (Kieras, 1992): three experiments to examine the cognitive aspects of diagrammatic displays (of engineered systems) for use in interfaces for decision support systems and expert systems for managing complex systems; the major factors of interest were: topological content of displays, mainly represented by the extent to which structured relationships are revealed visually, and availability and visual presentation of state information; sketches for the three experimental designs employed: (1) between-subjects factor: three display conditions (no diagram, static diagram, and dynamic diagram), and within-subjects factor: the different problem situations; (2) between-subjects factors: topological versus nontopological factor and three levels of state information, resulting in a 2 × 3 design with six groups; (3) between-subjects factor: good versus bad display condition, and within-subjects factor: 20 problems, with subjects doing each problem in random order; the measures used included accuracy in responses, task completion times, response sequence quality (based on categories of sequences that had been judged to be good or poor), plus some other time-based measures (response choice, reading, observation).

Notice that this study is related to the subject of interface structures (Chapter 4) and how visually displayed and reinforced structures inherent to the information objects represented within the task domain can enhance/support user performance.

Then, just as graphics experts have been interested in comparisons of light pens, mice, and other input devices for years (e.g., Foley *et al.*, 1990), researchers in HCI are motivated by new device options to continue to ask questions about them. A recent sample:

- *Touchscreen versus mouse use* (Sears and Shneiderman, 1991): three experiments to examine the effects of three different selection devices (mouse, nonstabilized touchscreen, and stabilized touchscreen) on user performance; the other (within-subjects) variable was target size (four different rectangular targets); the experiments used different combinations of the above; in each case, every subject was tested with respect to all devices and target sizes; the basic

measures were selection time, number of errors, and user preference rating.

A number of other types of input or input devices have been compared,
e.g., voice and touch (Bierman *et al.*, 1992), touch-typing with stylus
(Goldberg and Richardson, 1993), and multidimensional input devices
(Jacob and Sibert, 1992). The performance of speech recognition devices
has also gained attention, e.g., with regard to its accuracy subject to fatigue
or voice drift (Frankish *et al.*, 1992). Also considered have been noninter-
active input alternatives, e.g., optical character recognition (OCR) (Cushman *et al.*, 1990).

Finally, a variety of other studies look more at the general relationships between users and computers, with special regard to qualifications
and effects. An example:

- *Interface characteristics versus user skill level* (Trumbly *et al.*, 1993): an
  experiment to determine whether the matching of interface characteristics with the knowledge level of the user can improve user
  performance; two interfaces were constructed for the needs of
  novice and experienced users, respectively, based on varied interaction technique, use of color, types of error messages, degree of
  help, etc.; the experimental treatments were categorical variables
  (matched and mismatched); performance was measured using task
  completion time, user accuracy/error ratio, and "simulation game
  profit."

Notice that these evaluations clearly imply selective approaches, in
that they focus on particular features or techniques representing the
computer/interface, and/or factors representing the user. Then, the goal is
to examine their relationships, preferably toward suggesting cause-and-
effect patterns. However, unlike some of the relatively informal approaches
(e.g., involving heuristic evaluations) described in Section 8.3.1., the
studies outlined above tend to be more formal. In the context of experiments, they use the factors that represent different HCI objects in the
testing of hypotheses on whether and how such variables (independent)
may influence performance (dependent variables). "Performance" levels
and comparisons depend on the "measures" chosen. A great variety of
experimental designs (Chapter 3) provide the formal organizational
framework to enable the experimenters to structure their experiments in
ways that are likely to produce credible results.

Further, with regard to the distinctions outlined at the beginning of
Section 8.2, the evaluation approaches typically involve either objective or

subjective data. As far as choice of measures is concerned, the basic measures discussed in Chapter 5 certainly come through very strongly. Indeed, that gives support to our assertion (e.g., in Chapter 7) that HCI evaluation is in need of more complex and interesting measures, constructed with reference to the SEE aspects hierarchy and validated as appropriate.

8.4. Methodological Distinctions

It is instructive to consider all types of evaluation with regard to not only their differences, but also their commonalities. What do they have in common? Let us reflect on the various techniques and tools, including the many "measures," that we have covered in the chapters up to this point. All of them are parts of our preparation for defining a general HCI evaluation method. That method is based on the following assertion:

- Regardless of the evaluation purpose, objectives, scope, and type, any reasonably objective evaluation, even if it relies on subjective data, can be reduced to and described as being fundamentally dependent on measure(s).

For the types of evaluation profiled in Section 8.3, this claim is supported by the studies cited. For example, Nielsen and Molich (1990), in determining that aggregated evaluators (or evaluator groups) using the heuristic method produce better evaluation results than do individual evaluators with the same method, based their conclusions on measures like "average number of problems found," "distributions of problems found," and "proportions" (i.e., ratios) of problems found to number of known problems. The "average number," as a basic, descriptive statistic, was also prevalent in Karat and colleagues' (1992) empirical testing study; and "proportions" or "ratios" were also used by Nielsen (1992) in comparing six interfaces and by Lewis et al. (1990) in relating the number of task paths predicted (or observed) against the total number available. Each such study involved the identification, detection, and measure-based manipulation and transformation of the fundamental data, namely "numbers of problems" in usability.

The above-stated claim is also supported by other types of evaluation:

1. *Descriptive*: determining how well any HCI object or feature performs in and of itself requires
   - Measurable data, and/or

- Otherwise collectible data (e.g., opinions, observations).

Both types of data lead to the use of measures, including sums, averages, distributions, and ratios. Also, in both cases, an evaluative conclusion is contingent on having established goal values (e.g., accepted standards or comparative thresholds). The conclusion is then based on how significantly better or worse (than some established or maybe arbitrarily decided goal value) the evaluated interface system performs.

2. *Predictive* or *Explanatory*: determining the effects of varying the values of one or more variables, representing an HCI object or feature, on the performance of some other HCI object also requires
   - Measurable data, and/or
   - Otherwise collectible data

about how the performance (response variables) changed (or can change) and how significant the changes were (or can be). Again, measures (e.g., averages for the number of data values measured or observed) are necessary, and the measures are compared (statistically analyzed) with respect to different levels and combinations of input factors.

As suggested earlier, the explanatory type of evaluation can also be a variation of one of the other types, or a hybrid combination, depending on exactly what is to be explained and how (in)formally that is to be done.

Notice that the major types of evaluation do have commonalities. Both the diagnostic type and the descriptive type appear to be most consistent with descriptive statistics (Definition 3.2) in that they involve various fundamental but nevertheless meaningful measures. Many of the measures described in Chapter 5 are relevant. However, as advocated in Chapter 7, many more interesting, descriptive measures are conceivable and likely to become useful, especially for the descriptive type of evaluation, if we learn to construct, test (validate), and utilize them.

Another example of the descriptive type is the interface acceptance test characterized in Section 7.3. But it can also involve other types, e.g., the diagnostic type—to detect errors, the explanatory type—to explain the test results (including why the errors occurred), and the predictive type—to determine specific interface changes required to improve its test results.

It is also interesting to observe that the usability "problem identification" methods described in the previous section are based on having a list of interface problems to be detected, using a method for finding them, and counting the number of (each type of) problems detected. But notice that then they need to compare the results with those of other methods. Thus, they involve both (1) fundamental descriptive measures, e.g., sums, averages, percentages, distributions, and (2) the need to have a similar set of values, resulting from another method, to compare against. Without the latter, it is difficult to decide what ratio or percentage of problems detected is good or bad. (It is noteworthy here that we must distinguish the performance of the interface being evaluated from the comparative performance of the methods used to determine that interface performance!)

What about the predictive type and also the explanatory type? As they are described above, they seem more closely associated with the use of "inductive statistics" (Definition 3.3) gathered in conjunction with experimental designs, followed by data analysis and hypothesis testing. That means that the tools and techniques of Chapter 3 are especially relevant. But the fact is that the kinds of measures identified with descriptive statistics (e.g., mean values) are also critically involved and tested, along with more complicated measures (e.g., regression formulas). On the other hand, experimental techniques can also apply to the other types of evaluation (descriptive, diagnostic), e.g., through population sampling techniques required.

In other words, the major types of evaluation indeed have much in common, although they might use the techniques and tools to different extents and with different emphases. Particularly relevant for the purposes of this book is the fact that measures really supply the basic, underlying mechanisms in all (objective) evaluation methods for enabling evaluative decisions on test results. This is true whether the evaluation is enveloped by very rigorous empirical design procedures or not.

It is very evident from the literature that the HCI community must continue to improve and extend the already proposed methods and endeavor to develop new and better alternatives. The latter should include methods that are not just intent on detecting problems; evaluations that assess a variety of performance features and attributes of an interface, in a manner transcending the existence of usability problems, should also be available.

Having a variety of evaluation types and methods available, as if in a shopping list or catalogue, may ultimately be best for serving the diverse needs of HCI evaluation. The choice will depend on exactly what is being evaluated and why. Diversity in evaluation approaches, methods, and means is clearly indicated. This is also confirmed by coverage in Chapter 9 of the evaluation of user stress and satisfaction. However, given the theme of this book, it should not be surprising to the reader that the main method being advocated has as its premise the use of measures. At the same time, its dependence on measures (and relevant tools and techniques)

156   CHAPTER 8

is variable, as should be evident from the description in the following section.

8.5. A Measures-Based Evaluation Method

A general method for evaluating an HCI design is modeled in Fig. 8.1. It is analogous to the method that was outlined for HCI design (Treu, 1994). But, while the design method is "driven" by principles and factors that cause the determination of interface features, the evaluation method is "undergirded" by measures and other indicators that can be used to assess the existence, appearance, and behavior of those features. As reviewed in Chapter 2, HCI design and evaluation methods must really be closely linked. The results of the first are evaluated by the second, thereby producing feedback for redesign. To the extent possible, this close linkage should exist in parallel, that is, with the design process directly influenced by intermediary evaluation results.

Let us discuss the steps of Fig. 8.1, with reference to the sections or chapters providing more details. Based on whatever inputs are provided by management, during the preparatory Step A, the evaluation purpose (Definition 6.3) and objectives (Definition 6.4) must be carefully delineated, in Step B. This must be done with regard to what is(are) to be the object(s) of evaluation and, hence, its total scope (Definition 6.5). Having this information will enable the evaluator to tailor the remaining steps of the method accordingly, rather than wandering through them with inadequate direction and then obtaining results that are really not responsive to (management) expectations. The evaluation purpose may require an assessment of whether and how well the specified design principles were met.

After knowing about evaluation purpose, objectives, objects, and scope, as discussed in Section 6.2, the evaluator can attempt to determine, in Step C, the type(s) of evaluation (Section 6.2.2) that is(are) most appropriate. Further, closely associated to choice of type is the question about which evaluative aspect(s) (Section 6.2.3) is(are) to become involved.

Then, in Step D, the evaluator must determine the kind of evaluative data that can be responsive to the indicated type of evaluation and to the SEE aspects identified as important. That is, if, for example, it is required that an interface be evaluated with regard to whether it contributes to greater user productivity (implying at least efficiency but maybe also synergism and/or effectiveness), then it must be possible to obtain evidence on that subject. For the example, the type of evaluation is likely to be

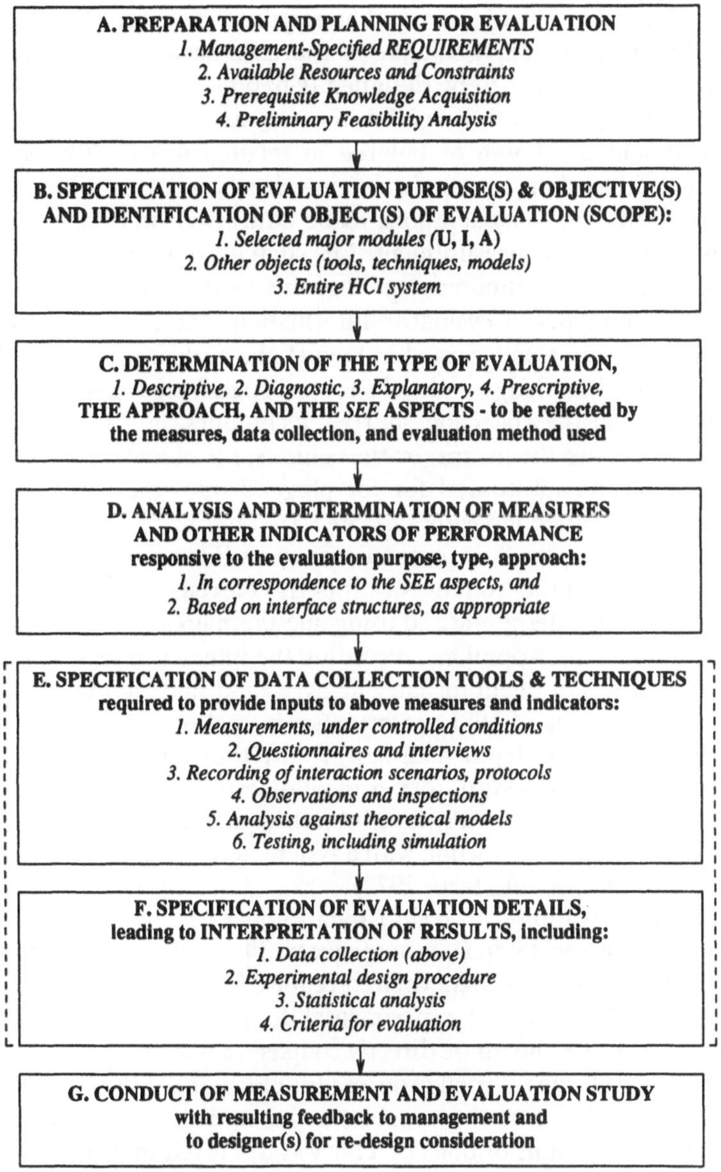

A. PREPARATION AND PLANNING FOR EVALUATION
1. Management-Specified REQUIREMENTS
2. Available Resources and Constraints
3. Prerequisite Knowledge Acquisition
4. Preliminary Feasibility Analysis

B. SPECIFICATION OF EVALUATION PURPOSE(S) & OBJECTIVE(S) AND IDENTIFICATION OF OBJECT(S) OF EVALUATION (SCOPE):
1. Selected major modules (U, I, A)
2. Other objects (tools, techniques, models)
3. Entire HCI system

C. DETERMINATION OF THE TYPE OF EVALUATION,
1. Descriptive, 2. Diagnostic, 3. Explanatory, 4. Prescriptive,
THE APPROACH, AND THE *SEE* ASPECTS - to be reflected by the measures, data collection, and evaluation method used

D. ANALYSIS AND DETERMINATION OF MEASURES AND OTHER INDICATORS OF PERFORMANCE responsive to the evaluation purpose, type, approach:
1. In correspondence to the SEE aspects, and
2. Based on interface structures, as appropriate

E. SPECIFICATION OF DATA COLLECTION TOOLS & TECHNIQUES required to provide inputs to above measures and indicators:
1. Measurements, under controlled conditions
2. Questionnaires and interviews
3. Recording of interaction scenarios, protocols
4. Observations and inspections
5. Analysis against theoretical models
6. Testing, including simulation

F. SPECIFICATION OF EVALUATION DETAILS, leading to INTERPRETATION OF RESULTS, including:
1. Data collection (above)
2. Experimental design procedure
3. Statistical analysis
4. Criteria for evaluation

G. CONDUCT OF MEASUREMENT AND EVALUATION STUDY with resulting feedback to management and to designer(s) for re-design consideration

FIGURE 8.1. Measures-based evaluation method.

predictive or explanatory. What kind of evidence should be obtained? The evaluator must consider the entire repertoire of available HCI measures and other indicators, in order to select those that will output the responsive values. This assumes of course that requisite data are measurable or collectible (Chapter 3). If suitable measures/indicators are not available, new versions may have to be designed (Chapter 7).

According to Step D of Fig. 8.1, the measures or indicators of performance should be chosen or tailored in relation to the SEE aspects of interest and based on any applicable interface structures. The evaluative aspects clarify the considerations to be addressed; interface structures organize and enable measurement. The contents of Chapter 7, therefore, can become a major, innovative part of this kind of evaluation method.

Given the types of evaluative information that are to be generated, using the measures determined in Step D, the evaluator must, in Step E, utilize his/her knowledge and skills toward specifying (selecting, modifying, designing) the collection sources, techniques, and tools to be employed. These are the means, or the vehicles, for obtaining the data that will, in turn, be substituted for (or plugged into) the variables in the measures and other indicators of Step D. The major alternatives were described in Chapter 3 as prerequisites to evaluation. A range of possibilities exist, including conduct of properly controlled experimental measurement studies, designing and using questionnaires and/or interviews to obtain and tally user opinions, recording the interactive session scenarios (of transactions) in detail for later analysis, and making expert observations or inspections of HCI performance in real time. Other techniques available are the in-depth analyses against theoretical models and the conducts of various kinds of (experimental) tests including simulations. A more unusual, but potentially fruitful technique is the unobtrusive stimulation of the user in interaction with a system, toward measuring the user's reactions to the stimuli (Treu, 1972).

But, only planning to collect data (Step E) for use in the selected measures/indicators (Step D) is inadequate. The evaluator should know in advance the quantity of data desired/required (e.g., sample sizes), in the context of well-established experimental design procedures. This means that Steps E and F should be directly coupled and carried out in parallel. Included must be any formal ordering (or blocking) of the data collection and analysis relative to the variables to be studied as representative of individual and groups of objects. This was discussed in conjunction with the experimental design phases outlined in Fig. 3.3. The evaluator must know both the order in which data should be obtained and, then, what to do with those data. This is what Step F is about. It also means that statistical analysis must be part of the evaluator's (or evaluating team's) expertise (Chapter 3). Furthermore, even after the measured values and statistical analysis results are determined, it is essential to know how to interpret them. This task is elaborated next.

8.6. Interpretation of Results

Any and all data collection/measurement efforts should be carried out carefully and lead to careful analysis of the data. This should be true not only for formal methods, but also when the approach/method is relatively informal. Statistical analysis techniques should be selected as conducive to supporting the type of evaluation (e.g., descriptive or predictive). Numerous resource books are available, as mentioned in Chapter 3. It is not feasible to review the techniques here.

Results of such analysis can serve as inputs to evaluative decision-making. This means that the following are necessary:

1. *Presentation of results* should be in a meaningful, understandable format, to enable the ultimate evaluator to assimilate, compare, etc., whatever data have been produced.
2. *Criteria for evaluation* (Definition 6.12) should accompany the results; they should be appropriate for the kind of evaluation conducted and the data produced.

The point about presentation of results relates to organized recording and representation, in meaningful and visualizable form, of the data collected and analyzed. It assumes that the raw data (basic level of hierarchy, Section 7.2) have been accumulated and that they or their averages, variances, standard deviations, etc., have been plugged into variables of higher-level measures selected for a particular evaluation. Then, the values of measures and other indicators can feed into evaluative decision-making schematics, such as those illustrated generically in Fig. 8.2.

Alternatively, those values can be employed in the context of hypothesis testing, within formal experimental design procedures. In the latter case, well-known test statistics are available to help the evaluator in analyzing various relationship patterns among or between data values. For example, he/she can determine whether a value (e.g., a mean) or whether differences in values are significant at some level of probability. However, when the type of evaluation is more descriptive in nature, other criteria are needed.

For that purpose, Fig. 8.2 displays three schematics that are dependent on criteria for evaluation. If such criteria are not available in some

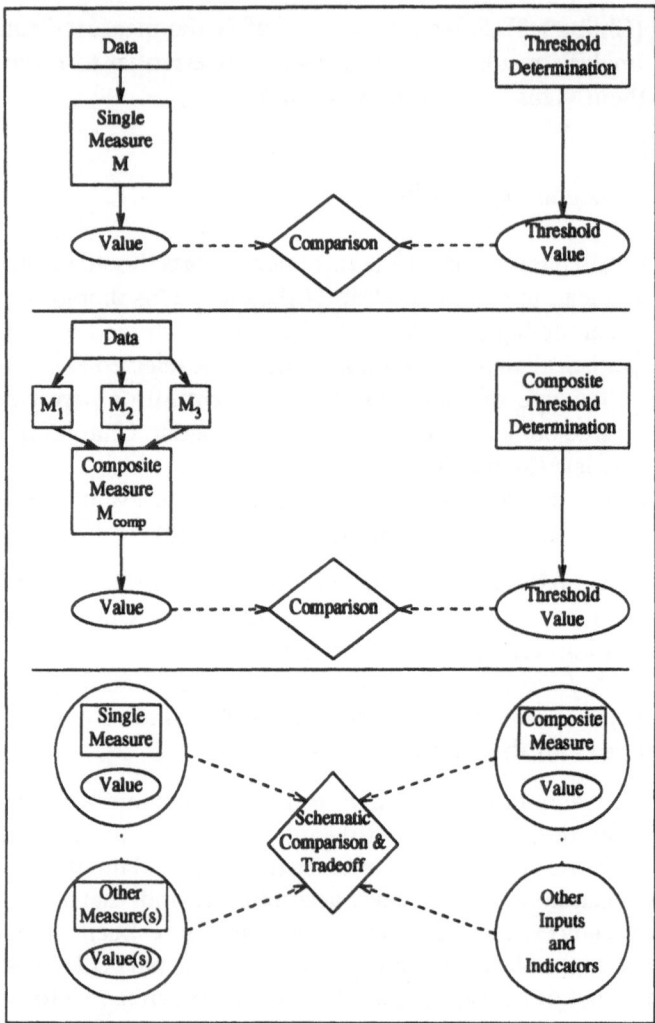

FIGURE 8.2. Schematics for evaluative decision-making.

form, the evaluative decision may have to be purely subjective, perhaps based on the whim of the evaluator. There are two basic types of criteria for evaluation:

1. *Threshold-oriented*, enabling comparison of the value of a measure (at whatever level of the SEE hierarchy) against some established threshold, standard, or statistic.

2. *Decision-oriented*, in which the evaluator takes into account all significant inputs, perhaps from a variety of sources, and considers their trade-offs.

For the first type, a standard threshold may not be available. Nevertheless, it is possible to take advantage of a value produced for another interface or interface feature, thereby obtaining the equivalent of a threshold value for comparison (Section 6.5). If a certain measure value, e.g., for user productivity, exhibited by Interface A, is less than, equal to, or greater than the equivalent value for Interface B, that obviously carries implications for the relative performance of Interface A. Alternatively, someone (e.g., the evaluator, or the responsible administrator) may have to make a judgment on whether a value is good or bad.

Comprehensive evaluation was indicated in Section 8.2 as one kind of distinction in evaluation approach. When it applies, multiple values may have to be produced across a range of different measures and indicators. If so, the interpretation step (Step F) requires the equivalent of a multi-input decision schematic, as also shown in Fig. 8.2. Such a schematic can be used to guide the evaluator to reach a judgment on the existence and performance of a composite design feature, or of a collection of features.

Evaluation criteria may include priorities or weightings indicating which values are more significant than which other ones. When feasible, it is helpful to develop a *summative* result, or a composite "figure-of-merit," belonging to Level 4 of the SEE hierarchy of measures described in Chapter 7. Such a figure-of-merit consists of a function of multiaspect measures, each with assigned weights, as illustrated in Section 8.8. The function might be a summation or some other collective formula that relates the input values and weights in a manner producing a meaningful composite value. The outcome of such a figure can be useful especially when the values for comparable interfaces are available, thereby enabling relative evaluation.

8.7. An Evaluation Studies Profile

Having the opportunity to be personally involved in HCI evaluation studies should tend to enhance one's knowledge about such work and hence one's feeling of being qualified to analyze and (even) critique the work. Several prototype studies were presented in considerable detail in the companion book (Treu, 1994), but with emphasis on their design. In this section, their evaluations are profiled among a selected set of interface

162   CHAPTER 8

evaluation studies (in which the author participated personally). The
studies are listed briefly in Table 8.1. The point behind this profile is *not* to
suggest that the reader try to locate and analyze the cited publications.
Indeed, the intention is rather the opposite; the studies enable a convenient, retrospective illustration of the use (and nonuse) of the evaluation
method advocated in this chapter.

The seven studies are characterized with reference to Steps B, D, and
E of the evaluation method of Fig. 8.1. Step B is represented simply by
referring to the design principles (Table 2.1) that were of primary interest
in the designs, thereby suggesting that evaluative information was to be
determined on whether those principles were satisfied. This point is itself
an oversimplification. Especially in evaluations involving operational (application) systems (e.g., Studies 1, 3, and 4), there were typically also other

TABLE 8.1
Critical Portrait of Seven Evaluation Studies

Study I.D.	System interface	Step B: (primary) design principles	Step D: measures or indicators used	Step E: techniques and tools used
1	CIRC (Treu, 1967b)	Responsive (content) (P35)	Precision, recall, and also errors	Questionnaires and interviews, analysis
2	Transparent Stimulation (Treu, 1972)	Satisfying (e.g., P39)	User ratings, along with indicated reasons	On-line recordings and measurements
3	NMM (Abrams and Treu, 1977)	Responsive (in time) (P36)	Time-based, lengths, rates	On-line measurement, recordings
4	NAM (Treu, 1982)	Uniform (P42)	Expert opinions	Protocol recording, analysis
5	GIGL (Bornique and Treu, 1985)	Adaptable (P3)	User opinions, preferences	Protocol recording, analysis
6	SAUCI (Tyler and Treu, 1989)	Adaptive (P4) Context-providing (P13)	Task completion, number of errors	Protocol recording and analysis; questionnaire
7	N-CHIME (Treu et al., 1991)	Facilitative (P20) Context-providing (P13) Unconstraining (P41) Adaptive (P4)	Expert and user opinions	Cognitive walkthroughs

underlying purposes behind conducting an evaluation. But they need not be mentioned here.

The next column in Table 8.1 indicates the measures that were utilized in the studies. Notice that some of them were indeed objective in nature, e.g., for Studies 3 and 6. For example, some results of Study 6 are summarized in Table 8.2. It compares the numbers of user errors (M22) and the task completion times (M7) for the SAUCI (adaptive) interface with the nonadaptive alternative. Results indicate considerable reductions by SAUCI of the errors committed, while the reductions in the times required to complete the task exercises are not as significant.

A figure-of-merit is illustrated later on (next section) with regard to Study 3. As will be evident, data like those of Table 8.2 are conducive to use in a figure-of-merit approach to presenting evaluative results.

Other evaluations were primarily dependent on gathering and analyzing user opinions about preferred interface features, e.g., Studies 5 and 7. Study 1 was mostly about the performance of the application module in retrieving relevant information for the user, rather than performance of the user-visible interface as such. However, very carefully designed flowchart models were used, as logical, guideline tools and screening devices, to support the analysis of the performance data collected.

Study 2 had and still has the potential for much more interesting evaluation results. However, at the time, the task of observing and measuring HCI in real time, coupled with collection and analysis of massive amounts of data, was almost overwhelming. The interface in Study 4 was evaluated more with regard to whether several expert users found it (the "uniformizing" intermediary) to work as promised, rather than to consider collection and analysis of more objective data for measures representative of uniformity.

Collection and examination of interaction protocols was used in several of the studies. That approach has been extensively critiqued and

TABLE 8.2
Comparison of Adaptive versus Nonadaptive Interfaces[a]

Task exercises	User errors (M22)		Completion time (min) (M7)	
	SAUCI	Nonadaptive	SAUCI	Nonadaptive
Document preparation	1.7	4.7	46.2	56.8
Programming	2.3	5.3	29.8	39.2

[a]This table represents part of a table from Tyler and Treu (1989) reprinted with kind permission from Academic Press.

defended in the literature (e.g., Newell and Simon, 1972; Mack *et al.*, 1983; Ericsson and Simon, 1984). In spite of its limitations, it was and remains popular among HCI researchers. As discussed with regard to the current evaluation approaches and methods in Sections 8.2 and 8.3, it is much more reliant on the expertise of the evaluator (of the protocols) than it is on statistical significance reflected by the resulting data. The analysis of recorded protocols is like a special form of after-the-fact cognitive walk-through by a knowledgeable person, to determine what went right and wrong.

In all seven studies, especially those involving prototype interface implementations (the last six), the test and evaluation phases typically came late in the study period and required considerable additional human and other resources. As a result, they normally received less attention than they should have. Specialized versions of cognitive walk-throughs were used in several studies (2, 4 through 7), although that method is only indicated in Table 8.1 for Study 7. The interface developers and/or HCI experts utilized goal-oriented protocols on behalf of target users to assess whether the interface was performing correctly and according to design requirements.

A few more details about the evaluations in the last two listed proto-type studies might be of interest here. For Study 6, the evaluation was conducted using human subjects (Tyler, 1986). Exercises were created and assigned to subjects both with regard to utilizing the available UNIX-based commands and to completing the two prescribed tasks. Subjects who had little knowledge of UNIX but were familiar with VAX/VMS were recruited from introductory computer science courses. Three subjects were used to test each of two interfaces, one SAUCI (adaptive) and one nonadaptive. All six subjects had roughly equivalent computer-relevant backgrounds, interests, and abilities. Brief, written descriptions of the interface layouts and operations were developed and used for training. Selected results are shown in Table 8.2. With reference to the distinctions in approach made in Section 8.2, the evaluation approach represented by Study 6 is selective in nature, dependent on objective data (supplemented with subjective opinions), formal in the experimental design organization employed, and resulting in data particularly relevant to the efficiency branch of the SEE hierarchy. The type of evaluation is partly predictive (with regard to improvements that can result from changed capabilities) and partly descriptive (in describing how much better one interface is than another).

For Study 7, a formal evaluation of the adaptive capabilities of N-CHIME was not feasible. Instead, and as mentioned earlier, the developers conducted special cognitive walk-throughs, using prespecified inter-action scenarios (protocols) to determine and demonstrate (to technical experts and managers) that the interface was working as designed. In addition, informal assessment of its performance was carried out using a group of graduate students in computer science. That effort led to generally positive feedback (Sanderson, 1991). The students were positive about certain features, such as the adaptively provided guidance and suggestions. On the other hand, some of them, who were N-CHIME novices but experts in computer science, expressed concern over some adaptively made decisions about what to do next, thereby taking away their feelings of control. Such reservations confirmed one of the "prob-lems" expected with this kind of interface. As a consequence, the designer should feel obliged to iterate the design with attempts to alleviate isolated user concerns. For our interests in illustrating evaluation methods em-ployed, Study 7 made it possible to arrive at percentages of the sample users who experienced and were able to articulate either positive or negative features. In summary, it represents an evaluation approach that was very selective, dependent on subjective data, informal in the technique employed, and resulting in data pertaining mostly to the synergism aspect of the SEE hierarchy. It represents a type of evaluation that is purely descriptive in nature.

In fact, most of the seven studies involved evaluations that were (mostly) descriptive in nature, and most were relatively informal in their conducts. Four of them were dependent on the collection and use of (mostly) objective data, while the rest utilized opinions resulting from user experiences or expert analyses. Several also contained elements of the diagnostic type, e.g., trying to identify problems. Only three of the studies actually set up formal experimental designs to enable the generation of predictive results. But they were limited in success in doing so.

Thus, the profile represents something of a mixture of evaluation types, approaches, and methods. In a way, that seems reasonable. On the other hand, the profile appears to be somewhat inconsistent with the structured approach advocated in this book. In retrospect, a number of the studies could have been and should have been better structured, more comprehensive, and more systematic in what was done. HCI evaluation is more easily talked about than carried out. The evaluation stage is, in a sense, more difficult than the design. This was already implied in the discussion (Section 8.3) of methods currently in use. Particularly expen-sive and time-consuming is empirical testing (e.g., Jeffries et al., 1991).

Nevertheless, it is essential that the state-of-the-art of HCI measure-ment and evaluation be advanced, by:

1. *Comparing and improving the methods* that are currently available and being examined (Section 8.3).
2. *Describing the methods* that are being used, in concise and understandable terminology and format, for consideration by others; Sweeney and colleagues' (1993) framework, specifically oriented to usability evaluation, is a useful step in that direction.
3. *Insisting on development and use of evaluation methods*, in conjunction with authorized HCI design efforts, whether sponsored by industry or government agencies.

The second suggestion can be accomplished by relating an evaluation to the steps of an evaluation method, such as the one in Fig. 8.1. Portraits of the evaluation effort are implied by the entries of Table 8.1. With suitable elaborations and extensions, such capsule descriptions should be minimal requirements to be met by evaluators as a matter of routine.

8.8.   Figure-of-Merit Example

For Study 3 (Table 8.1), data resulting from 69 user sessions with operational systems were measured and analyzed (Abrams and Treu, 1977). We utilized selections of measures based on time (Table 5.1), lengths (Table 5.2), and rates (Table 5.3). Where appropriate, each of the mean, standard deviation, median, 90%, and 95% values was calculated and tabulated.

The resulting data are of course out-of-date by now. But we can demonstrate how similar data could be utilized in a hypothetical example. Suppose that an evaluation team has selected the following factors as most important in representing how well an interface is performing for the user. Assume that the selection is based on guidelines from management and inputs from users. Corresponding measures are identified by the labels used in above-cited tables.

1. *Productivity*: the number of tasks the user can complete in some specified period of time (M24); this is deemed most significant and is assigned a weight of 3 (the highest).
2. *User errors*: the number of mistakes made by the user in carrying out a task (M22); this is assigned a weight of 2.
3. *Effort imposed on user*: the amount of time the user typically has to spend thinking about and preparing for the next input (M5), coupled with entering (e.g., keying in) that input (M6); the conjunction of these two values is assigned a weight of 1.

Notice that as the values of these three performance factors increase, they become more favorable in the first case and less favorable in the other two cases. Also, one can argue that increases in the latter two are likely to have detrimental effects on the productivity factor. But to keep the example fairly simple, we are ignoring such interaction.

Now, suppose that the mean values listed in Table 8.3 resulted from Interface A for the measures selected. The numbers were picked to facilitate calculation. We use a figure-of-merit formula like the one described in Section 5.4. Therefore, the mean values cannot simply be multiplied by their respective weights and then added. That would be like adding apples and oranges. Instead, we must incorporate (1) the positive/negative interpretations of increases/decreases in each factor individually and (2) relate each factor's value to some baseline, or standard, that is considered minimally acceptable, i.e., a threshold. However, we treat Interface A itself to represent the "standard" for comparison. Hence, relating each of its values against itself (in Column 3 of Table 8.3) is very easy.

With Interface A treated as the standard, an increase in M24 from 20 tasks to 21 tasks or more should have a favorable impact on the figure-of-merit for any interface compared against it. On the other hand, increases in the other two measures should be unfavorable.

So, suppose that the same measures are used to evaluate Interface B, and it is to be compared against Interface A, the standard that supplies the threshold values. Table 8.4 shows this comparison. Because the last two factors get better as they decrease in value, they must be compared against the threshold in a manner opposite to that used for the first factor. Notice that for Interface A, after normalizing its values (i.e., comparing the interface against itself as the standard), the total figure-of-merit calculation leads to 6. According to Eq. (5.1), this value can be divided by the sum of weights to normalize to 1. For Interface B, even though productivity is

TABLE 8.3
Figure-of-Merit Calculation for Interface A

Measure label	Mean (A) # of units	Ratio (R) (A) ÷ Std	Weight (W) or rank	Product R × W
M24	20 tasks	1	3	3
M22	10 errors	1	2	2
M5 + M6	30 seconds	1	1	1
Total				6

TABLE 8.4
Figure-of-Merit Calculation for Interface B

Measure label	Mean (B) # of units	Ratio (R) (B) ÷ (A)	Weight (W) or rank	Product R × W
M24	15 tasks	0.75	3	2.25
		(A) ÷ (B)		
M22	5 errors	2	2	4
M5 + M6	30 seconds	1	1	1
Total				7.25

reduced by 25%, the fact that the number of errors is reduced by 50% more than compensates and the total result is greater than 6. Dividing out the sum of weights (6) results in a figure of approximately 1.2.

The example runs the risk of division by zero, if the number of errors goes to zero. Therefore, other ways of assessing improvement or degradation relative to a threshold value must be considered. For example, one can take the increment or decrement in value and relate that to the threshold (Exercise 8.14).

8.9. BE³ST Approach

The general evaluation method that has been developed in this and previous chapters has as its "common denominator" the use of measures. Those measures were categorized as corresponding to the various nodes of the SEE aspects hierarchy (Section 7.2). One distinct purpose was to convince the reader that all HCI evaluation methods share the use of measures, although those measures may differ significantly in complexity and meaning.

This view is to enable the evaluator to arrive at evaluative conclusions not only with regard to selected objects or features and their performance comparisons; it should also be possible at higher levels of attention, with regard to composite groupings of objects and features, potentially encompassing the entire HCI system. Suitably tailored composite measures, representing each SEE aspect and also any meaningful combinations or interactions, were suggested as potentially useful.

The method we have proposed includes the possibility of assessing the impact or effect that a measured level (or composite figure) of HCI performance might have on the organization that is likely to either benefit or suffer from that performance. However, to accentuate explicitly that prospect, the approach labeled "Benefits based on Efficiency, Effectiveness, Effects and Synergism Testing" was developed. Although its acronym (BE³ST) sounds too presumptuous, its purpose is nevertheless noteworthy. The intended thrust is depicted in Fig. 8.3. The "Effects Measures" represent one further category of measures to be defined. They are measures that can variously take into account the following:

- *Resources* (e.g., personhours, hardware and software costs) required to sustain a particular level of performance, or to enable an increment in that level to be attained;
- *Performance levels* determined by means of measures in the three SEE categories and their combinations, using appropriate evaluation methodology (defined in this and previous chapters).

By being able to incorporate in the evaluation both the required resources and the resulting (corresponding) performance levels, the measures (and all of the methodology surrounding them) can provide indications of

- Effects that can result, from using the cause-and-effect relationship between changing the resources in HCI (human and computer) and thereby causing increases or decreases in the performance; and
- Benefits that can be derived by the organization (i.e., management) from those effects.

Actually, some of the measures discussed in Chapter 7 already implied an ability to discern measurable effects, e.g., in user productivity, by changing one interface feature to another one preferred by users. So, the SEE hierarchy can feed directly into the BE³ST approach outlined here. But the latter, in turn, suggests the outward-looking perspective of not

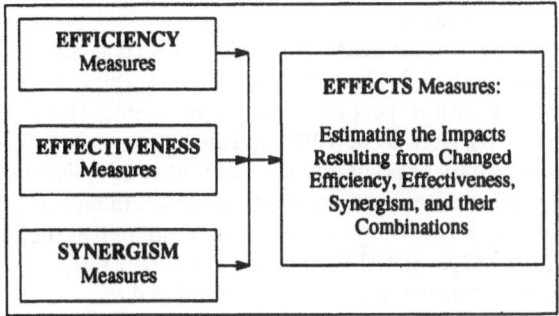

FIGURE 8.3. The BE³ST measures categories.

merely carrying out SEE-based evaluations for purposes of determining whether or not an interface works well or can work better. It, therefore, highlights the additional challenge awaiting evaluators of HCI: what good are the improvements, which normally translate into required additional resources, to the organization? Are the prospective effects, i.e., benefits, worth the investment in additional resources? Such cost–benefit analyses are of course of great interest in business and industry. Some HCI researchers have addressed such analysis to limited extents (e.g., Nielsen and Phillips, 1993), while also acknowledging how difficult it is. It is not feasible here to pursue the topic any further. Yet, the reader should recognize it as a logical follow-on to the measures-based method that is proposed in this book.

Exercises

8.1. Given the evaluation methodology developed, look back at the five methods outlined for IS&R systems in Section 1.4 and characterize them with respect to the major distinctions that have been identified.

8.2. Repeat Exercise 8.1 for each of the four current evaluation methods (described by Jeffries *et al.*, 1991) outlined in Section 8.3.

8.3. For each of the four methods referred to in Exercise 8.2, how does/should the evaluator decide whether the interface is performing well, poorly, etc.? Do you think that evaluation criteria, similar in format to Fig. 6.2, can be used? If yes, how? If not, how might Fig. 6.2 be adapted to be useful for each method?

8.4. Do you think that the discrepancies (indicated in Section 8.3) among investigators on which current usability evaluation methods are most effective are explainable? What might be the reasons/causes behind the different results and opinions about them?

8.5. Read Roberts and Moran (1983) and the subsequent critiques of their methodology by Allen (1985) and Borenstein (1985). Do you agree? Explain.

8.6. Using the four distinctions in approach outlined at the start of Section 8.2, characterize the four usability evaluation methods of Section 8.3. Tabulate and summarize your results.

8.7. One of the four current methods outlined in Section 8.3 is called "usability testing." The method displayed in Fig. 8.1 is to enable testing and evaluation of an interface with respect to whether it is "usable" (Principle P44), "well-organized" (P31), "consistent" (P12), and any one or more (in combination) of the other principles listed in Table 2.1 and other such listings. Select one of those principles (other than usable) that sounds interesting. Then, outline the steps of Fig. 8.1, starting with Step B, in terms of how they are affected by the design principle stated (within the evaluation purpose). Also, suggest some suitable measures that should be employed.

8.8. Repeat Exercise 8.7 for another, very different choice from Table 2.1

8.9. In Section 8.6, two basic types of criteria (threshold-oriented and decision-oriented) are identified. Are both of these compatible with the format of an evaluation criterion portrayed in Fig. 6.2? For each, explain which components of that format apply and how.

8.10. It seems apparent from the discussion of the measures-based method that the more meaningful and "powerful" the measures (Step D), the easier should be the evaluator's critical role of reaching evaluative conclusions. In everything said about measures in this and previous chapters, what characteristics of a measure are most likely to make it meaningful and powerful?

8.11. In informal evaluation methods, including unstructured, cognitive walkthroughs to determine how well, generally, an interface works, do you think that the evaluators use at least some kinds of (conceptual) measures, even though they might not be explicitly identified as such? (Note: even a simple detection of the existence of an interface feature, or its subjective comparison against another, can lead to a binary result; is this a very basic "measure"?)

8.12. The figure-of-merit example tabulated in Section 8.8 allows for very amorphous contributions to the total value resulting from a set of measures and their respective weightings. As a result, very differently performing interfaces can attain the same total merit value. Is that result reasonable? Are there potential problems with it? If so, can they be resolved? Explain.

8.13. Construct your own figure-of-merit example, to include (a) a good mixture of at least six measures, (b) with at least one measure from each table in Chapter 5, (c) with some measures having positive interpretation, and others negative interpretation, as their values increase. Identify each measure as to whether it mainly reflects performance of the U-, I-, or A-modules, individually or in some combination. For each measure, select a reasonable value and assign a relative weighting. Accept the values selected as the standards (i.e., thresholds) for comparison. Let the values represent Interface S. Then, hypothesize three very different types of performance for Interfaces A, B, and C. Calculate and discuss the resulting total merit figures. Do they seem useful and reasonable (a) in relation to Interface S and (b) when compared against each other?

8.14. Rework the figure-of-merit example in the text. Use instead the differences between measured values and standard values. Those differences can be interpreted as "distances" from the standard, either in the positive or negative direction. How does this view affect other elements of the formula? Do the weightings have to be interpreted differently or given different values? For example, what happens if the distance between measured and standard values is zero?

8.15. As pointed out in Section 8.3, the current evaluation methods are largely oriented to identifying and ranking problems (with respect to how they affect usability) and then detecting them in an interface. Read Karat et al. (1992) and some related papers. Do you see any relationship or correspondence between the measures characterized in Chapter 5 and the interface problems to be detected? Which, if any, usability problems (a) could be determined using a measures-based method, (b) must be determined using walk-through and other related methods (because the measures-based method is inadequate or ineffective)?

8.16. The planned detection of problems in interface evaluation tends to conjure up a rather negative view of the evaluation task. Discuss whether and how it might be possible to transform it to an activity with a positive outlook, while essentially accomplishing the same objectives.

8.17. Read Sweeney *et al.* (1993) and compare the framework of terms developed by them for usability evaluation with the terminology developed in this book for HCI evaluation in general.

SPECIAL TOPICS

Various topics in the first three parts of this book can be refined and expanded considerably. This is illustrated by the four special topics addressed in this part. In Chapter 9, one particular design principle (from Table 2.1) motivates the modeling and hypothetical measurement of user satisfaction, based on the conjecture that user (dis)satisfaction is correlated with measured user stress. In Chapter 10, the topic of interface structures is extended to encompass user-visualizable objects represented in different "spaces" at and behind the interface. Chapter 11 treats visualization as a kind of interaction style and compares it with DMI and VR styles with regard to amount of required user mental involvement. Finally, Chapter 12 revisits interface structures once more, with emphasis on formal evaluation of their utility.

STRESS AND USER SATISFACTION

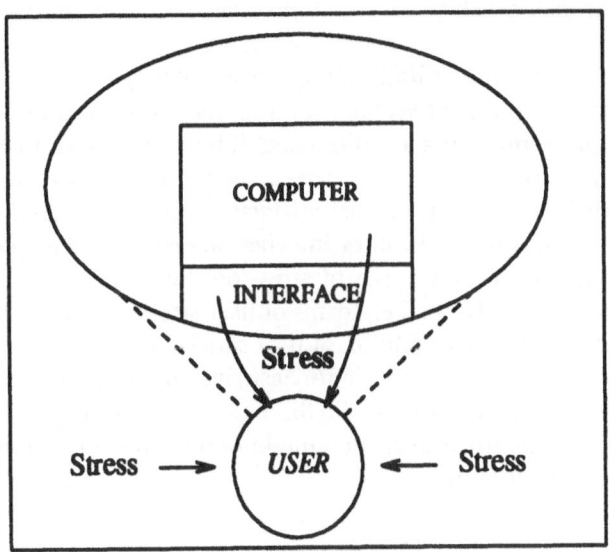

9.1. Overview

It is possible to measure various quantities about a user's interaction with a system, such as frequencies of command usage, task completion times, and user think times (Treu, 1975a; Abrams and Treu, 1977). This was discussed in Chapter 5. Values of such measures can reflect the design complexity of interaction language and how well a language is known by certain users, when compared with other users who are more or less experienced. But they say nothing about attainment of user satisfaction with interface features. Satisfying the user is one of the high-level principles of interface design.

In part because of the difficulties in determining whether users are truly satisfied with an interface, much attention has been paid to the concept of system friendliness. Many users and computer advertisers like to refer to "user-friendly" interfaces. Friendliness implies something good about the interface hardware and software, not about the user. It has to do with being on good terms, amicable, supportive, and nonhostile. Presumably an interface that is friendly is also satisfying to the user. However, a computer could be designed to exhibit many friendly traits and still fail to satisfy the user in what he/she is trying to accomplish. That is analogous to dealing with a very friendly person who, in spite of some commendable qualities, may have disruptive and even annoying effects on another person. System friendliness should, therefore, not be viewed as a surrogate or substitute for user satisfaction. It can, however, be a cause or contributing factor.

This chapter presents a different approach to trying to ascertain user satisfaction. First, in the next section, the problems with asking for user opinions and observing users are discussed. That is followed, in Section 9.3, with a cause-and-effect model, based on the conjecture that user stress, or lack thereof, causes user (dis)satisfaction. Various types of factors in and around the human–computer interface are suggested as potential causes of a range of different types of stress on the user.

In Section 9.4, the effects (i.e., forms of user stress) are hypothesized as being linked to a special definition of user satisfaction. Some methodological considerations for determining/measuring the stress data are outlined in Section 9.5. Finally, Section 9.6 discusses how this kind of correlation between stress and (dis)satisfaction might become useful, especially in very high-stress job situations.

9.2. Problems with Opinions

Asking the user directly, by interview or questionnaire, is one important means for collecting data about satisfaction. This was summarized in Chapter 3. Chin *et al.* (1988) prepared and tested a useful set of questions designed to elicit the user's level of satisfaction. However, because of the subjective nature of user opinions, a more objective source of evidence on how good or bad the user feels about interface features and performance would be helpful. It could confirm, clarify, and possibly contradict opinions. While pure user opinions are important, there are problems with after-the-fact questions posed of the user, including (1) a user having difficulty discriminating among different technical features or articulating which one does what, (2) a user not remembering exactly what happened and when, and (3) generalization of user opinions across the duration of an interactive session. Further, if an evaluator attempts to question the user during a session, it must be done very carefully to avoid disruptive effects that can influence the resulting data. In any case, user opinions, if employed by themselves, can produce less than reliable judgments on how "satisfying" the interface appears to be.

Another technique is to conduct real-time observation of the user, to see whether he/she exhibits various emotions (e.g., anger, frustration, happiness). These may be symptomatic of the user's current level of satisfaction. But users are very different regarding how they show their feelings, and it is extremely difficult to draw conclusions based on such observations alone.

It is preferable to measure the user directly, if possible, and then to utilize the other means (questionnaires, interviews, observations) in confirming or explaining the results. If a means for detecting both favorable and unfavorable user reactions to interface stimuli were available, using any reliable physiological indicators, those critical points could be analyzed in correlation with relevant user explanations. In that sense, any objectively measurable data would be complementary to results from more subjective sources. If such data can be obtained, we should at least be able to compare one interface feature with another across different systems.

9.3.   Cause-and-Effect Model

The basic premise is that human stress or lack thereof in HCI causes user (dis)satisfaction. It may not be the only cause, but it is nevertheless a potentially significant contributor to whether or not a user is satisfied with/ by a computer interface. Toward gauging user satisfaction with various interface features, the approach presented in this chapter involves the following general steps (Mullins and Treu, 1991):

1. Study the *nature and causes of human stress,* especially in the context of computer-related job situations, in order to develop a categorization of cause-and-effect relationships
2. Consider *user (dis)satisfaction* as the result or the effect of a number of possible causes, including interface features and performance
3. Characterize the *multifaceted nature of user satisfaction,* in preparation for separating out its more intangible components
4. Hypothesize a general *conceptual measure of (dis)satisfaction* (based on 2 and 3 above) and relate it to psychological stress (based on 1 above)
5. Take advantage of the available *technology and methodology for measuring human stress* in other areas of application
6. *Tailor that methodology* for application to humans interacting with computers

This chapter is generally organized according to the above sequence of steps.

Types of Human Stress

We all know what it feels like, but let us define it:

Definition 9.1. **Human stress**: pressure, force, or strain on the mind or on other parts of the body; internal forces interacting between contiguous parts of the body (including the mind), caused by external forces.

Stress comes in a variety of forms and affects different people differently. The literature provides extensive coverage of types of stress and of how humans differ in reaction to stressful situations and stimuli. Asterita (1985) described how the body reacts to increased levels of stress through changes, such as in the autonomic system and the neuroendocrine system. The type of stress we are interested in (neutral stimuli) may be caused by a change in expected events or by totally unexpected events. A change from what is expected causes a heightening of functions in the autonomic system (Frankenhaeuser, 1980). The amount of heightening decreases with repeated exposure until the subject becomes habituated, ceasing to react (Levine *et al.*, 1978).

Of course, people react in different ways. There are two basic categories for the stress reaction exhibited by people: Type A and Type B (Haney and Blumenthal, 1985). The Type A person is characterized as more aggressive, competitive, and impatient. He/she generally shows a greater increase in sympathetic reactions than do Type B persons, who cannot be classified as Type A. Further differences, even within one individual, depend on the amount of stress and the person's current mental and physical state. Stress normally causes sympathetic reactions like increased heart rate, blood pressure, and blood flow to the organs.

Human expectations also play significant roles at the computer interface. What a computer user expects or needs is not necessarily what he/she gets. Computer technology tends to increase the required pacing, workload, and information-processing demands made on its users. These changes result in stress, especially as persons get older (Czaja and Sharit, 1988; Salthouse, 1985). Indeed, the discrepancy or imbalance between demand and user capability forms a basis for the occurrence of stress (Cox and Mackay, 1981). Thus, given that interactive computer tasks are largely characterized by their information processing requirements, Czaja and Sharit (1988) assert that assessing the potential for stress requires an understanding of the relationship between the cognitive demands of the task and the information processing requirements imposed on the user. Those requirements can be categorized as follows. As a user concentrates on accomplishing a certain task with a computer, he/she must be able to conceptualize, visualize, and process the required information objects and actions. We can refer here to the different knowledge representation spaces and to the interspace mappings to be discussed in Chapter 10. For simplicity, we distinguish only the (1) *interface* space, in which the user must directly see, perceive, comprehend, and process whatever information and instructions are displayed, and (2) the *logical* space, represented by the *task domain*, which may be conceptualized by the user as being operative in the software implementation behind the visible interface. These two spaces are included in the multispace model of Fig. 10.2. Both can be studied with regard to their effects on the user. For example, Graf and Krueger (1989) have investigated how the display screen layout as well as the tasks involving different cognitive requirements affect the user's eye movement. However, the structures and procedures that pertain to the task domain (e.g., the goal structures) may or may not be consistent with the corresponding representations and actions in the interface (e.g., the device structures), as was illustrated by Kieras and Polson (1985). If they are not, a user's expectations are not met, and stress is likely to result.

Stress Causes and Effects

The potential causes or causers of stress in the interface are the interface features (Mullins and Treu, 1991). Their effects on the user can be characterized with the model of Fig. 9.1. The word "feature" (and any specified relationship between/among features) is used here to encompass both its definition and its performance, in comparison with what the user expects or needs. First, there are three types of stress causers (labeled SC) that can affect the user's mental state. Each type involves a discrepancy between the level of cognitive complexity inherent to the computer-based implementation and the user's ability or capacity for handling it:

SC1: Perceived (visual) interface features, to be viewed, utilized, and processed by the user;

SC2: Logical task domain features, to be conceptualized, visualized, and processed by the user;

SC3: Any discrepancies, or incongruities, in the mappings between the task domain features (e.g., how a task must be carried out) and the interface features (e.g., how its logical procedure is presented or confirmed visually)

A number of researchers have studied the effects of factors such as task clarity/difficulty and increased mental workload on user stress (e.g., Sainfort and Lim, 1989; Hart *et al.*, 1987). In addition, if the user can do nothing to change the way things are done, or to exert control over "what

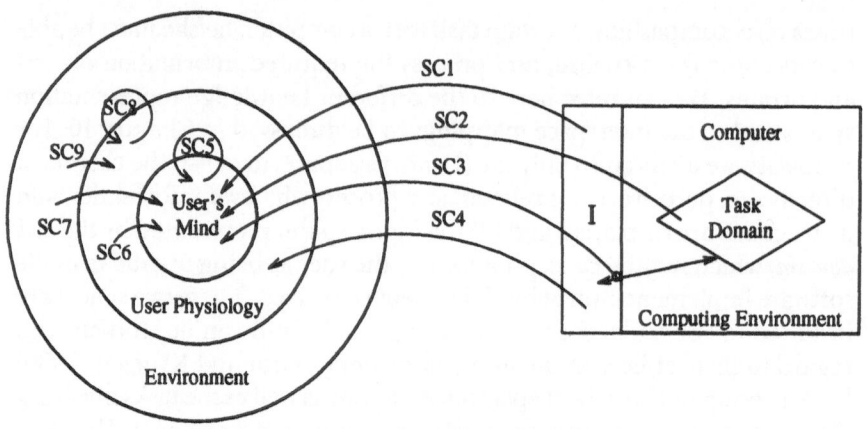

Arc	CAUSE	AFFECTED STATE	Examples
SC1	Perceived interface features	mental	screen layout
SC2	Logical task features	mental	invisible editor clipboard
SC3	Correspondence between task space and interface	mental	edit task structure on display mismatches logical task plan
SC4	Physical interface features	physical	input device, font (size), brightness
SC5	Psychological factors	mental	personal job performance; concerns about career
SC6	Physiological factors	mental	(indirectly) fatigue, back pain
SC7	Environmental factors	mental	competition with peer employees; life events in family
SC8	Physiological factors	physical	hunger, thirst
SC9	Environmental factors	physical	room lighting, temperature; area noise

FIGURE 9.1. A cause-and-effect model. [Reprinted from Mullins and Treu (1991) with kind permission from Taylor & Francis.]

goals, what plans, what kind of feedback" may be desired (Frese, 1987), stress will result.

Computer-based task demands on the user are generally dichot-omized as imposing either physical or cognitive requirements (e.g., Smith, 1984b). SC1, SC2, and SC3 emphasize those features that relate mostly to human cognition. But, to enable HCI, they necessarily must be coupled with interface features that are physical in nature. These range from the characteristics of the display screen (e.g., brightness, font size, color, glare), to various input devices (e.g., keyboard, mouse, joystick, tablet), to the physical layout of the components of a workstation, in relation to the physiological characteristics of the user. A number of studies of the effects of physical interface features on visual discomfort (e.g., Marek *et al.*, 1988; Miyao *et al.*, 1988; Lee *et al.*, 1988) and on musculoskeletal discomfort and postural stress (e.g., Zwahlen and Adams, 1988; Hobday, 1988) can be found in the literature. Spatiotemporal characteristics of the user's eye movements and viewing distances can also be related to the user's working posture and resulting fatigue (e.g., Saito, 1987). This category of potential causes of stress affects the physical state of the user:

SC4: Physical interface features, upon which the user's eyes, hands, motor functions, etc., are dependent.

The four categories identified thus far pertain directly to the relationship between the user and the computer. Unfortunately, those are inadequate to define all of the possible sources of stress that affect users. The user's mental state is also influenced by (dis)satisfaction with personal job performance. Thus, since stress and lowered productivity have been found to be related (Zavala, 1984), that kind of stress tends to feed on itself. This means that a user who is already stressed because of other causes (SC1–SC4), tends to get worse as a result of observing that his/her performance is decreasing. It is aggravated even further by the user's negative feelings about the job (Kumashiro *et al.*, 1989) and by user worries about future career prospects (Sainfort and Smith, 1989).

The user's mind is also influenced by physiological factors. Some of these may result from office ergonomics, and hence are related to SC4 above. For example, health complaints, such as back pain, add to psychological stress (Lim *et al.*, 1989). User fatigue, accumulated from a variety of causal factors in the workplace, also takes its toll in terms of stress (Dainoff, 1984; Marek and Noworol, 1987). A transitivity rule must be operative here, with respect to cause SC4 defined above. The physical features of the interface that influence user physiology are, in turn, contributors to mental stress.

A further group of stress causers that affect the user's mental state involves environmental factors. Included are concerns about the social/competitive situation at work, with regard to peer employees, or about the employer monitoring an employee's work by computer (Smith, 1984b; Smith *et al.*, 1987). It can also involve distress events that have nothing to do with work, e.g., a death in the family.

In summary, the additional three categories of stress causers are only indirectly, or not at all, linked to the computer interface. They are:

SC5: Psychological factors, including worries about personal job performance

SC6: Physiological factors, which work via a transitive mechanism to transmit effects of physical interface features (SC4) and other factors (SC8 and SC9 below) to the user's mind

SC7: Environmental factors, including problems with peers, family, etc.

Finally, two further categories can be identified as affecting the user physically and, because of transitivity, also mentally. They are distinguished from the other causes by being independent of the characteristics of the computer, the user, and their interaction. These causes are (relatively) controllable and can be eliminated or ameliorated by external resources or actions. For example, user hunger and thirst can be overcome by food and drink. Likewise, a poorly illuminated or noisy work room can be rectified by changing those conditions. Thus, these stress causes are:

SC8: Physiological factors, e.g., hunger

SC9: Environmental factors, e.g., room lighting

Figure 9.1 uses cause-and-effect arrows to portray how the above-defined nine types of stress causes affect the user. Illustrative examples are indicated in the legend.

9.4. Basis for Satisfaction

It is now useful to divert our attention from user stress, as presented above, to the potential causes of user satisfaction, or dissatisfaction, with a computer system. The user communicates with the application/task domain via the interface. He/she also relates to the environment. Within that context, cause-and-effect relationships develop between the computer-generated behavior at the interface (or behind it) and the user's satisfaction with that behavior. The level of satisfaction or dissatisfaction can, therefore, be assumed to be the effect of some cause(s). Furthermore, a user's feeling of satisfaction somehow results from mental processes applied to what happens, and to what circumstances exist, in the interface or during the interaction with it. Indeed, it seems very reasonable to consider adoption of the same cause-and-effect model that was created for stress (Fig. 9.1). But now, we interpret the effects to be states and levels of user (dis)satisfaction.

The causes, SC1 through SC9, can be grouped as shown in Table 9.1. First, we assume that the user's mind (level of satisfaction) is affected *directly* by those causes that are attributable to interaction with the computer. These causes are *external* to the user. They are the events, behaviors, and characteristics that

TABLE 9.1
Categorization of Causes[a]

Cause	Influence on user's mind	
	Direct	Indirect
External (by computer)	SC1, SC2, SC3	SC4
Internal (within user)	SC5, SC6	SC8
External (other sources)	SC7	SC9

[a]Modified from Mullins and Treu (1991) with kind permission from Taylor & Francis.

1. Do (or do not) exist or occur at the user-observable interface (SC1); examples are screen organization, command mode, interactive system performance, etc.; they generally involve the features that tend to be common to different tasks; they organize and facilitate interaction.

2. Are associated with the task domain and also the task environment, which affect the user whether or not they are apparent at the interface (SC2); examples are the results of an editing operation on a file, success of a retrieval operation on a database, clarity of explanation of errors detected during program compilation, etc.; they generally involve the more substantive features representing the concepts, structures, and functions of the task of interest.

3. Represent correspondences between the task domain and the interface (SC3); these indicate whether user expectations on how things should work in the task domain (SC2) are confirmed, or reinforced, in what happens in the visible interface (SC1); examples: when certain steps in a stored procedure are included or omitted (at least from user-expected feedback); when the number of data units displayed is consistent with the user's command; and when the structure of knowledge representation, e.g., vertical, is the user-preferred choice.

Other external causes that affect the user's mind directly, but which are not associated with the computer, include such events as disruptions from other people in the area (SC7). In addition, two categories of direct effects on the user's mental state are related to user-*internal* causes, namely SC5 and SC6. These are indicated in Fig. 9.1 by the feedback loop on the user's mind and by the link between user physiology and the user's mind. All three groupings are listed in the middle column of Table 9.1

Certain *external* causes influence the human mind *indirectly*. They involve intermediary effects on user physiology with consequent transitive influence on user psychology. An example is computer-caused eye strain (SC4) resulting from small type font or excessive screen brightness. Other such external causes are SC8 and SC9, with examples indicated in Fig. 9.1. Unlike SC4, the latter two are independent of the computer. These groups are listed in the right column of Table 9.1.

Ideally, causes SC5 through SC9 (in Rows 2 and 3 of Table 9.1) should be eliminated, to enable exclusive attention to the causes of user (dis)satisfaction attributable to the computer (with the exception of SC6, in part, which transmits the effects of SC4 to the mind). If those causes can be eliminated or at least minimized, our analysis of the user-interface situation can take advantage of the well-known stimulus–response model utilized in behavioral psychology. An "input" to the user can be interpreted as a stimulus, or (sequential/parallel) pattern of stimuli, issued by the interface (Treu, 1972). The user's response or "output" is then a command or answer to the system, combined with any associated reactions. In this chapter, such a model is useful for measuring user reactions to interface stimuli. The reactions contain the information that can reveal the user's level of (dis)satisfaction.

How specifically or how broadly the stimuli can be identified depends on how refined or discriminating the measurement methodology becomes. If an effect (on the user) can be ascertained, it is of course desirable to determine its cause as specifically as possible. However, because of the multitude of potentially influential factors involved in the user–computer interface, simplifying assumptions are necessary, leading to relatively general kinds of evaluative conclusions. To compare two different interfaces, appropriate controls have to be imposed, such as holding the task domain constant (SC2 in Fig. 9.1). As a result, the comparison may reflect only certain visible features of the interface (SC1), such as the screen organization and the interaction techniques, and whether or not those features are consistent (SC3) with the expected goal structure of the task in the task domain (held constant).

A Measure of Satisfaction

To enable us to take advantage of the cause-and-effect model (Fig. 9.1) in assessing user (dis)satisfaction, we must know more precisely what the latter term means. A dictionary definition is:

Definition 9.2. **Satisfaction**: the fulfillment of conditions, demands, desires, and hopes.

For a computer user, we supplement that definition as follows:

Definition 9.3. **User satisfaction**: the fulfillment of conditions, demands, desires, and hopes in a computer user's attempts to reach some goal.

The user should have a *describable* purpose or objective in using the computer. Therefore, a user who expects to be "fully" satisfied, while attempting to reach his/her computer-aided goals, is theoretically imposing very stringent requirements on the computer.

User satisfaction should not be treated as if it were one homogeneous quantity. Its above-defined components must be recognized and those which are specific and realistic enough for measurement purposes must be determined. The components are:

1. *Goal(s)*: what the user aims to accomplish with the computer via its interface, within an application of interest and based on selected tasks; the other four components (2 through 5 below) are to varying degrees supportive of achieving the goal(s).
2. *Conditions*: with respect to known physical and psychological needs of the user, to be served by the interface; example: the screen and interactive devices should be organized according to whether a user is right- or left-handed.
3. *Demands*: with respect to what the user thinks is necessary and realistically possible in the computer; example: because the user is very familiar with a certain editor (e.g., vi), he/she expects it to be available.
4. *Desires*: with regard to what the user strongly wishes to get done (even if beyond reach); example: the user has limited time available, but would very much like to complete the entire, extensive editing job, e.g., on an important paper or report.
5. *Hopes*: with regard to a user feeling that what is desired (4 above) is possible and will happen; example: in compiling and executing a complex program, hoping it will be error-free; also, while working on some task, wishing for an important e-mail response from a supervisor or colleague.

The above can all be interpreted as user factors (U-factors) that can/should influence interface design. Conditions and demands fall into the category of user expectations. Desires and hopes belong in the more fuzzy area of wishful thinking. However, they may or may not exceed user expectations, depending on how knowledgeable the user is in what the computer can do.

Measurement efforts must be restricted to the more clearly describable user goals and associated conditions and demands. With respect to a selected subset (or parts, or functions) of the interface, this expectation-specific satisfaction is defined to be the fulfillment of a user-identified goal, given the ith set of *Condition*(s) and the jth set of *Demand*(s):

$$SAT = USER\ SATISFACTION = Fulfillment\ of\ Goal_u|\{Con\}_i\ AND\ \{Dem\}_j \quad (9.1)$$

This equation, as a measure, is conceptually appealing. But, without further definition and refinement, it is of very limited practical value. For one, it needs a unit of measurement or at least a scale for comparison. A percentage or ratio can be useful here. Assuming that SAT represents a variable level of fulfillment, ranging from 0 to 100%, we can define the ideal or complete user satisfaction to be

$$SAT_C = 100\%\ Fulfillment \quad (9.2)$$

while the more realistically achieved level of satisfaction is

$$SAT_{Ai} = Actual\ \%\ Fulfillment \quad (9.3)$$

for the ith interface being evaluated. Then, we can refer to

$$D_i = SAT_C\text{-}SAT_{Ai} = 100\text{-}SAT_{Ai} \quad (9.4)$$

as the difference or shortfall in satisfying the user on Interface i. This D_i can be interpreted to be the part that contributes to *user dissatisfaction*.

It is unclear how large D_i has to become in order to swing the balance for a user from being satisfied to being dissatisfied. If it is only 10%, the user may regard it as a minor irritation, considering that 90% of his/her expectations were fulfilled. On the other hand, if the shortfall is 50%, it probably is viewed quite differently. In any case, our focus is on *relative* stress levels, that is, on the shortfall, drop, or increase from one level to another, rather than trying to measure stress in some absolute sense.

Therefore, the value of the ratio, involving Eqs. (9.4) and (9.3),

$$R_i = (100 - SAT_{Ai})/SAT_{Ai} \quad (9.5)$$

may be more closely associated with a user's switching from a state of being satisfied to becoming dissatisfied. Perhaps if that ratio approaches and exceeds an empirically determined representative value, e.g., 1, the satisfaction scale flips from the positive to the negative side. The thresholds at which this occurs probably differ greatly among users.

If it is possible to ascertain what the shortfall is, at least in relative terms, it would enable direct comparison of Eq. (9.3) and (9.5) for different interfaces. But we need a way to measure either the level of satisfaction or the shortfall. To do that, we must be able to directly observe and physically measure either the phenomenon (i.e., satisfaction or dissatisfaction) itself or some causally related phenomenon for which the relationship is well known, thereby providing an indirect measure of the original phenomenon.

Human stress, as discussed in Section 9.3, is such a causally related phenomenon. It unfortunately focuses on the negative rather than positive effects in HCI. But, on the other hand, technology enabling its measurement is available. Using Definition 9.1, we interpret the human user as experiencing the effects of external forces (from the computer interface), which cause irritations, frustrations, and disappointments in the user's mind. These effects, in turn, trigger internal forces. Technology enables the measurement of effects resulting from those internal forces, e.g., changes in blood pressure.

Before considering such measurements in detail, the following is presented as a conjecture:

A correlation exists between some function F of the satisfaction shortfall, i.e., $F(D_j)$, and the measurable stress level experienced by the user. As a result, the relationship between level of satisfaction and level of stress should be obtainable.

A number of functions are candidates for F. For example:

$$F = c_1 \times R_i + c_2 \quad \text{for some constants } c_1 \text{ and } c_2 \quad (9.6)$$

The constants are dependent on other factors, such as user type, tolerance, and patience; they must be empirically determined. Then, any abnormal user stress measurements, or peaks, obtained during interaction with a particular interface, could be used to (1) identify the particular feature of the interface, or at least its surrounding context, that was the cause, and (2) gauge at what appropriate threshold value the negative response was triggered, assuming that relatively steady (nonfluctuating) baseline measurements are available for the satisfied user state.

How sensitive and discriminating this stress-based measurement approach could become remains subject to extensive experimental work. Available technology and methodology suggest that it does have the potential for useful application.

9.5. Measurement Conditions

Assuming the above-stated conjecture is correct, a relationship exists between the amount of stress a user is experiencing and that user's level of (dis)satisfaction. In particular, a high level of stress would seem contrary to user satisfaction. It implies that the user is, in some sense, not satisfied with the system in question. Relatively low stress levels are harder to interpret as they may indicate complacency or resigned acceptance (habituation). To probe into these questions, the conjecture must be converted into a hypothesis for testing under well-controlled experimental conditions. Experiments must be designed to discourage the user's acceptance of features that are not satisfying. Then, given the hypothesis and also valid candidates for the Function (9.6), we need to develop effective means for measuring user stress.

Available Technology

The measurement of stress has traditionally been performed by chemical means. This rather invasive technique is one of the oldest (Selye, 1980). Stress in humans induces physiological changes, e.g., increased heart rate, blood pressure, respiration, and skin conductance. Recent studies of such changes include the work by Itoh *et al.* (1989), relating heart rate variability resulting from subjective mental workloads (in flight simulators), and the work of Yoshino *et al.* (1989), relating skin resistance reflex and level to mental load and consequent user error rates.

Other techniques are noninvasive, such as direct observation of the subject by a trained observer and questionnaires to determine stress levels. Questionnaires may be used both before and after a subject is exposed to the suspected cause of stress (e.g., Guynes, 1988). Likewise, questionnaires to determine user satisfaction (e.g., Chin *et al.*, 1988) are administered only at the end of the test session. It seems preferable, in a fairly long HCI session, to utilize means to measure stress/satisfaction on a more frequent (incremental, periodic, or critical incident) basis.

Those means come from the field of psychophysiology (Martin and Venables, 1980), and specifically from polygraphy, the technique for determining truthfulness based on physiological indicators of stress. Polygraphy has been criticized for (1) inaccuracies related to inadequate operator training, (2) failure to discriminate extraneous effects, and (3) invalidity of the basic premise. The first of these applies to any such technique; the second can be addressed in the HCI situation, as discussed in Sections 9.3 and 9.4; the last one does not apply to HCI-related use, because we are not attempting to determine truthfulness, only relative stress levels in user responses to system features. Further, the less than perfect lie detector rate cited for experienced polygraphers is considered poor, because of the consequences of a single failure in its normal use. Measurement of computer-caused stress, however, would not rely on a single reading or a single user. Instead, trends and averages over a test population would be of interest. In any case, a false determination for any user would not have a personal, catastrophic effect.

Two general alternatives are available for measuring a subject's physiological stress reaction. The first uses traditional polygraphy equipment, or some newer variation (Asterita, 1985; Martin and Venables, 1980), to measure heart rate, blood pressure/flow, respiration rate, and electrodermal activity. This technique provides continuous, accurate data needed to avoid user interruptions, but it has the disadvantage of physically constraining the user and thus can itself cause stress. Further, the measurements are cumbersome and time consuming, requiring a qualified expert to interpret the output (traces) of the instruments.

A different technique is often used by polygraphers, either separately or in conjunction with the traditional techniques. It uses Psychological Stress Evaluators (PSEs), or voice stress analyzers. It is based on the assumption that stress induces various changes in the musculature of the throat, causing measurable FM vibrations in the voice. These devices have been shown to be nearly as accurate as traditional lie detector methods in determining truthfulness (Fuller, 1976). Detractors use the same arguments against this device as against traditional polygraphic techniques. But, once again, the arguments do not apply to the measurement of user satisfaction/stress. This method is much less threatening, if somewhat less accurate than the others. The user need not even know these data are being collected. However, some interruptions may be required, if the subject is less than ideal at the think-aloud method.

While the subject's stress level can be objectively determined, the causes of the induced stress are more difficult to identify. As discussed in conjunction with Fig. 9.1 and Table 9.1, the potential causes of stress that are not related to the computer should be removed or at least minimized. This must be reflected in the design of the experimental methodology employed.

Data Collection Tools and Techniques

A general framework for determining user stress should actually combine the above-indicated measurement techniques with other techniques or methods that can complement and substantiate the results. This is consistent with the discussion of tools and techniques for data collection and measurement in Chapter 3. Most techniques that have gained acceptance for gathering empirical data come from user-interface experiments and psychology. None is new, and each is accompanied by a body of evidence suggesting its potential usefulness.

To enable comprehensive analysis of stress measurement results, the following profile of data collection techniques and tools is relevant and should be utilized to the extent possible:

1. Administering a questionnaire to determine the Type (A or B) of the individual user, prior to the experiment
2. Administering a questionnaire to determine the current level of stress in the user, both before and after the experiment

3. Administering a questionnaire or interview to determine the user's subjective level of satisfaction
4. Direct observation of the individual using the interface, keeping a written log of all significant observations
5. Making a high-quality audio and visual record (videotape) of the experiment for later reference and analysis
6. Maintaining a time-stamped, keystroke level log of the user's entire session
7. Using a question-and-answer protocol, a variation on the think-aloud protocol method, to determine how the user feels at various points of interest; the user is only interrupted as necessary with simple questions about current interface features
8. Measuring physiological stress indicators, continuously if possible, or at least at selected times or when critical events occur; this should be done as unobtrusively as the technology allows

Experimental results of whatever subset (among the above) is selected should then be correlated in the analysis. The degree of correlation may be used as an indicator of quality of the data. The physiological stress indicators should, in general, match the findings of the questionnaires and observations. Causes of stress should be identified using the visual, keystroke, and observer logs in correspondence to the stress measurements taken at the same timepoints.

Time and funding constraints often limit the experimenter's ability to collect such comprehensive sets of data. The subset of techniques chosen should complement one another. For example, Techniques 3 and 5 provide a relatively inexpensive and effective combination.

Laboratory Setup and Control

The proposed type of experimentation requires closer control than is typical for experiments in HCI. An environmentally controlled laboratory setup is needed, with a minimum of distractions. The subject should be alone to reduce inhibitions and distractions. If possible, the subject should be observed (4) and video recorded (5) through a two-way mirror. A high-quality audio recording is also important, although this may be part of the video record. The subject should be made to feel comfortable in the laboratory and be made aware of an easy way to contact the observer.

The usual precautions should be taken to put the subject at ease with all aspects of the experimental method. Included should be practice sessions with the hardware in the experimental setting. If other means of gathering data are used, e.g., voice protocols (7), the subject should also have corresponding practice sessions. The more obtrusive means of gathering data require extensive use for habituation.

Exposure to specific interface features should be planned to elicit significant user reactions. In particular, it may be necessary to provide time for the user's stress level to return to a "normal" (or baseline) level, to enable more accurate determination of the stress caused by a particular event. Repeated exposure may be used to verify responses, taking care to avoid habituation while allowing the user time to comprehend and learn. Control events (events that are known to cause stress) may be used as further points of comparison. Also, users should be tested with the same interface. Large amounts of data from different users allow "averaging" of results to find trends, without permitting any particular individual to unduly influence the outcome.

To isolate the causes of stress that may interfere with the findings (see Fig. 9.1), environmental causes (SC9) can be eliminated by adequate design of the laboratory. Physical effects (SC6 and SC8) are avoided to the degree possible by preventing fatigue (except as may be caused via SC4) and by remaining sensitive to the physical needs of the subjects. Psychological effects (SC5) are minimized by making the subject cognizant of, and comfortable with, the purpose of the experiment. In particular, the subject should understand that mistakes are to be expected and are, indeed, an essential part of the data being collected. Also, subjects under undue psychological stress related to life events (SC7), e.g., a death in the family, should be disqualified. To the degree that SC8 and SC9 can be eliminated as causes of stress, SC6 (psychological stress resulting from physiological effects) may become the transmitter to the mind of the physiological effects in the interface (SC4).

The general experimental procedure includes noting those significant events that may force a deviation from the above (e.g., a loud noise or reported physical discomfort). The specifics must be determined in context, however, because the design depends on what is being compared. For example, when comparing two interfaces for overall user satisfaction, it is not appropriate to interrupt the user (to allow stress levels to return to a baseline state) or to use control events since these may affect the results. Repeated exposure may, or may not, be appropriate when comparing entire interfaces.

9.6. Potential Usefulness

With ever more computers used in critical applications, such as in air traffic control and in process control in the nuclear and chemical industries, user stress and satisfaction are likely to become increasingly important. In such applications the user is required to work with the interface over extended periods of time. It is essential, therefore, that appropriate measurement techniques be developed. Measurement of user stress, and the correlated user satisfaction, hypothesized in this chapter, may aid in the design and evaluation of all computer interfaces. But it should be of particular importance for the large, high-pressure work environments.

Accurate, objective measurement of user satisfaction can aid in the comparison of alternatives, thereby clarifying design guidelines and supporting the engineering process. Such measures should be used in conjunction with, and may be viewed as complementary to, subjective assessments of user satisfaction resulting from the questionnaire approach (Chin et al., 1988) and Guynes's anxiety measure (1988). An effective, composite method offers promise of providing high-level, objective measurement useful to researchers as well as practitioners.

The measurement of physiological stress is only one technique among a number of data collection techniques to be used in combination for drawing conclusions about the user's satisfaction with elements of the user interface. Each technique or method has been used separately to accomplish specialized tasks. In combination, as proposed, a subset of techniques can serve to reinforce one another, thereby yielding an evaluation process that is more accurate and meaningful. It is assumed that the user can be isolated from causes of stress that are external to the interface. With careful selection of subjects and a proper testing environment, this seems reasonable. Most of the effects which cannot be avoided will be caught during the process of correlating the data, especially with the help of direct observation logs.

The basic premise of this chapter is that significant events at the user interface affect the user in measurable ways. Specifically, dissatisfaction with one or more aspects will cause stress, which, in turn, causes well-known physiological reactions. The literature on stress in computer-related jobs provides ample support for this premise. Yet, it remains to be shown that it holds for transient events at the interface and that other user-internal, interface-caused effects do not create interference. The latter problem is handled in the same way as extraneous causes of stress. The same process of correlating the individual data streams is expected to identify this type of interference. The former problem, measurement of transient effects, has been adequately demonstrated in the literature. Such data are routinely used to monitor patients in surgery and astronauts in space. Less well known is the work of Vidal (1973, 1977), who demonstrated the use of EEG monitoring as a technique for controlling the computer. A more recent illustration of using EEG to measure mental stress is reported by Yamamoto *et al.* (1989). Thus, it has been demonstrated that the types of events to be monitored can be accurately and objectively measured.

The material in this chapter is centered on modeling and interpretation of data representative of user stress and satisfaction. The proposed satisfaction measure obviously must be validated. The results obtained within the framework described must be compared with those produced by other accepted methods, such as direct observation and subjective user reports. Further verification should be possible by presenting the user with a purposely flawed interface (e.g., exhibiting unrecoverable errors, confusing display of information, and poor or incorrect help) and correlating the findings with the expected, intuitively correct results as determined by commonly accepted means. This kind of experimental work is both difficult and expensive to carry out. Nevertheless, it holds promise for producing useful help for designers who are expected to develop stress-minimizing and satisfaction-maximizing interfaces in pressure-packed applications of computers.

Exercises

9.1. Read Chin *et al.* (1988). How do they define "user satisfaction"? To what extent and how does their instrument consider user stress at the interface? Is it viewed as contributing to user (dis)satisfaction?

9.2. Prepare a critique of the nine categories of stress causers discussed in Section 9.3. Are any types of causes of stress not covered? As you place yourself into the position of a real-life computer user, and reflect on what might give you stress, are any of the categories outlined unnecessary or redundant? Explain.

9.3. Prepare a critique of Definition 9.3 and the general measure of satisfaction shown by Eq. (9.1). Do they seem reasonable? Do they seem realistic, in consideration of actually trying to "measure" satisfaction in that way?

9.4. Assume that the conjecture stated in Section 9.4 holds. Then, it should be possible to measure a user's stress level (in a carefully controlled manner) and determine (a) a user's corresponding level of satisfaction and (b) specific interface features or events that caused significant dissatisfaction. For both results, discuss whether the level of (dis)satisfaction determined is likely to be (a) dependent on critical incidents, rising and falling as different interactive features and events are experienced, or (b) cumulative, across all such features and events in an interactive session.

9.5. Consider Eq. (9.6). Again, assuming that the conjecture (stated in the text) holds, what factors might influence the detailed formulation of F, besides the instantaneous or cumulative (dis)satisfaction level? To what extent is the type of user likely to diminish or accentuate the user's stress level?

9.6. The focus on user stress unfortunately carries a negative rather than a positive connotation. Ignoring the correlation between stress and (dis)satisfaction proposed in this chapter, what would you independently list to be the factors that contribute to user satisfaction at the computer interface? Does your list encompass anything not included in Definition 9.3? Where does a very positive event (e.g., a surprising success at the interface) fit in? Such events should obviously contribute to user satisfaction. Do they also cause stress?

9.7. User satisfaction could be tied to the achievement of any of the user-oriented principles listed in Table 2.1. Does that mean that the use of technology and methodology for measuring user stress could be linked directly to determination of whether the design goals have been met? Explain.

VISUALIZABLE OBJECTS AND SPACES

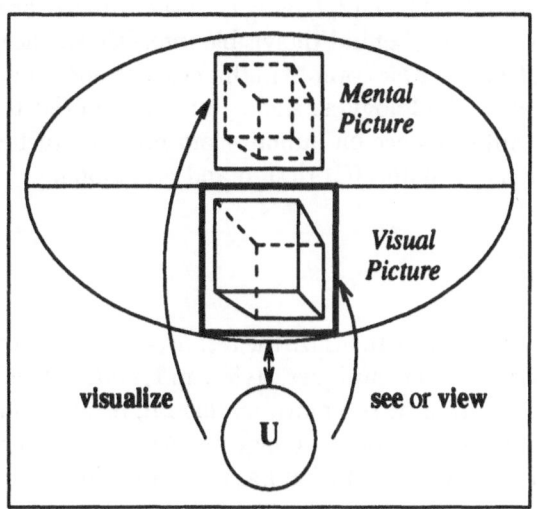

10.1. Overview

According to Chapter 4, interface structures reflect the knowledge representation patterns both of the human mind and of computer-based implementation. But how can they actually be utilized for HCI design in ways that can prove synergistic, effective, and efficient? The answer is contingent on having the designer and evaluator take deliberate advantage of what the user is able to conceptualize and visualize in the interface. In Section 10.2, several prerequisite definitions are presented. These are then employed, in Section 10.3, to describe an object-oriented, layered framework for visualization and, in Section 10.4, to characterize a multispace model encompassing whatever objects a user may visualize in HCI. Each of the spaces is defined.

One of the spaces is equivalent to the visible interface itself. It is the platform on which the contents of any of the other spaces can be revealed to the user. It is also where the user's mental images of any objects may be reinforced or made visible. These mappings to the visible interface are discussed in Section 10.5.

Finally, in Section 10.6, an application is used to illustrate the structure-based mappings from the various visualizable spaces to the user-visible interface surface. The topic of this chapter is pursued further in Chapter 11, with regard to the range of options in interaction style open to the designer in terms of mental and sensory involvement required of the user. That range spans the extremes of (1) making everything directly visible and manipulatable to (2) having the user visualize or imagine all or much of what happens behind the visible interface surface.

The visualization topic covered in this chapter does not explicitly deal with evaluation methodology as such. But the material is presented as having significant influence on human–computer interaction and, therefore, implications for both HCI design and evaluation.

10.2. Definitions

The user must be able to utilize the resources within a computer, given the available interaction techniques, styles, and modes (Treu, 1994, Chapter 6). This means that he/she must, in general, be able to transcend the relatively limited interaction language by trying to conceptualize and visualize what is going on and what has to be done in order to complete a job. Interface designers and evaluators should deliberately take this fact into account. The interface should be conducive to and supportive of user conceptualization and visualization.

These terms are defined as follows:

Definition 10.1. **Conceptualization**: the formation of concepts, including ideas, general notions, patterns, any objects, or classes of objects.

The use of the term "object" here is consistent with Definition 1.1. Examples of object classes are animals, triangles, and objects that move. Now, we can utilize Definition 10.1 to create images of the objects:

Definition 10.2. **Visualization**: (1) the formation of a mental image of concepts or objects that are invisible and (2) making that (or those) visible.

Figure 10.1 portrays the dichotomy suggested by this definition.

The reader might try it out: select your favorite animal object (e.g., a dog), form a mental picture of it, and sketch it on a piece of paper. The resemblance to the real object will vary (depending on artistic skills, etc.), but the above-indicated definitions are demonstrated. The first meaning

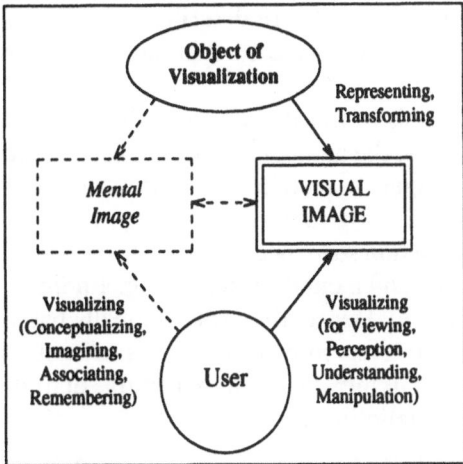

FIGURE 10.1. The visualization dichotomy.

of visualization is necessarily linked to conceptualization. The second meaning, namely making those concepts visible, *should* be dependent on the first meaning and, hence, also on conceptualization. Ideally, the images displayed at the interface should provide visual representation of the physical and logical patterns within and among the objects of a computer-based system, in a manner consistent with the mental pictures created by the human mind. A third meaning can be added to Definition 10.2. It is the hybrid of the other two, in that the user can see a displayed picture and envelope or extend it, in his/her mind, with other (invisible) images and changes. In other words, the viewer can transform a visible object in accordance with relevant knowledge (or mental images).

It is reasonable to ask what kinds of objects a user can visualize, in the sense of Version 1 of Definition 10.2, regardless of whether they subsequently are rendered visible on the interface surface, in the sense of Version 2 of that definition. Within a user's conceptual framework, a great variety of objects must be created, stored, retrieved, transformed, evaluated, and also discarded. These "objects" are constituents of the information, or knowledge, that the human mind must process. The notion that such objects are somehow "manipulated" in user–computer interaction is not new (e.g., Shneiderman, 1983; Hutchins *et al.*, 1986; Tauber, 1986). However, the nature of those objects and how they are represented, relative to the user's mind, require much more study. Consistent with the knowledge representation research (Rumelhart and Norman, 1988) discussed in

Chapter 4, conceptual objects are describable in *declarative* or *procedural* ways. The declarative category is further subdivided into *analogical* and *propositionally based* systems.

Because emphasis in this chapter is on how the user conceptualizes and visualizes objects, the analogical type of representation, dealing with mental or visual imagery (e.g., of a house), seems most important. But the user must also visualize logical constructs (e.g., House A costs more than House B) as well as action sequences or procedures (e.g., the steps required to construct a house) and mental strategies (e.g., finding a suitable contractor to build the house). Hence, the propositionally based and procedural systems are also of interest in considering visualizable objects.

For the latter, let us introduce another simple definition, pertaining to the object of visualization:

Definition 10.3. **Visualizable object**: any object (Definition 1.1) that the user can visualize, or for which a visual representation can be created, according to either or both versions of Definition 10.2.

It is thereby any representable information entity, or any component, member, step, or feature of such an entity. It may be user-conceivable in one of the following ways:

1. *Singly* or in isolation of any other objects
2. As a member of an unordered *set* of objects
3. Within a *pattern* of associations, or interconnections, between two objects (binary relation) or among more than two objects (n-ary relation)

Any set or pattern of objects can, in turn, constitute another object, at a higher level of definition. In general, different levels of objects are representable, ranging from the individual to the collective (as above), from the general to the specific, and from the abstract to the concrete. To illustrate, a user can visualize an individual "dream house," as if it were suspended in space. However, that house can instead be thought of as belonging to a class of houses, separately visualizable but all of the same type (e.g., ranch style). A particular house can, furthermore, be visualized as physically adjacent to (and at some distance away from) an existing house and also as being physically located in a pattern of houses in some housing development. The resulting "neighborhood" can then be visualized as a higher-level object, in a class of similar neighborhoods or in a physically definable pattern of neighborhoods. Although images of houses and neighborhoods illustrate the analogical category of knowledge representation, examples can be traced similarly for the logical and procedural alternatives mentioned above.

10.3. Hierarchy of Visualizable Objects

The above discussion leads to the definition of another model: an object-oriented, layered framework within which a user visualizes and manipulates objects. A diagram of the three-tiered model is shown in Fig. 10.2. Each tier is dichotomized into low-level and high-level alternatives. The user must be able to deal with all of them. The different types can be illustrated by continuing with the example of rooms, houses, and neighborhoods:

- **low_SINGLE**: a particular room, representing either a real, existing room or an abstract, imagined instance of a room
- **high_SINGLE**: a house (containing a low_SINGLE object)
- **low_SET**: m rooms (of low_SINGLE), similar or different, located in that house (of high_SINGLE) or spanning different such houses
- **high_SET**: n houses in a neighborhood (including the one of high_SINGLE); this can also represent n sets of rooms (of low_SET) or some logical combination of those sets
- **low_PATTERN**: one specific house (of high_SINGLE) is located to the left of another house (within high_SET objects); or a specific room (low_SINGLE object) is located above another room (within high_SINGLE object and among low_SET objects)
- **high_PATTERN**: a specific row of p objects within the neighborhood object (high_SET); or two vertical floor objects, each containing a specific subset of the multiroom objects (low_SET)

Types high_SINGLE and high_SET provide a certain kind of implicit (but indefinite) structure (S-structure, Fig. 4.4), in the sense of general constituency or composition of their respective lower-level objects into collective objects. Types low_PATTERN and high_PATTERN, however, are intended to specify structure among component objects in explicit form.

In addition to the relationships already suggested by the above example, the following pairwise relations apply to the six object types. These associations are also portrayed diagrammatically in Fig. 10.2.

- Types *low_SINGLE and high_SINGLE*: the latter can be transformed into the former; this "downward" transformation can be repeated to whatever level of generality or composition desired and possible. Alternatively, the low_SINGLE object can be partitioned or refined, if desired and possible, into two or more component objects also of low_SINGLE type, thereby transforming the original object "upward" into a high_SINGLE object.

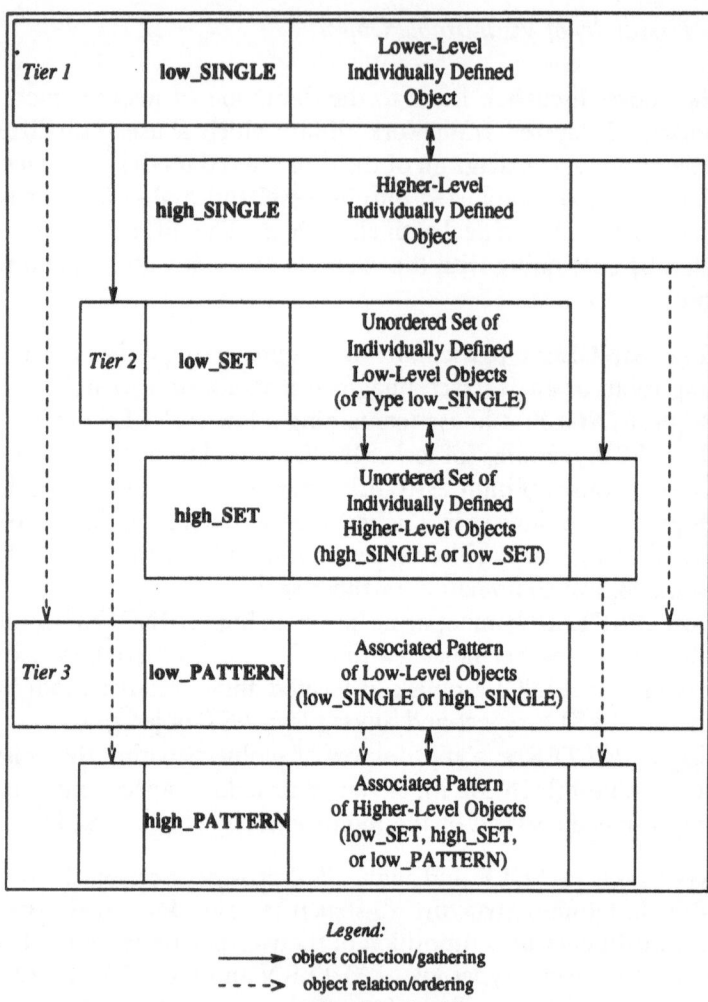

Legend:
———▶ object collection/gathering
- - - -▶ object relation/ordering
◀——▶ up/down transformation

FIGURE 10.2. Three-tiered relationships and transformations among conceived object types.

- *low_SET and high_SET*: contain individually defined objects (low
  _SINGLE or high_SINGLE, respectively) at some level of definition. A high_SET object can be transformed downward to a low
  _SET object, contingent on redefinition of the lower-level types of
  objects. For example, the neighborhood must become a high_SIN-
  GLE object, while the house becomes a low_SINGLE object. Likewise, low_SET objects can be transformed into high_SET objects,
  assuming again that the lower-level objects are suitably redefined

(e.g., the low_SINGLE object might become a wall, the high_SINGLE a room, and the low_SET the four walls in the room).

- *low_PATTERN and high_PATTERN*: with explicit association patterns among the individually defined objects (low_SINGLE and high_SINGLE) as well as the sets of objects (low_SET and high_SET) that are extremely variable, depending on the kind(s) of interface structures (Chapter 4) deemed applicable.

To summarize the above,within each tier of the object-oriented framework (Fig. 10.2), both a lower-level and a higher-level definition of objects apply, confirming the *upward and downward transformation* mobility that is present in the human mind. From Tier 1 to Tier 2, the process of object *collection* or *gathering* into composite, unordered sets takes place. This is done for both lower-level and higher-level objects, based on some criteria, such as measures of similarity or any common attributes among members of a set. Then, from both Tiers 1 and 2 to Tier 3, the process of imposing explicit patterns of physical or logical *relation* or *ordering* among objects can be invoked.

Table 10.1 indicates the rooms and houses example plus two other examples, involving text strings and also personal and family names and relationships. Still another example of the model framework emphasizes a different kind of relation among objects to be conceptualized. Instead of focusing on inanimate things such as houses and rooms within them, or on names of people (individual and families) and relationships among them, it deals with definitions and relationships among individual and species of animals.

- *low_SINGLE*: a particular cat
- *high_SINGLE*: a species of cat, e.g., lion or tiger
- *low_SET*: a number of cats (of low_SINGLE) belonging to a species (high_SINGLE) or spanning different species
- *high_SET*: two or more species of cats (high_SINGLE) in the genus *Panthera*
- *low_PATTERN*: one particular cat (of low_SINGLE) has the same color as another one; the tiger species (high_SINGLE) is larger in build than the lion species
- *high_PATTERN*: several of the cats of low_SET are siblings (i.e., a litter); two particular species of cat (high_SET) share the same habitat

As the user's conceptual focus moves up or down the scientific classification hierarchy, corresponding transformations among the object types must take place. For example, if the user replaces the different species in

202

CHAPTER 10

TABLE 10.1

Objects of User Visualization

Type	Basic unit, level, and pattern	Characteristic user orientation	Examples
low__SINGLE	Information object, concept, entity, component, process, at low level of definition	To an individual or isolated object	(a) alphabetic character (b) personal name (c) room
high__SINGLE	As for low__SINGLE, but at a higher, composite level	"	(a) word (character string) (b) family name (c) house
low__SET	As for low__SINGLE, except for n such objects, associated in a set	To multiple, unordered objects (similar or different)	(a) letters in alphabet (b) names in a family (c) rooms in a house
high__SET	As for low__SET, except for n higher-level objects	"	(a) words in a sentence (b) families among relatives (c) houses in neighborhood
low__PATTERN	Two objects that are related spatially, temporally, logically, . . . , resulting in an ordering[a]	To a pairwise association between objects (similar or different)	(a) one letter precedes another (b) one family is friends with another (c) one house is left of another
high__PATTERN	As for low__PATTERN, except for three or more related objects[a]	To pattern(s) of association among the objects	(a) Sequence of words (sentence) (b) hierarchy of family names (c) specific row of houses

[a]Objects may be similar (as peers) or they may differ (e.g., in containment: a "process" object within a "network node" object; or the "1993 year" object within the "20th century" object)

"Genus *Panthera*" in high__SET with different genus in "Cat Family—Felidae," then the other object types must be redefined upward accordingly. (See the exercises for computer-related applications of the model.)

Different object types are expected to require different visualization efforts of the user. An individually defined object should be more easily visualized than an unordered set of two or more such objects. The latter, on the other hand, may or may not be more difficult than a specific pattern of objects. It depends on the nature of the objects and the complexity of their relationship pattern. Determining the impacts of object types on visualization effort, especially if they are somehow measurable, can be of interest to interface evaluation. The kind of impact to be studied of course depends on evaluation purposes, etc., as discussed in Part III. Primary attention at this point is on how an object, of whatever type, may be represented differently in different "spaces," producing different effects on the user's visualization.

10.4. Spaces for Object Representation

Both physical and logical considerations may pertain to the different types of conceivable objects. In general, it is important to distinguish whether the information objects and relevant associations exist in the real world, or in some logically structured domain, or in computer hardware/ software representation, or by visual representation on the interface screen, or in the conceptual space of the user's mind. Accordingly, we can give a general definition for the space in which visualizable objects are contained:

Definition 10.4. **Visualizable space**: the conceptual, logical, or physical domain within which visualizable objects are defined.

Every such object is assumed to "occupy space," exhibiting some degree of *spatial extent.* This is expected of images represented with analogical knowledge (Kosslyn, 1980; Shepard and Cooper, 1982), but is also assumed to be necessary for logically and procedurally defined objects. For the latter, spatial extent implies various logical distances such as "number of steps" or "number of levels" between logical constituents.

As implied above, five visualizable spaces are especially relevant to HCI. They are individually defined as follows.

Definition 10.5. **R-space**: the *real* world domain, encompassing objects or patterns of objects that exist in physically measurable form, with regard to dimensions, shape, weight, temperature, color, etc.

Definition 10.6. **L-space**: a *logical* domain, covering objects that exist only in logical form and that are measured in terms of logical distances; or that give logical representation to objects existing in R-space, including values and relations resulting from (or approximating) the physically measurable characteristics.

Definition 10.7. **S-space**: a *software and database* domain, defining objects that exist in their own right within a computer implementation, e.g., with distances between storage locations; or to assist in representing objects in L-space and, therefore, also R-space.

Definition 10.8. **I-space**: the visual *interface* domain, portraying visually (or graphically) any objects or patterns of objects from R-, L-, or S-space; or to display user-input objects conveying currently envisioned contents of U-space (see below).

Definition 10.9. **U-space**: the domain created by the *user's* mind, mapping into/from any of the first three above-listed spaces, with or without (effective) intermediary help from I-space.

The first letters of each of the five spaces obviously were chosen for mnemonic utility, based on the respective key words printed in italics. Consistent with Definition 10.2, the user is not only able to see, or view, what is displayed at the interface (I-space) as well as what is real and physically measurable (R-space), if that exists and is in view; the user may also visualize objects in any of the other spaces, even if they are not displayed (or not displayed properly) in I-space, and even if they don't exist in R-space.

Figure 10.3 shows how these spaces relate to each other and how they correspond to Chang's (1989) distinctions between physical and logical pictures. Table 10.2 illustrates the spaces, using both real tree and logical (family) tree objects. R-space is being restricted to physically existing objects and physically distinguishable (measurable) characteristics, e.g., color. Hence, a set of trees is necessarily ordered, or in some pattern. Logical characteristics of physical objects (e.g., their names) are consigned to L-space.

Actually, each of the other spaces could be interpreted to have its own (surrogate) R-space. For L-space, it could be the physically marked, pencil-on-paper representations; for S-space, the computer hardware storage locations and patterns; for I-space, the touchable screen area and what it displays for user viewing; and even for U-space, the brain cells and the patterns of associative storage in human memory. However, the physiology of the brain is not of interest here. Also, because the major responsibility for visualization support is assigned to I-space, any "real" representations pertaining to L-space and S-space are, in effect, merged with the I-space model. For example, any L-space approximation of a tree should also be viewable in I-space, as should be a (logical) layout of memory locations containing the stored representation of that tree.

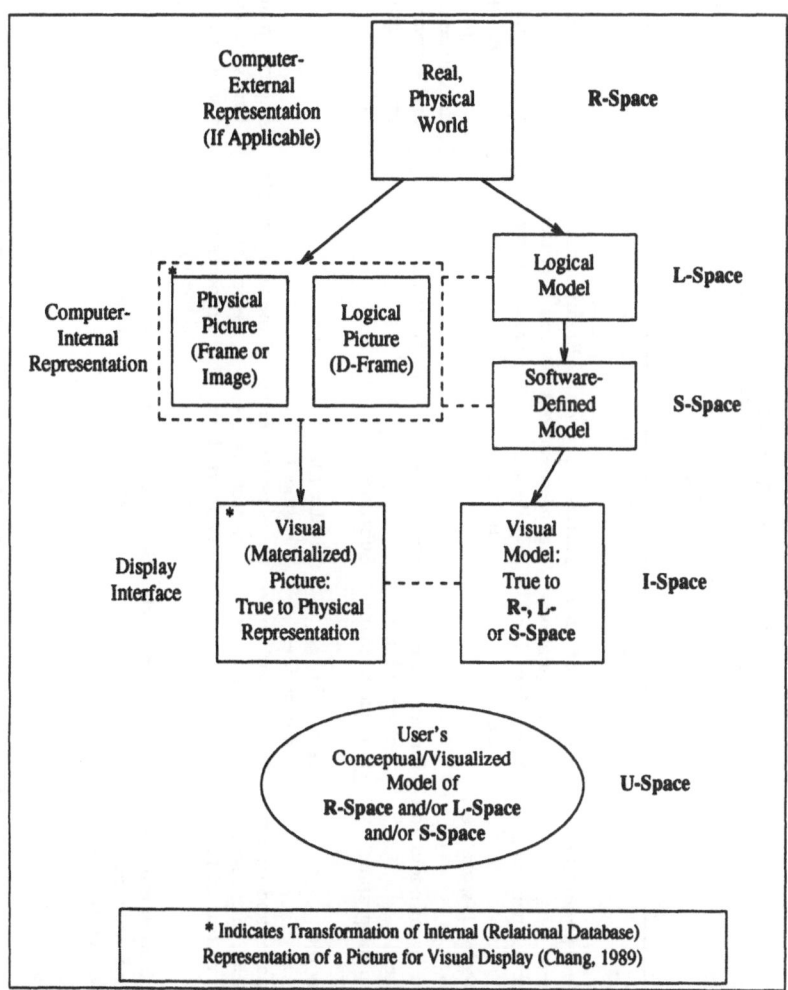

FIGURE 10.3. User's conceptual space in relation to the R-, L-, S-, and I-spaces. [Reprinted from Treu (1990) with kind permission from Academic Press.]

TABLE 10.2
Making Objects Visible for the User

Object exists or defined in:	Single object	Pattern of objects	Object component	Object feature	Means for representation or expression
R-space	A tree	Row of n trees	Branch or leaf	Greenness (of leaf)	Through real, physical existence
L-space	Approximate representation of R-space tree	Sequence of such approximations	Partial representations	Feature name or classification	With R-space measurements and relations
	A family tree (L-space origin)	Several family trees	Specific tree branch	Branch name	Using symbols, language, predicate logic
S-Space	Either R-space or L-space tree, defined by				Using computer storage data structures, algorithms and software, according to representative L-space data
	(1) Linked list of nodes and branches	Linked sequence of linked lists	Indexed sublist	Attribute or label	
	(2) Bitmap for graphic display	Multiple bitmaps	Subraster		
	(3) Display file	Several linked display files	Display file segment		
I-Space	Displayed images and features in pictorial, diagrammatic, graphic, or textual forms	Same as for single object (as supported by S-space)	Same as for single object (as supported by S-space)	Same as for single object (as supported by S-space)	Using computer and video hardware and software for visual display of any of the above
U-Space	Any above object(s) conceptualized and visualized	Same as for single object	Same as for single object	Same as for single object	Using human thought processes, memory, vision, perception
	(1) Independently without I-space				
	(2) In conjunction with I-space				

aModified from Treu (1990) with kind permission from Academic Press.

10.5. Mappings to the Interface

The reason for including U-space as a distinct space is that, for purposes of research, it can give separate identity to the very complex conceptual framework of the user. U-space transcends and reflects the other spaces. Because it contains visualized object representations, it qualifies as a space in its own right. Although it is extremely variable because of individual differences in cognitive and memory skills among users, the definition of U-space lends itself to studying the different abilities to conceptualize and visualize objects, with or without assistance from I-space (Table 10.2).

The U-space is equivalent to a composite, structured "visual space" (Chang, 1990) that encompasses both of the following

1. *Mental Picture*, resulting from visualizing the information objects and patterns in one or more of R-space, L-space, and S-space
2. *Visual Picture*, resulting from S-space supported creation of information objects and patterns that originate in R-space and/or L-space for user viewing in I-space

A U-space representation, then, involves the construction of a mental picture that is either preceded or followed by rendering it visible to the user in I-space. If the visual picture in I-space comes first, it may assist the user in creating a mental picture in U-space. Consistent with the dual role attributed to U-space, the I-space model should be bidirectional. It should enable both output to the user, by making objects visible (realistic, etc.), as well as input from the user, to create, manipulate, etc., the visual objects.

According to the second definition of visualization (Definition 10.2), a pure U-space representation of an R-space object is only possible if the user sees the object directly, in its physical form. Even then, limits in vision and perception might somehow distort the object. An alternative, near-approximation of an object in R-space is to present it via video camera (or its logical equivalent) in I-space. This is R-space visualization *with I-space help*. Any other representations of R-space objects are considered as belonging to L-, S-, or I-space.

There is one exception to this rule. It is implied by the mental picture–visual picture dichotomy (Fig. 10.1) outlined above. According to the first definition of visualization, a user with the required ability is free to visualize in U-space any of the other four spaces, including R-space. This is visualization *without I-space help*. It enables user creation of R-space entities (e.g., a tree, a dog), at least in approximate forms, and without directly seeing them.

In a sense, a U-space representation of any object in the other spaces is a special kind of conceptual L-space model. It could be defined as some logical combination of the R-, L-, and S-spaces, as seen through and constrained by any visualization facilities provided by I-space. Among the potential problems that can be isolated (or diagnosed) during interface evaluation is the user's frustration about not getting I-space confirmation of images, in a manner consistent with what he/she visualizes.

Also, as a result of the different spaces defined, the user may have mode problems, that is, problems distinguishing which of the four spaces (other than U-space) is currently invoked. This depends on the interface design and on the user's depth of understanding, interest, and reasons for using (see below) the information system. A novice user may only want to see and manipulate surrogates of R-space or L-space objects and do so in as simple a manner as possible. He/she may prefer to be shielded from the space-dependent technical details. A more knowledgeable user, however, may want to probe into the accurate and detailed representations and compare their task-specific effects.

10.5.1. Object Existence and Utility

The user may visualize the objects and patterns of objects as they exist in any one or more of the other four spaces. This is illustrated by Table 10.2. Whether or not the user does (or can do) this intentionally and reasonably correctly is dependent on the user's mental characteristics, including capacity and inclination toward structured thinking and problem solving.

The mere *existence* of an object or pattern of objects in a certain space may not justify its mental representation in U-space. Its *utility* may be the dominant factor in determining whether that mental effort should be carried out. That is, the user relates (in U-space) to objects in one of the other spaces depending on the purpose of the interactive application. This can be illustrated with an analogy to an on-line conferencing situation. If a user (the conference leader) wants to organize, at minimal cost, a real (physically together) meeting of participants (the objects) in some city, then the participant locations and distances from the selected site matter greatly. Technically, the R-space model, visualized by the user independently, or an L-space surrogate of it, seems appropriate in this case. If instead the on-line conference is to probe into locally implemented policies on some issue (e.g., what is true for a participant in Los Angeles versus one in New York), then the location factor combined with local, enveloping context may have important implications. Physical distances may not matter. In other words, only selected aspects of the R-space model are important. If, on the other hand, the conferencing topic centers only on soliciting participant opinions on some question that is independent of factors like participant location, distance from others, and contextual environment, then none of the above R-space factors may affect the outcome. A logical (L-space) model, associating participant objects with their opinions and recording them (in S-space) for later analysis and retrieval, may be the appropriate choice.

10.5.2. Desirable Visualization Features

The computer user must somehow create meaningful mappings between object-oriented U-space models and the corresponding information objects and patterns that exist or are defined in R-, L-, or S-space, and ultimately in I-space. But, besides being dependent on personal knowledge and mental abilities, the user is at the mercy of whatever functionality is designed to support I-space. If only one mode of visualization is available, pertaining to one space, the user may be seriously constrained. The situation is aggravated even further if that one mode is not representative of any space or is inappropriately structured. On the other hand, if multispace mode versatility is provided through I-space, and if this is done in a well-structured and user-conducive manner, the user has much greater visualization powers available in the system. This becomes even more attractive if it is coupled with user freedom to experiment and determine which representations happen to be most convenient and effective. Terms like versatility, attractiveness, and freedom in visualization should some day become subject to the kind of evaluation methodology presented in previous chapters.

Above-indicated features suggest that both designers and evaluators of interfaces must learn to understand the characteristics of the user's mind, to the extent feasible. This means that multimode (or multispace) visualization support should be provided through I-space, but in a task-specific manner and only as needed and preferred by the user. Clearly, this has implications for the choice of interaction style, as discussed further in Chapter 11.

10.6.   Multispace Visualization

In Fig. 10.4, the user (U-space) is situated on the left, viewing/visualizing I-space and the other spaces behind it to the right. From the perspective of the user, this setup is itself representative of an H_z-structure (or an $H_z + O$ hybrid), suggesting a lateral distance, or "interface depth," as discussed in Chapter 4. The lower half of the figure outlines an example of a user

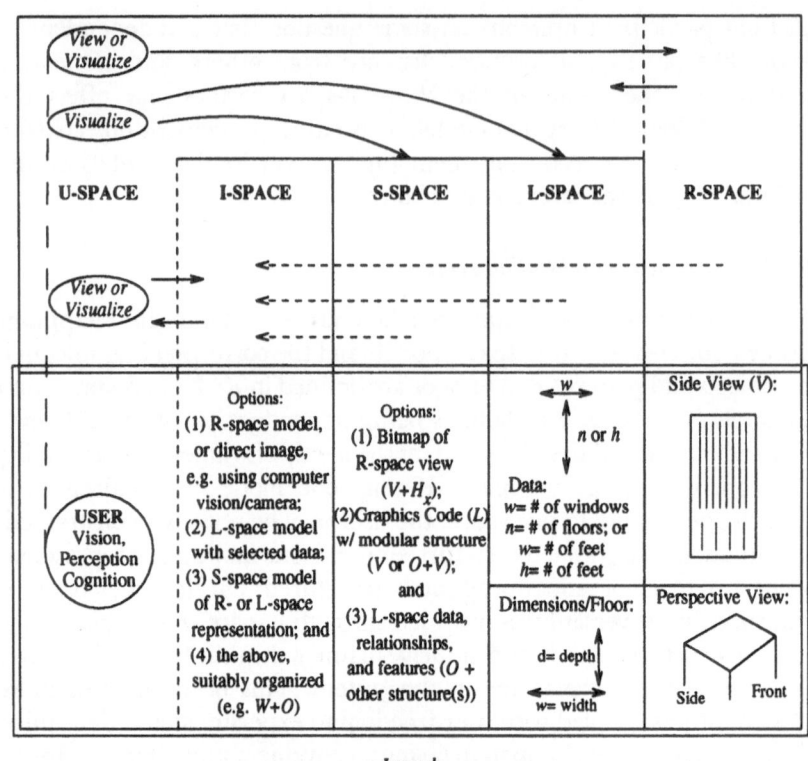

FIGURE 10.4. Multispace object representation and visualization. [Reprinted from Treu (1990) with kind permission from Academic Press.]

visualizing an object represented within the multispace model (Treu, 1992). The user is considering the layout of an n-story office building that an architect (maybe the user) has designed. The primary representation in this case is analogical, but propositionally and procedurally based representations and applications can be treated similarly, as discussed in Section 10.7. Some interface structures that apply in each of the four spaces (other than U-space) are indicated. Depending on the user's current task and interest, any one of the four spaces, or some combination of them, may be the object of the user's attention. Suitably structured access to all spaces should be made available. This example includes potential user viewing, in I-space, of a building existing in R-space. To do so, special camera equipment would have to be available, and resulting images would have to be displayed within a region of the interface surface. The possibility of using the virtual reality style for user viewing is also relevant. But there are different versions or degrees of virtual reality, ranging from realistic motion pictures (representing R-space) to realistic computer-generated, dynamic imagery. In the latter case, the presentation really comes from L-space and S-space, rather than R-space.

Besides stratifying the application into the different visualizable spaces, the primary purpose of the example is to indicate how different structures may be appropriate for different purposes. But sometimes a structure and its orientation (e.g., vertical versus horizontal) may not be as important to a user as having the same structure used for the same purpose and under similar circumstances. That is, the structure chosen and presented at the interface should correspond to the structure and mental orientation that the user has learned to expect for the type of task-specific representation involved. It should be utilized on a consistent basis. It is also necessary to adapt to user differences. The nonexpert user should be shielded from structures in S-space. However, the more sophisticated user may want to have direct, visual, and logical access to all technical details and patterns. In that case, a "coverup" approach may be totally unacceptable. In other words, structural mappings should preferably be individualized, to adapt to the particular knowledge and preferences of each user.

In summary and analogous to Kieras and Polson's (1985) hypothesis, designers should endeavor to create effective correspondences between pairs of structures situated in different spaces. And evaluation should ideally be able to certify such correspondences and detect situations in which mismatches exist. Mismatches should be avoided, unless they are essential because of incongruities between patterns or because a novice user's U-space demands simplified versions. In general, the I-space representation of R-, L-, and S-space models should be conducive to and consistent with what the user visualizes and expects in U-space. This is a very difficult design challenge. Among the prerequisites for meeting it, designers and evaluators must understand the different kinds of interface structures. This topic is addressed further in Chapter 12.

10.7. Software Visualization

Thus far, this chapter has considered the visualization of whatever objects might be of interest to the user. As suggested by the general definition of "object" and as mentioned in a number of places, those objects can come in many different forms and types. Included is the software variety, which is of great interest to computer scientists. So we are concluding this chapter with a characterization of software visualization, relating it to the multispace model presented in Section 10.6.

Although visualization seems to have become popular only recently, it established roots years ago. Computer graphics actually provided the initial impetus for what computer scientists now call visualization. The ability to display 2-D and 3-D objects at the user interface, ranging from static diagrams, symbols, and plots to dynamically transformable and realistic objects, patterns, shapes, surfaces, and scenes, was a remarkable improvement over previous methods. Graphic images are clearly more conducive to the mind of the human user.

But most such efforts focused on visualizing objects generated by user applications of computers, such as the representation of a car in computer-aided design and the display of performance data using a histogram. Techniques for visualization of the *software* responsible for those graphic objects were relatively ignored. The programs were normally visualized by means of sequential listings of code, preferably in a modular pattern. Further, the traditional flowchart was used when available. The modular organization of programs, combined with flowchart diagrams, gave early evidence in favor of visual (or visualizable) support mechanisms that could render the software more understandable to both developers and users.

The need for software visualization has gained increasing attention over the last decade. Motivating factors include: (1) greater sophistication in the computer applications being implemented, leading to (2) more complex requirements for analysis and optimization in software design, especially to take advantage of (3) high-performance computer architectures and environments. Thus, in a sense, the more powerful types of computer technology are stimulating computer scientists into becoming more intensely interested in visualization models and techniques that can enhance the human user's capabilities.

However, computer scientists have tended to view visualization almost totally in terms of "making objects visible," i.e., the second version of Definition 10.2. It is now becoming more recognized (e.g., Price *et al.*, 1993) that both versions are necessary in order to address the topic comprehensively and with greater likelihood of achieving desired results.

The dichotomous interpretation (Fig. 10.1) is important because evaluation of the effectiveness of a visualization technique depends on how well the visible object corresponds to a user's already existing mental images and/or facilitates the user's creation and understanding of a new mental image of an object. Conversely, we must ask whether and how the user's (preconceived) mental image of an object can be used to influence the creation and also the modification of a displayed object. In other words, visualization should be evaluated with regard to both its output (to the user) and its input (from the user). A visualized object is, therefore, not only subject to static representation; it must also be changeable and, furthermore, it should preferably be possible to invoke any changes in real time, under either computer or user control.

With regard to computer-based representations, the objects of visualization include not only the myriad of entities (of different data types and multiple media) that are defined within computer applications; they also include the components and models of the computer hardware and software supporting those applications. In this section, our interest is in objects that are specifically software-based or software-oriented. A considerable variety of only such objects exist. To deal with them systematically, we distinguish the abstract-level representations (e.g., algorithms) from the implementation-oriented representations (programs).

Definition 10.10 **Program visualization**: visualization in which the objects are computer programs, including the code (programming language statements) and any data (data structures), both in their static representations and in their dynamic behaviors.

Definition 10.11 **Algorithm visualization**: visualization in which the objects are abstract-level representations, models, or specifications of program objects.

Consistent with Price *et al.* (1993), our definition of *software visualization* is then the union of program visualization and algorithm visualization. Within those subcategories, the usual distinctions apply, based on user needs to visualize either *systems* software or *applications* software, or some combination of those two.

Using the above-indicated distinctions in definition, it is possible to illustrate different objects of interest and their existence in or dependence on different spaces (Section 10.4) by relating to the multispace model shown in Fig. 10.4. We utilize that model again in Fig. 10.5, thereby providing insight into the different types of representation that may be applicable to any particular software object and also the interactions (among representations) and transformations for visual presentation at the interface.

Although software visualization, as defined earlier, seems to involve the conjunction of S-space and L-space, the user may actually have to visualize objects representing any of the first four spaces, in addition to creating images in his/her mind. The challenges facing researchers are (1) to determine how to represent an object in each of some subset of the R-, L-, and S-spaces, (2) to transform the representation(s) for effective presentation and visualization by the user via I-space, and (3) to enable

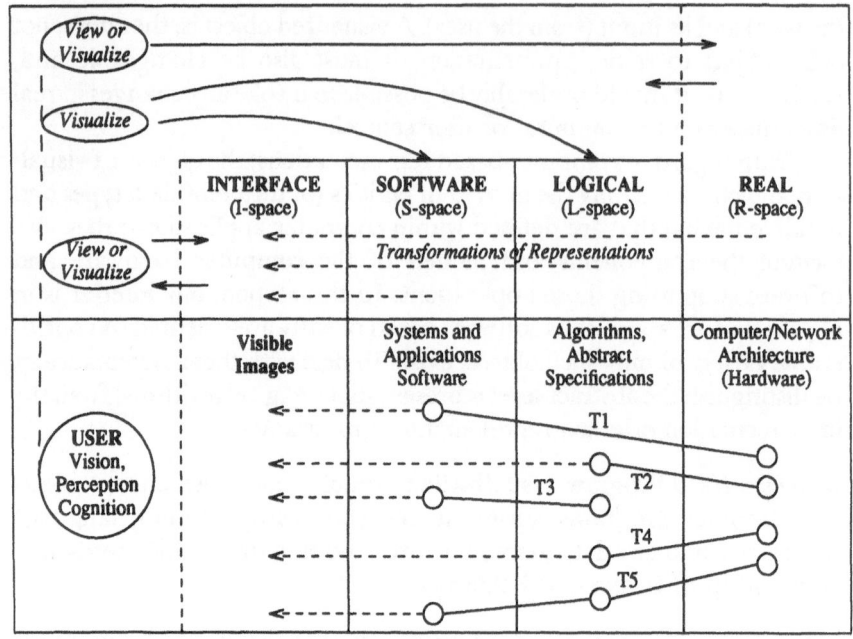

FIGURE 10.5. Example visualizations of software objects.

effective user interaction with the resulting visible object(s). Included is the interest in meaningful animation of objects at the interface, such as of algorithms (e.g., Stasko *et al.*, 1993).

The labels T1 through T5, in Fig. 10.5, refer to different possible visualization-intensive combinations or transformations that can be reflected by software objects. Example objects are:

T1: *programs*, represented in S-space, e.g., programs involving parallelism (e.g., Dow *et al.*, 1992) and the need to optimize them; such program structures are also significantly dependent on the corresponding algorithms (L-space) and especially on parallel hardware architectures (R-space).

T2: *algorithms*, represented in L-space, e.g., for purposes of scheduling (e.g., Mossé, 1993) to evaluate performance using step-by-step animation; such algorithms are designed to schedule the CPUs, disks, memory, etc. (R-space), in single- or multi-resource configurations within operating systems.

T3: *programs* (S-space), for purposes of creating representations in L-space, e.g., by means of the parsing and extraction of the "meaning" of a program from its embedded comments (Massari *et al.*, 1993).

T4: *systems*, existing in R-space, such as computer networks, for purposes of producing meaningful representations in L-space, e.g., the graphic model suggested by Fig. 11.2.

T5: *systems* and *networks*, existing in R-space or planned in L-space, for purposes of modeling (L-space) and creating software (S-space) to support simulation and animation of model outputs (Treu *et al.*, 1991).

With regard to the last object listed above, labeled T5, the modeling and simulation of computer systems and networks is a potentially effective method for analyzing and predicting performance. But the process of modeling, in preparation for simulation, requires considerable user creativity and ability to conceptualize and visualize the systems that are to be modeled.

The prototype interface system we developed is specifically designed to provide the user with interactive visualization support. To enable a user to create an original model of either a real or a hypothesized system, a graphical editor was designed to utilize basic symbols (representing processes, resources, entity flows, etc.) in the construction of a graphical model on the visible screen. Then, the resulting visual representation can be transformed automatically into a shell of the corresponding simulation program (implemented in a new, process-oriented simulation programming language, HSL) that is structured to facilitate such transformations. Thus, a (partial) program visualization can be produced and also viewed at the interface, based on the logical, graphical representation originally created by the user. This capability is particularly useful for persons who are not skilled simulation programmers. But the graphical models themselves are effective in supporting the visualization needs of all users, ranging from novice to expert. Further, all models, whether graphical or program-based, can be added to a library and retrieved for future user reference.

In addition, the simulation phase is supported by means of a dynamic form of visualization. That is, as a programmed model is executing, the increasing and decreasing lengths of queues (waiting for critical resources) can be represented visually and animated.

Visualization Factors

The taxonomy of software visualization presented by Price *et al.* (1993) is based on the following six "categories": scope, content, form, method, interaction, and effectiveness. The first two, scope and content, delimit the software objects to be visualized. We already talked about them above. The other four factors are briefly discussed below.

Visualization form relates to the characteristics of presenting visual images, including the display medium used, the style of output (e.g., static or dynamic), its appearance (e.g., shapes and colors), and also multiple views. A computer interface must have the capabilities and flexibility needed to represent objects of visualization in variable forms, utilizing both static and dynamic displays, including motion and animation where appropriate.

However, one element of form in which we are especially interested in this book is the study of structures that underlie the various representations to be visualized. Interface structures were defined in Chapter 4. Such structures are essential ingredients of the object representations in different spaces (Fig. 10.5) and the transformations between/among them. Ultimately, they can significantly affect the visualization form seen by the user. They also influence the *interaction* techniques and styles (e.g., DMI) to be employed, to ensure that the user can have suitable control over the visualization. Included should be capabilities for interactive manipulation and navigation through the structured images.

The form and interaction features of visualization contribute to its *effectiveness*. As asserted at the outset of this section (and in Chapter 4), a visualization is unlikely to be effective if it is not conducive to the way user's think, or to the way in which users conceptualize, perceive, understand, create, and use visual images. This means that visualization should not be produced in an arbitrary manner, without suitable structure and without careful attention to the meanings conveyed by the visual objects and patterns of such objects.

Finally, the visualization *method*, according to Price *et al.* (1993), encompasses certain style and connection considerations. The style questions include: will the visualization be hand-coded or use a library of visualization tools? Will it be fixed or be produced automatically? The connection question relates to how a specified visualization is actually implemented (or instrumented) in software. For example, does it require invasive insertions in the code, contrary to software engineering principles? Or can it work as a nonintrusive tool that can be wrapped around the code?

It is obvious that there will not be any shortage of potential visualization objects for which human–computer interfaces can be designed and evaluated. Among the important research objectives for HCI investigators will be to determine the most *effective* ways of representing, transforming, and presenting visualization objects in support of users needing synergistic, effective, and efficient ways to interact with computer software. Special emphases should be placed on (1) visualization form, including underlying structures and visual semantics, and (2) visualization method, including tools to support both automatic and user-directed generation and modification of visual objects. In order to evaluate the effectiveness of alternative forms and methods, for any type of object, we must conduct experiments with users as subjects. The results, over a period of years, will surely advance the state-of-the-art of both HCI design and evaluation.

Exercises

10.1. Suppose you have a mental picture of a structured computer program you must write. If you have a diagrammatic interaction technique available, you could convert that mental picture into a diagram displayed in one window. Assuming that you have already written two (of three) required procedures, you can also have images of those in your mind (in approximate line-by-line detail) and request that they be made visible in another window of the screen. (Also, the high-level program structure diagram could highlight the boxes or other symbols representing procedures already completed, e.g., with color coding). But the third (not yet written) procedure you can only visualize, in general form, by creating a mental picture of it. Given the situation outlined, discuss the relationship between and relative importance of the two versions of Definition 10.2.

10.2. For Exercise 10.1, which interface structures would you use in visualizing (a) the total, high-level program structure and (b) each individual procedure? Why?

10.3. Assume that the computer application involves your being supplied with five well-defined variables (or values), labeled A through E. You are to use them in a mathematical expression to calculate some result. At which levels of the three-tiered model (Fig. 10.2) would you visualize the objects involved? Explain.

10.4. Repeat Exercise 10.3 for the retrieval of information, relevant to Subject Terms A, B, and C, from an IS&R system or a DBMS. The subject terms are initially a set of visualized objects.

10.5. Assume that you are editing a text file. You are conceiving and/or visualizing objects in each of the following contexts: (a) replacing a word in a sentence with a different one; (b) correcting the spelling of a word used repeatedly in several different sentences, spanning two or more paragraphs; (c) moving a paragraph to another position in the text. For each case, identify a level from the three-tiered objects model (Fig. 10.2) that seems most applicable, and discuss whether you could transition up or down in the model to carry out other related editing operations in the same context.

10.6. For each of Exercises 10.3 through 10.5, identify the interface structures that you would/could use in visualizing the objects, both (a) in your mind and (b) in displaying them on the interface screen.

10.7. Construct a realistic interactive situation involving (a) display of several window and menu objects, (b) visualizing the file objects in your directory object, to decide on which one(s) to output in selected windows, and (c) editing a selected file, i.e., debugging a computer program (written in some language), in preparation for compiling and executing it. Does each of the three aspects of your interactive work require a separate instantiation of the three-tiered visualization model (Fig. 10.2)? If not, why not? If yes, do the different instantiations have to be integrated somehow? In either case, discuss how the different visualization models (and relevant structures) might make the user's mental work easier or more difficult.

10.8. For Exercise 10.7, distinguish the three different aspects of the interactive work with regard to which visualizable spaces (Definition 10.4) must become involved. To what extent is your answer dependent on how knowledgeable the user is?

10.9. How could you extend the interactive situation of Exercise 10.7 so that the user would be required to visualize objects in all of the defined visualizable spaces (Definitions 10.5 through 10.9)?

10.10. For each of (a) novice users and (b) experienced users, what are the likely consequences of representing objects in I-space (for some application) that have no resemblance to relevant representations in *any* of the other visualizable spaces? Such an approach can result either from deliberate efforts by the designer or from poor interface design. Under what circumstances, if any, might it be justified to have a user work with visible representations (objects) at the interface that are totally illogical or unrelated to objects in the intended application? Can you cite an example of such design?

10.11. Construct an example similar to the bottom half of Fig. 10.4 for the application of CAD&E, specifically designing an electronic circuit board. Include identification of appropriate interface structures for each space.

10.12. Repeat Exercise 10.11 for the application of computer programming, by designing a computer program in some procedural language. Take into account the software visualization material presented in Section 10.7.

INTERACTION AND MENTAL INVOLVEMENT

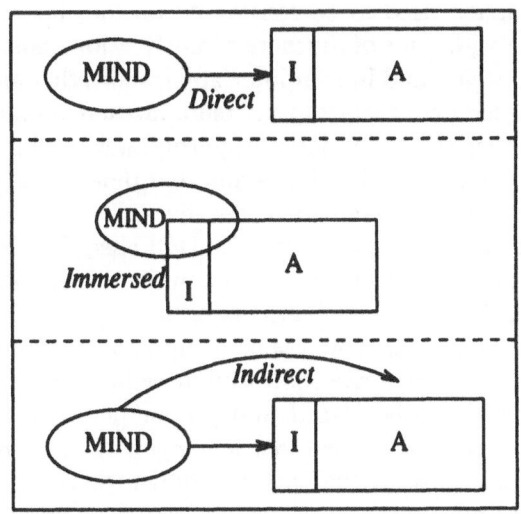

11.1. Overview

The development of HCI design and evaluation methodology throughout this and the companion books has emphasized the treatment of user and computer as a combined system. Words like "partnership" and "synergism" are employed, and interdependence between the two information processors is stressed repeatedly. At times it probably sounds akin to a marriage, whether voluntary or forced, between two rather dissimilar entities. The cause-and-effect model makes clear that the enabling and constraining factors of the two, in combination, have determining effects on the feasibility of creating interface features and achieving desirable levels of performance. In other words, for the union to work out with reasonable success, both have to do their parts; both must be prepared and participate in the interaction.

But all of the above is based on the unstated presumption that the users are willing, although possibly limited participants in the partnership.

Maybe users do not want to be that "involved." The pin-on buttons that were handed out to attendees at computer conferences years ago, reading something like "MY COMPUTER UNDERSTANDS ME" (supposedly better than one's spouse), are probably not valid for many people. Some have an outright dislike, even hatred, for computers and interacting with them. On the other hand, some persons may use a computer as a surrogate companion and aspire to become a closely linked and harmoniously functioning combination.

Such discussion used to be considered on the "farfetched" side of things. But now, with some of the more recent developments in interaction techniques and styles, and in computer applications that are on the near horizon (e.g., home-based access to and manipulation of unlimited, audio-visual resources via the "information superhighway" and using television and computer interfaces), the above-indicated thoughts become increasingly pertinent and are no longer provocative.

The point of this chapter is that the HCI specialist should view the potential of human–computer interaction in its totality, not in a myopic way conditioned by personal experience with certain limited design options. He/she should understand the basic ingredients of interaction techniques and styles, but then rise above and move beyond them. Ultimately, the whole topic has to be placed into proper perspective, with *highest priority given to the needs, preferences, and rights of the human user*. Not everyone will want to use "virtual reality"; neither will everyone want to use DMI. We must understand the major choices, their pros and cons, and tailor the user's extent of involvement in appropriate and discretionary ways.

Section 11.2 defines a model based on five key variables or dimensions, according to which the degree or extent of human involvement in HCI can be characterized. It is followed by discussions of three major alternatives, namely direct manipulation (Section 11.3), virtual reality (Section 11.4), and indirect, visualization-based interaction (Section 11.5). Section 11.6 presents an example using the visualization-based style, and Section 11.7 defines and discusses a measure of "conceptual distance" and how it might impact the user's mental efforts in HCI. The chapter concludes with some observations.

11.2. Dimensions of Involvement

The degree or extent to which a user becomes involved in HCI can be discussed in terms of the relevant physiological and psychological factors. But interaction is not only dependent on what the user is able to do physically (e.g., with visual acuity; arm–hand dexterity) and mentally (e.g., with logical reasoning); it is also influenced by the user's background and inclinations as well as the nature of the application of interest. In other words, the entire profile of U-factors mentioned in Chapter 2 can give a pretty good idea on how qualified and predisposed a user might be to get "involved" with a computer for application-specific purposes.

And that is not all. The reader is probably anticipating that the user's involvement is also contingent on what the computer is capable of doing. The kind and amount of support provided by the computer clearly impact what can/must be expected of the user. The interface may be designed to keep the user relatively uninformed and even uninterested in greater involvement. This can happen, intentionally or not, if the interaction style makes everything at the interface appear to be self-explanatory and straightforward and, hence, perhaps rather routine, unchallenging, and even boring.

Another possibility is for the interaction style to be anything but boring. It might insist on a certain kind of involvement, which, in the extreme, forces the user into a "straightjacket" of having to do things in a prescribed way only. The style itself may actually be attractive but difficult for the user. The main problem is that the user may have no options, such as turning to a less demanding technique which places greater responsibility on the computer side of the interaction.

On another extreme, the interaction style might foster variability and freedom of choice as to the degree of involvement with which a particular user is most comfortable. The choices might vary depending on the user, the user's current mood and inclinations, and the nature of the task at hand.

The following five variables constitute a model that seems reasonable for portraying the degree or extent of user involvement in HCI. In brief, consider that interaction with a computer requires each of the following:

1. *KNOWLEDGE* ABOUT THE APPLICATION DOMAIN, distinguishing (a) computer-dependent from (b) computer-independent knowledge
2. ABILITY TO *EXPRESS* the application-specific actions, objects, and qualifiers, in terms of the language being utilized
3. ABILITY TO CONCEPTUALIZE AND *VISUALIZE*, focusing on forming mental (imagined or imaged) pictures of objects
4. *SENSORY* AND MOTOR FUNCTIONS, with particular emphasis on the visual, audio, and haptic channels
5. *INITIATIVE* AND ASPIRATION, especially to advance in knowledge and skills, based on appropriate challenges and stimulation;

in part this connotes whether a user can/must be active (aggressive) or passive in pursuit of completing computer-aided work.

The first three variables represent important aspects of the human mind and its abilities to represent knowledge. Having application-specific knowledge subsumes the need to have it in (human) memory and being able to utilize it; utilizing it implies being able to express it and to communicate it via action–object patterns; conceptualizing and visualizing objects and actions here refers to being able to do so within the user's mental framework. The latter is not equivalent to viewing the object on a display screen (see Definition 10.2). The fourth above-outlined variable is self-explanatory. It is prerequisite to the workings of the other three. Users tend to be quite different in all four of these variables.

We could add the variable of human intelligence (or intellectual capacity) to the model. It certainly varies greatly among users, and it can be argued as important to a user's potential for becoming more deeply involved with a computer. But, for our purposes, consideration of intelligence is neither desirable nor necessary. The first three dimensions of the model (knowledge, expressiveness, and visualization) are sufficient for representing mental capabilities.

The fifth variable is rather different. Regardless of how sharp the user might be with regard to the first four variables, he/she may or may not be motivated or stimulated enough to want greater or more demanding involvement. It depends on such factors as whether success and career advancement are deemed important, especially for persons whose jobs are contingent on the use of computer technology.

All five variables, mnemonically identified by the acronym KEVSI, can be treated as factors representative of user capabilities, i.e., the U-factors. For each one, we can assume a simple ranking of the demands made on a user by a particular interaction style. Suppose we use 1 for lowest and 10 for highest demand. Then the following profile for some anonymous interaction style,

KNOWLEDGE: 3
EXPRESSION: 3
VISUALIZATION: 1
SENSES: 5
INITIATIVE: 1

implies that the user can be very passive, must exhibit fairly intense use of sensory and motor functions, but with low demands for knowledge of the application and for ability to express it in language. Also, there is no need to form mental pictures independently of what is viewable on the screen. Presumably the latter is possible because the application is very simple or the computer does everything necessary (via its output channels), including giving the user self-evident instructions and cues at each step on what to do and what to do it to.

The implications of this example are clear: either *the user* must have minimally acceptable capabilities for each variable of the model or

1. The capability is obviated because *the application* does not demand it, or
2. *The computer* must have a corresponding capability in support of the interaction, either
   • To reinforce or enable what the user must do, or
   • To complement or compensate for what the user does not have or is unable (or unwilling) to do.

Thus, the KEVSI model boils down to representing the mutually supportive or complementary situation between user and computer in interaction. It turns out, therefore, that the model is not only useful for characterizing the degree to which the user becomes "involved"; it also gauges to what extent the interface, or the interaction style being used, is capable of supporting different degrees of user involvement. In other words, the variables of the model collectively also provide an evaluation of interaction style.

The next three sections describe three major interaction styles with reference to the KEVSI model and its implications for what the user is expected to do. The three categories are labeled surface-level interaction, sensory immersion, and interface-transcending styles. Reasons for that terminology should become apparent.

11.3. Surface-Level Interaction

The interaction style based on traditional, command line techniques (without special forms of assistance and direction from the computer) requires the user to be rather knowledgeable and to be able to express the actions and objects by means of frequently cryptic and illogical sequences of words and parameters. The need for users to visualize those command objects and structures is substantial, although this fact was relatively unrecognized in years past. That was partly because of the serious lack of visual/graphic support provided by interfaces, which can encourage and reinforce command visualization efforts.

With regard to use of sensory and motor functions, the users only need to view the text displayed and key text in by hand. So, pure command line interaction neither makes much demand nor causes much excitement in the sensory category. Finally, the last variable of the KEVSI model is definitely critical to basic command line style. If a user wants to succeed, in spite of high demands in each of K, E, and V, while simultaneously working in a less than exciting sensory mode, S, he/she necessarily has to be highly motivated and show considerable initiative, I. No wonder that many people were turned off by computers and became resistant to having them invade their work environments.

But advances in computer technology have significantly enhanced the repertoire of interaction styles and features possible. Especially influential have been computer graphics, including color, microminiaturization of componentry, personal computers, and workstation configurations, often including multiple media for I/O. As a result, HCI researchers took appropriate advantage and created interestingly different, user-oriented interaction techniques and styles.

One style that has really caught on is DMI. Over nearly a decade of use, it has become symbolic for many people of the ideal type of interaction. It has almost become a de facto standard (Buxton, 1993) that designers aim to emulate.

Let us look at it with reference to the KEVSI model. By definition, a user of a DMI is expected to contribute as follows:

K: Not much knowledge should be needed; the amount that is necessary should be easily learnable.

E: Within the context of continuously displayed objects (e.g., icons) and available actions on those objects, the user *should be able to express* (i.e., select, gesture) everything that is required.

V: Because the objects are directly displayed and manipulated, the user need only *view* them; the need for visualization, in the sense of forming mental pictures independently, should thereby be minimized.

S: A much more extensive range of sensory and motor skills is necessary than for the traditional command line interface, although the amount of keying in of text by hand is of course reduced significantly if not eliminated; the user must not only see and perceive the displayed objects in their 2-D and even 3-D (with perspective depth) layouts, but also be able to select and manipulate them with various physical devices; recognition of distinct audio outputs (e.g., as feedback cues) may also be necessary.

I: How much motivation and initiative are required for the user to become prepared and involved? Not too much, in view of the facts that K is low, E and V can be handled within that low-knowledge context, and S tends to make the interaction fun and exciting (for a while, at least, until things become routine).

Some researchers have started to question the performance of the DMI style (e.g., Morgan *et al.*, 1991) and to ameliorate some of its problems, e.g., confusion in expressing clearly the semantics of objects (Rohr, 1990). Several investigators have carried out comparisons of DMI interfaces against command-driven interfaces. Eberts and Bittianda (1993) did so with regard to user preferences about corresponding mental models. Svendson (1991) basically determined that the "user friendliness" that is engendered by the DMI is accompanied by sacrifice: it tends to reduce the user's problem-solving ability. In effect, the user can get certain things done without having to think very deeply about what is going on.

Thus, we have apparently progressed from an interface style that was perhaps too demanding of the user to a style that may be appealing and effective for certain applications but, at the same time, too undemanding. It fosters a relatively superficial or surface-level interaction, which may not be very conducive to stimulating (many) users to become more knowledgeable about computer technology, i.e., of what goes on behind the visible surface. This point relates to the multispace visualization model of Chapter 10.

But, besides the attribute of superficiality, the DMI style has also been criticized for being seriously inadequate with regard to enabling expressiveness (variable E) for certain applications. As Buxton (1993) has pointed out, DMI principally supports specification of objects and actions by (visually based) demonstration rather than by description. As a result, the user can be severely hampered in trying to describe a required action, e.g., in CAD of a large logic array. Buxton says that DMI is "woefully weak in supporting the articulation of the type of Boolean or conditional expression required."

Yet, the reader should not misunderstand the purpose of this discussion. Development of DMI has been very important to HCI and computer users in general. It has demonstrated various positive features of computer use and contributed to having many people accept computers in both their work and home environments. But it is time to look at the result very objectively, to realize its strengths and weaknesses, and to create alternative styles that may be partly dependent on DMI but provide future designers with a rich assortment of choices.

11.4. Sensory Immersion

In a manner somewhat analogous to the development of DMI, virtual reality (VR) hit the HCI scene several years ago and made a big splash. It is also becoming very popular, although far fewer people have access to it compared with the DMI interface at the same stage of development. That is obviously because of the special hardware/software required (e.g., Foley, 1987), although it is possible to configure a VR interface at fairly reasonable cost (e.g., Pausch, 1991). Also, substantial software (programming) effort is needed to implement VR applications (e.g., Shaw *et al.*, 1992), especially if the interaction is to be of high graphical quality.

VR undoubtedly represents a significant development. Several sectors of our society, including the medical and nuclear industries, are considering its potential for providing real-time "visualization" support for critical, computer-aided applications. Even the possibility of performing surgery on remotely located patients is being hypothesized.

How does VR measure up in terms of degree of user involvement? The variable of the KEVSI model that is most critical to its success is:

S: Immersion of the user's sensory and motor functions within a seemingly real, visual 3-D space.

VR is not a singular concept; it actually encompasses a range of capabilities reflected by different values of S, which depend on how deeply the human senses are drawn into the application. On one extreme is a relatively detached user viewing of something that looks very realistic; on the other extreme, the user is thoroughly involved in (or enveloped by) that apparent reality. This general range is confirmed by the following historical account.

For many years, the human mind has been tricked into believing that the changing images on a TV screen or at a computer graphics interface are continuous, even though they are in fact sequences of discrete images that are displayed repeatedly at a rate too fast for the mind to distinguish. The mind simply manages to blend them into each other, or fuse them into a continuously changing image or scene. The result is the illusion of continuity, which is one significant constituent of realism. Computer graphics experts take advantage of that illusion in creating remarkable animations of objects, processes, and scenery displayable via computer interfaces and duplicated in some highly successful movies.

Related is the ability to make the mind perceive depth in objects and scenes that are displayed on a 2-D surface. Using appropriate perspective depth calculations, the user gains the illusion of depth along the third dimension of a perceived 3-D space, even though the space (or medium) is technically 2-D. Other techniques used for rendering computer-generated images increasingly realistic in appearance include hidden line/surface removal, color and shading, shadows, close approximations of irregular and curved surfaces and their textures, reflections and refractions, high-lighting according to light sources, etc. (Foley *et al.*, 1990).

Notice how important the human sense of vision is to the kind of realism achievable. It channels visual data to the human mind. The latter fortunately (for our purposes here) submits to the illusion of reality that is created by the data. However, the mind is still situated comfortably in a position *external* to the apparent reality produced on the display screen. That is, as in the traditional mode of a person watching a motion picture in a movie theater or on TV, the viewer remains safely seated, away from the action depicted, unless he/she allows the mind to project him/herself into the scenery by imagining personal presence and involvement.

The latter possibility became increasingly likely with the advent of broad-screen movies played in old-time theaters. The more extensive and intense (relative to the viewer) the visual spectrum or panoramic view appeared, coupled with powerful audio channels (some emanating from clearly distinguishable directions, in stereo), the more likely it was for the viewer to be "suckered" into the scene and feel included in it.

It was natural, then, to take one more step. Disney World in Florida created an interesting experience for visitors seeking total audiovisual immersion. People could stand in the middle of a large, round room, which was darkened except for the 360 degrees of coordinated moving pictures displayed on the surrounding walls. The sensation was amazing to visitors. Without really exerting any conscious mental effort, the audio-visual sensory inputs in such an arrangement are interpreted automat-ically by the mind. A genuine feeling of reality results. Even an ill feeling in the pit of one's stomach can be caused in such an environment if, for example, the surrounding movies depict a swooping-down airplane flight or a roller coaster in which one is riding.

Thus far, several alternatives have been indicated along the spectrum of VR possibilities. They have ranged from user perception of continuity and depth at the interface, with the user remaining independent of the scenery and relatively uninvolved, to the user being immersed in an audiovisual space in which the mind becomes totally (and involuntarily) involved. We can now follow the natural progression to a full-blown VR style in HCI. It requires the capturing and encapsulation of all of the above-indicated capabilities within computer-assisted hardware and sup-portive software in a manner that can immediately surround the user and the user's primary senses. The latter of course must include the audio-visual effects that can be provided via headgear enclosing the user's eyes.

In addition, special handgear is added to enable the user to use the haptic channel as well, by carrying out "pretend" (virtual) touching and manipulation of objects perceived in the enclosed medium of the headgear. Appropriate input signals from such devices inform the computer of the object being manipulated and the details of the user's actions in such manipulation.

That, in essence, is what the fully developed, user-involving VR style of interaction with a computer-based application is about. As stated earlier, the variable S of the KEVSI model is most critical to it. What about the other variables?

K: Knowledge required of the user is very much dependent on the application involved; if the application is "architectural design" and the user can get a guided tour of some modern architecture, he/she may just "go along for the ride" and enjoy; on the other hand, if the VR application should involve medical surgery, the user (physician) better be extremely knowledgeable in the application, and the "virtual" reality design better be extremely accurate, fail-safe, and close to "real" reality.

E: The same is true for this variable as for K above; some applications may not require the user to "express" or articulate a whole lot; the user may simply be able to experience the audiovisual expressiveness of the computer implementation; on the other hand, expressing oneself by means of hand-controlled gestures and manipulations, possibly even complemented by selected forms of speech, can be very demanding and draining, especially when critical, stress-inducing applications are involved and when the VR facilities are less than comfortable.

V: Deliberate visualization, in the sense of intentionally forming mental pictures, is in effect obviated by VR; that is, the sensory immersion is so extensive that, assuming that the mind is carefully and comfortably synchronized with the computer-generated, audiovisual dynamics, it is automatically and completely involved.

I: Does the user need to be active and show initiative? Again, this depends on the type of application; if the computer does all of the work, the user is able to benefit from the results while expending little personal effort (other than being there and letting the sensory facilities do their thing); on the other hand, if the VR application is demanding (in K and E), the user may have to conjure up considerable initiative and motivation.

The last point is especially revealing. Many users are likely to experience discomfort in, if not stressful resistance to, submitting themselves to the VR illusions on a regular basis. It tends to imply a kind of giving up personal control. It is one thing to undergo a fantasy experience through an exciting movie or a guided tour; it is another matter to conduct significant, computer-assisted work via VR as a matter of routine. The stresses reported by/for computer workers can already be severe, as discussed in Chapter 9. They could get much worse.

But it is too early to tell; the jury on VR is still out. As was said for DMI, VR is serving a very useful purpose and will undoubtedly occupy a specialized role in the range of interaction styles available for HCI designers. The recommendation in this book is to treat it as such. It is one among a number of options. It too should not be viewed as the ultimate and end-all solution to interface designs.

11.5. Transcending the Surface

Unlike DMI and VR, the primary focus in the third illustrative interaction style is on user involvement through visualization (variable V). The multispace model presented in Chapter 10 is used to describe it. The user is assumed to be able to visualize, in the sense of constructing mental images of objects existing in each of the following spaces:

- *R-space*: real, physically measurable representation
- *L-space*: logical representation of R-space and other objects
- *S-space*: software- and database-instantiated representations of L-space and R-space objects

Notice that these are all "behind" the visible interface surface (e.g., see Fig. 10.4). The interface medium, named I-space, is directly viewable (the second meaning of visualization). Thus, in the extreme, if a user has minimal I-space support (e.g., basic command line interaction), his/her mind (U-space) is obliged to transcend the interface surface by visualizing, via mental pictures, the objects and actions required within an application.

The reader may conclude immediately that this style surely is not very good. It sounds like the antithesis of DMI. However, one drawback of DMI, as pointed out in Section 11.3, is its relatively superficial nature and the resulting shallowness in knowledge expected of the user. So, let us keep our options open. We have many stylistic choices available. If the user wants (or is required by someone) to become more deeply involved in an application, it should be possible to do so. Perhaps an "indirect manipulation interface," or IMI, is desirable at least for selected parts of an interaction. It is also useful for developing a better understanding of the major stylistic directions available to interface designers.

The three styles portrayed in this chapter, namely DMI, VR, and IMI, are summarized with regard to the KEVSI model in Table 11.1. It is evident that the IMI alternative has a generic profile of ratings at the opposite extreme (mostly) of those representing DMI. The table entries for IMI assume, for the sake of emphasis, that the user is practically doing everything on his/her own, i.e., with little support from the interface. That is of course not very realistic, especially in view of the types of assistance (in K, E, and V) we are now capable of providing.

One approach is to consider interaction style as a design feature resulting from custom-tailoring. That is, the DMI, VR, and IMI options can be used in hybrid combination, either in succession or in parallel, to serve the changing needs and preferences of users with respect to involvement in different stages of interaction. Thus, instead of being restricted to a singular style, the user could have the option of switching modes. Selected integrations of styles might also take place. For example, a DMI style interface can enable (or necessitate) the user to select an IMI or a VR style object in order to pursue the corresponding avenue of interaction until a local goal (e.g., task completion) is reached.

Assuming that an integration of styles is desirable, it seems best to select one style and utilize it as the baseline for modification or enhancement with one or more other styles. Accordingly, the next section considers a network-oriented visualization example using the IMI style. It is done with reference to the multispace model of Chapter 10. The example is followed by definition and discussion of space-dependent "conceptual distance" in Section 11.7. The use of such a measure in the mapping of visualized objects to viewable objects at the interface is hypothesized. For purposes of object viewing, appropriate help from the interface is essential. Included must be the introjection of other techniques, e.g., graphical, and other styles, such as DMI and VR.

TABLE 11.1
Summary of Major Styles

Style	Knowledge (K)	Expression (E)	Visualization (V)	Senses (S)	Initiative (I)
DMI	Low	High (in limited context)	Low	Medium	Relatively low
VR	Variable	Variable	Sensory-immersed	High	Variable
IMI	High	Variable (depending on interface help and language used)	High	Low	Relatively high

11.6. Visualization Example

Consistent with Definition 10.2, any knowledge objects relevant at the interface are either visualizable in the sense of mental pictures constructed by the user, or visualizable in the sense of being viewable. If the separations between visualizable objects are logically defined, e.g., in terms of logical layers or links, a viewable model (I-space) should be easily available. But if distances between objects are based in R-space, the I-space representation can present difficulties. These may be due to the limitations of either the interface or the user. The fact that display screens are very limited in physical size tends to make proportional images of patterns of objects inconvenient, if not impossible. If for no other reason, there may not be enough pixels in the x- and y-directions to enable the digital representation of an object that is much larger in one dimension than in the other.

A network-oriented example (Treu, 1990) highlights the user's needs. Visualization of an R-space representation is often served well by an L-space model. The other spaces, S-space and I-space, play supporting roles in visualization, depending on the nature of the task and the interaction style available.

An R-Space Pattern

Consider the model of Fig. 11.1. The user communicates via an interface with some collection of objects. Within the user's network-oriented perspective, the objects could be any computer-based resources (e.g., hardware devices, software processes, database systems) or human resources (e.g., other users or collaborators) that are available in a network-wide information system domain. Or they could be retrievable information entities (e.g., documents, surrogates, facts) that are defined more abstractly (e.g., in terms of relevant subject areas). Any of these resources could be situated within one network node or distributed over two or more nodes in some pattern.

Within R-space, the situation is as follows. At time point t, each object, o_i, has an identity (including object type and other attributes) and one or more relationships to other objects. Each object in R-space also has:

1. A real (physically measurable) distance from the interface surface: $\mathbf{RD}_t(I,o_i)$.
2. A real distance from every other (similar or different) object: $\mathbf{RD}_t(o_i,o_j)$. If two objects (e.g., files or processes) reside in the same node, the physical distance between them may be assumed to be zero or some logical, structure-based quantity.

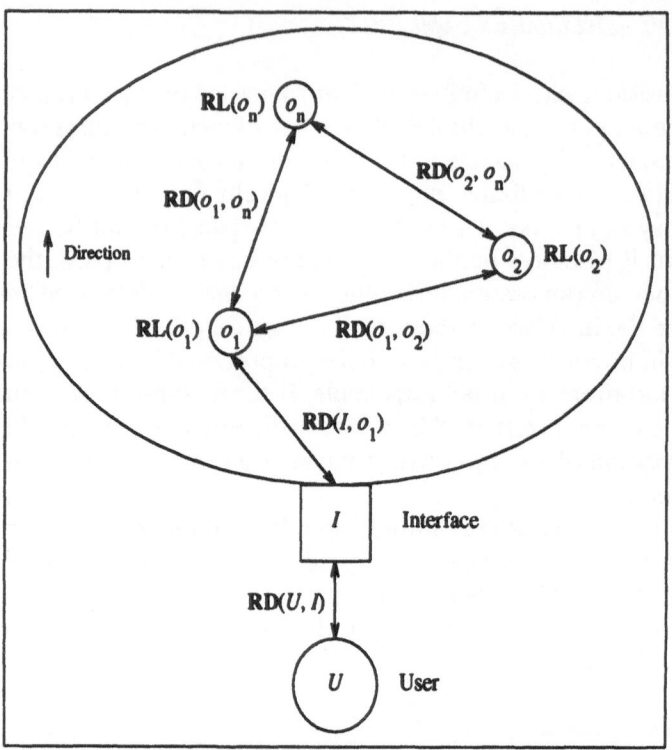

FIGURE 11.1. Model of user interaction with network-based patterns of real information objects. [This figure and Fig. 11.2 are reprinted from Treu (1990) with kind permission from Academic Press.]

3. A real (physically identifiable) location in the network domain: $RL_t(o_i)$. The locations of this and other objects, combined with their pairwise distances (as in 2 above), determine a topological (geometric) map.
4. A real context for an object's location, within its physical or logical environment (e.g., a file within the operating system of a node): $RC_t(o_i)$. This is not shown in Fig. 11.1. (Note: for simplicity, the t subscripts are also omitted from the figure and the remaining text.)

Of interest now is how the R-space model can be usefully mapped into a model visualized by the user (in U-space). Depending on the user's level of knowledge of the network, and contingent on his/her application-specific interest in using it (i.e., its utility), the "real" locations and distances may or may not be significant. For some applications and some users, especially those who are novices, treating the information system as if it were a black box may be adequate. For others, the ability to take advantage of real object location and distances can produce more insightful interaction with the system.

But, even for the latter type of user, two approaches exist for conceptualizing real objects. At one extreme, the user can try to learn and remember object identities, their relations, and the physically accurate coordinates and distances among them. If successful, the user's mental image (first version of Definition 10.2) would be equivalent to the physically correct conceptual map, in terms of real locations (RLs) and real distances (RDs) depicted in Fig. 11.1 It exemplifies a mapping from R-space to U-space. However, that may be neither realistic (to expect of the user) nor beneficial enough (to the user) to warrant the required mental effort. Most users may find it either impossible or worthless to remember precise distances among objects. Therefore, even if the existence criterion (Section 10.5) calls for an R-space representation, the utility criterion may suggest an easier option.

The L-Space Alternative

An alternative is a logically correct, conceptual map, which only attempts to retain the essential relationships among objects, with respect to *relative* locations, distances, and directionality. It is portrayed in Fig. 11.2. It illustrates a mapping between L-space and U-space, under the assumption that the L-space model is valid, i.e., it represents the R-space objects correctly in terms of those logical relationships that satisfy user requirements. The user now need not remember distances in miles and directional angles in degrees. Instead, according to the relationships outlined in the legend, the user can simply conceptualize an object (e.g., o_2) and visualize it as being more distant from the interface than another object (o_1), and to the right of it, with regard to an assumed orientation and reference node (e.g., o_n) within the logical conceptual map.

Many variations on such conceptual maps can be defined, depending on user-preferred relationships among objects. However, some set of relations must be applicable. This is to ensure the retention of an adequately representative spatial layout, at least with logical dimensions. The objects of interest to the user should normally not be permitted to remain unstructured, unless that is exactly what the user wants. Taking advantage of structure tends to minimize cognitive processing (Rosch, 1978). Either in physical or logical terms, structure enables consistent transformation of a U-space model of objects in R-, L-, or S-space to the visual, graphical display surface (I-space), and vice versa. For the above example, I-space

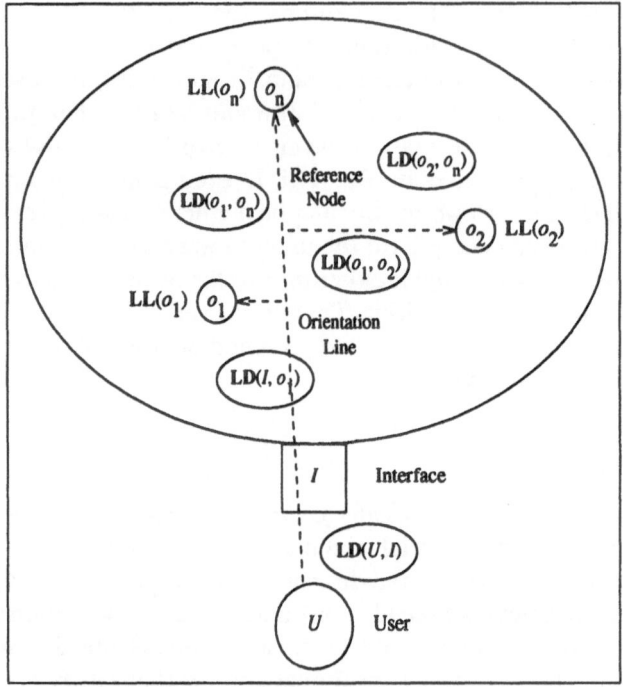

Legend:

• $LL(o_n)$ = Selected reference point (for orientation purposes) located in nearly straight-away direction "ahead" of the user in U-space;

• $LL(o_1)$ = Slightly to the left of $LL(o_n)$ and about half as far away;

• $LL(o_2)$ = To the right of both $LL(o_1)$ and $LL(o_n)$ and somewhat further from I than $LL(o_1)$;

• $LD(o_1,o_2)$, $LD(o_1,o_n)$, and $LD(o_2,o_n)$ seem nearly equal in U-space;

• $LD(I,o_1)$ is slightly shorter than any of the other inter-object distances.

FIGURE 11.2. Model of user interaction with logically interpreted pattern of objects.

could help by displaying either the R-space pattern (Fig. 11.1) or the L-space pattern (Fig. 11.2). The choice depends on the aforementioned utility criterion and the capabilities of the user.

11.7. Conceptual Distance

One more definition:

Definition 11.1. **Conceptual distance**: a measure of (1) the physical or logical separation (cd_s) or nearness between any two conceived objects or parts thereof and/or (2) the strength of correspondence, association, or relationship (cd_r) between them, as these are reflected in the functioning of the human mind.

This compound term may be considered synonymous with an association link between two objects, characterized by specified relational attributes. It is hypothesized to have significant influence on mental effort. On one hand, it depends on the structural characteristics of the mind. Its impact, however, is determined by the context of the user's mental activity, focus, and locality, that is, whether the user is visualizing objects only in I-space or in R-, L-, or S-space, with or without help from I-space (Chapter 10).

Viewing and manipulating objects only in I-space are essential ingredients of the DMI style. "What you see is what you get" interfaces have been analyzed in terms of the *directness* they are supposed to provide (Hutchins *et al.*, 1986). One aspect of that feeling of directness is *distance*, involving "a relationship between the task a user has in mind and the way that task can be accomplished via the interface." *Semantic* distance is distinguished from *articulatory* distance. The other major aspect is *direct engagement*, which is a qualitative "feeling that one is directly manipulating the objects of interest." The distance notion is, furthermore, characterized using Norman's (1986) "Gulf of Execution" and "Gulf of Evaluation," which are the unidirectional gaps between user goals/knowledge and the system-provided level of description (which the user must deal with), and vice versa. The feeling of directness is suggested to be "inversely proportional to the amount of cognitive effort it takes to manipulate and evaluate a system" (Hutchins *et al.*, 1986). That is, the shorter the distance between user and system, as supported by the interface, the less distance needs to be bridged by the user's cognitive efforts. Ballas *et al.* (1992) have evaluated the two major aspects of DMI style by building and comparing four different interfaces representative of the four combinations of low and high semantic distance and direct and indirect engagement.

Conceptual distance, especially cd_r, as defined above, is related to this notion of DMI distance, at least with regard to the (logical) distance (or difference) between the objects conceived by the user and the objects perceived and manipulated on the visible screen. But it is different in several respects. It is intended to address distances pertaining to visualizable objects and structures, not the totality and continuity of human–computer interaction. Hence, it is proposed only as a component measure that may contribute to the extremely complex problem of measuring and evaluating computer interfaces. Also, while dependent on the DMI, it is not confined to it. In fact, cd_s is specifically intended to gauge object distances in the IMI style of interface, for those users who want to conceptualize objects beyond the visible interface, or who must do so because the DMI is inadequate. Therefore, cd_s reflects object-oriented distances as they affect user visualization in U-space, based on representations both in I-space (e.g., DMI) and in R-, L-, and S-spaces (all subject to IMI), either with or without suitable support via I-space.

Because spatial extent and structure are prerequisite to measuring physical and logical distances, Version 1 of Definition 11.1 clearly qualifies. However, the association-based version of cd can also be placed into a spatial and structural context, e.g., using semantic networks and logical distances within them, such as the number of links between nodes. For the remaining discussion, a generic version of cd is used (i.e., the subscripts are dropped).

Depending on where (or in which of the five spaces) the information objects exist (or are defined) and are usefully conceptualized, the cd will differ and, hence, have correspondingly different effects on the user's mental effort required. The following terminology,

$$cd(o_i, o_j) | applicable\ space$$

is used to represent a measure of cd, between any two objects o_i and o_j, conditioned to the *applicable space*, i.e., in which the objects exist or are defined. Then, any instance of conceptual distance as visualized by the user (in U-space) must be a reflection of one or more of the following:

- Physical distance (R-space)—accurately represented:
  $$cd(o_i, o_j) |\ R\text{-}space$$
- Physical distance (R-space)—logically represented:
  $$cd(o_i, o_j) | (R\text{-}space\ AND\ L\text{-}space)$$
- Logical distance (L-space or S-space)—logically represented:
  $$cd(o_i, o_j) | L\text{-}space,\ or$$
  $$cd(o_i, o_j) | S\text{-}space$$
- Visual distance (I-space)—representing the logical distances in any of the other spaces:

$$cd(o_i, o_j) | I\text{-}space \text{ AND } (R\text{-}space \text{ OR } L\text{-}space \text{ OR } S\text{-}space)$$

The user must somehow abstract, derive, and visualize the $cd(o_i, o_j)$ based on information remembered (in human memory) about the corresponding physical or logical distances. For the application highlighted by Figs. 11.1 and 11.2, this mental process should become easier as the required representation moves from the physically measured (and accurate) distances to logical (and approximate) distances between objects. That is to say, the following relations should hold:

$$(cd(o_i, o_j) | (R\text{-}space \text{ AND } L\text{-}space)) < (cd(o_i, o_j) | R\text{-}space)$$

and

$$(cd(o_i, o_j) | L\text{-}space) < (cd(o_i, o_j) | R\text{-}space)$$

For other tasks, however, the opposite inequality may hold. For example, visualizing a complex R-space object, such as a human face, seems easier for the mind than would a nonrealistic L-space approximation of that same face. In other words, for that task,

$$(cd(o_i, o_j) | L\text{-}space) > (cd(o_i, o_j) | R\text{-}space)$$

unless the L-space is a true (although scaled) representation, in which case the following applies:

$$(cd(o_i, o_j) | (R\text{-}space \text{ AND } L\text{-}space)) = (cd(o_i, o_j) | R\text{-}space)$$

For the latter, the corresponding I-space display of the face should be very recognizable to the user.

In general, however, it is not clear what kinds of I-space models, with varying support of S-space storage structures and algorithms, may help or hinder user visualization efforts. For some tasks, e.g., visualizing the human face, a realistic graphical style and even a more advanced version of VR may be desirable. For other purposes, involving less realism in representation of objects but more directness in manipulating them, a DMI may be appropriate. Many different hypotheses could be suggested here as subject to experimental testing. In any case, the interface designer's objective should be to achieve the following:

$$cd(o_i, o_j) | I\text{-}space \text{ AND } (R\text{-}space \text{ OR } L\text{-}space \text{ OR } S\text{-}space) \ll cd(o_i, o_j) | (R\text{-}space \text{ OR } L\text{-}space \text{ OR } S\text{-}space)$$

In other words, the I-space representation of objects displayed for any of the three named spaces should facilitate the user's visualization, when compared with having no (or poorly designed) help from I-space. For example, displaying either Fig. 11.1 (for R-space) or Fig. 11.2 (for L-space) in an I-space window should make it easier for the user than having no visual help (pure IMI) or having the objects inappropriately or illogically listed on the screen.

Because user visualization in U-space potentially transcends and encompasses (logically) the union of the R-, L-, and S-spaces, the above equality can be simplified to:

$$(cd(o_i,o_j)|(I\text{-}space \text{ AND } U\text{-}space)) \ll (cd(o_i,o_j)|U\text{-}space)$$

This can also be interpreted to say that a user's independent input of visualized objects is likely to be more difficult than inputting those same objects with effective, visual I-space prompting or menu selection. Hence, a form of DMI, for example, should facilitate the process, as implied by the entries in Table 11.1.

Composite cd-based measures of mental effort, required for n-object pictures visualized in a particular space, can be formulated. An example is the summation of pairwise cd components:

$$CD_{total} = \Sigma\Sigma\,(cd(o_i,o_j)|\text{application space})$$

restricted to only those object pairs for which a meaningful cd exists. Critical analysis of this kind of formula prompts several important questions. Is literal distance, either in physical or logical units, directly or inversely proportional to the level of visualization effort? If directly, then the summation could become overwhelming, e.g., when the user must remember numerous R-space distances or when many different L-space objects are defined in widely ranging logical locations and levels of detail. However, in general, other factors become influential. They include the types of objects and associations, the number of required mental transitions among objects, and the nature of the user's task.

For example, consider a user visualizing two patterns of cities (Treu, 1990): {Akron, Cleveland, Oberlin} and {Cleveland, London, Calcutta}. If the visualization is motivated by wanting to determine the city nearest to Pittsburgh, it is clear that the first pattern, with a far smaller distance summation, would require far more effort than the second pattern. But if the task is to remember the interobject, R-space distances, the effort may be nearly equivalent. Further, this example also points out that a logical representation, using numeric distances explicitly displayed in I-space, can be preferable to presenting a correctly scaled R-space image. If the distances are nearly the same, the user would have difficulty distinguishing them.

Such interspace comparisons may render cd summations most useful. Whether the formula's value is greater or less than the corresponding L-, S-, or I-space value depends on obtaining valid, task-specific inequalities like those discussed earlier. Also, the formula must be extended for the many realistic applications involving objects in more than one space. An example is placing a telephone call in which the user visualizes the distance in R-space, but may be very dependent on information objects (e.g., various relevant codes) available through L- and S-spaces. It seems very likely that a task that involves objects in different spaces and the need to operate on them simultaneously (while transitioning between spaces) is considerably more difficult than a task constrained to objects in a single space. The desired I-space role then becomes the well-structured fusion (of a multispace task) into meaningful visual display. It is up to the interface designer to encourage and reinforce visualization, with suitable I-space support and using the differing object representations from the other spaces toward minimizing total visualization efforts. Suitable I-space support must include interface structure and interaction style.

Structure-Enveloped Mapping to the Interface

To achieve such interface design goals, appropriate logical structures (Chapter 4) must be employed in organizing the visual picture in I-space. To determine whether structures are helpful and conducive to the human mind, the following inequality should be assessed:

$$cd(o_i, o_j)|\text{I-space AND } (\textit{and other space(s)}) \text{ AND}$$
$$\text{structure} < cd(o_i, o_j)|\text{I-space AND } (\textit{the same other space(s)})$$

As discussed in Chapter 4, the association graph is useful for characterizing many types of objects in some relation (e.g., a semantic map; a network of cities). It becomes even more powerful, for purposes of user visualization, if it is used in conjunction with one of the other structures. For example, a V-structure superimposed on an O-structure categorizes the nodes of the latter into easily conceivable layers (and sets) of objects that exhibit some common characteristic. A graph can thereby be transformed into a hierarchy, e.g., a distributed network can be viewed as a hierarchical network, with a central controller at the highest layer and various other computers serving at other layers of functionality. The distance between any two adjacent nodes in the graph (or network) can then be represented by the purely logical quantity of "number of layers" separating them (Treu, 1989). This kind of structure-based reasoning for meaningful display of patterns of objects can be applied to other forms of object-oriented user–computer interaction.

The choice of structure to support user visualization depends on the type of object(s) involved. Logical interface structures are especially relevant when two or more objects are related in some pattern. Inherent layers are also implied by the definition of any specific object, with regard to level of specificity or generality, as well as any set of related but unordered objects which can share a particular structural layer.

Facilitating Visualization with Style

In Chapter 10, we were not yet prepared to discuss how different object representations, in different spaces, might require different levels of mental effort for their visualization. We can now summarize how *cd*-based visualization effort is likely to differ depending on various considerations (Treu, 1990):

1. The space in which the objects exist or are defined
2. The space in which object visualization is useful for the user
3. The type of software-provided (S-space) representation available for the objects
4. The nature of visual portrayal (I-space), especially whether it does or does not include meaningful visual imagery, and
5. Whether or not suitable interface structures are employed to envelope or orient the visual portrayal in a manner conducive to the user's mind

The last three considerations are critical ingredients of interaction style. Most of the discussion in this and the previous section relates to user visualization in the context of what was termed IMI. But now, we reiterate the need to supplement and facilitate the IMI style by means of other effective styles. While IMI should be recognized as an extreme option made available to (or required of) users who seek a deeper understanding of computers and computer-based applications, we obviously do not want users in general to be unnecessarily burdened and constrained.

This means that HCI designers should endeavor to provide well-structured interaction (Consideration 5 above) utilizing interface software (Consideration 3) that can represent the objects and their dynamics using meaningful imagery (Consideration 4). Depending on precise interpretation and refinement of these attributes and depending on the degree of user involvement (KEVSI variables, Section 11.2), the DMI style, the VR style, or some other style might be desirable. Or maybe some kind of hybrid style is indicated (see the exercises).

Individual differences among users are, as usual, extremely important in such determination. Users' minds are not uniformly equipped with mental compasses to enable easy orientation to any particular logical structure and interaction style. The ultimate objective of interface designers should be to individualize the visual interface beyond the commonalities among users, to adapt to user differences and peculiarities.

Illustrative is how people relate differently to geographical maps of cities, states, and countries. Some are able to look at a map and visualize the travel route from Point A to Point B, regardless of which direction they are currently (physically) facing. Others are known to have to turn the map (or the car) around to align their direction of travel, in order to have any hope of understanding and following the map. Still others have difficulty doing either of the above. Such "users" present special challenges to interface designers who want to reinforce human abilities to visualize object-oriented patterns.

Further, if the user is not (yet) knowledgeable enough to create and utilize a "conceptual map" or a task plan to carry out an application of interest, it is incumbent on the interface designer to construct and instantiate effective versions on the user's behalf. In a sense, this contrasts the IMI from the DMI. After starting out with a DMI style, the user should be encouraged to move toward more IMI-style interaction. The user's learning process may then work in reverse of the designer's process. That is, as a result of visual confirmation (in I-space) of the patterns of interacting objects in the system, the user can gain insight into what happens behind the interface surface and thereby learn to create and remember his/her own conceptual maps in the future.

11.8. Observations

Ultimately, we want to design and evaluate human–computer interfaces for the benefit of the human users. The numerous definitions, models, methods, etc., that have been presented have all been motivated accordingly. Some of the material (especially in Chapters 4, 10, 12 and this chapter) may be viewed by the reader as exceedingly abstract and too hypothetical. That is exactly what many people thought nearly 20 years ago about the suggestion that "required mental work" (Treu, 1975a) be taken into account in command language design. In the 1980s, however, user mental models, cognition, and related topics became standard fare in HCI.

People interacting with computers must expend considerable physiological and mental efforts to get things done. And computers are not people; they are controllable and can be altered to suit the needs of human users. If we want to progress to being able to take those user efforts and resulting by-products (e.g., stress) into account in more objective and deterministic ways, we must address all major, relevant factors, regardless of how vague and elusive they might seem to us at this point in time.

The different types of information objects (talked about throughout this book), the interface structures (Chapter 4) and the different spaces for object representation (Chapter 10), and the definitions of user-oriented measures (Chapter 5), including user satisfaction (Chapter 9) and also conceptual distance (this chapter), all are components of a design and evaluation framework that accentuates user thinking, visualization, feeling. After much more research, the major types and quantities of user mental effort involved in HCI will hopefully be determined and validated. These should include variables like (1) the number of objects to be visualized and/or displayed, (2) intraobject distances, due to internal shape or structure, (3) object contents, in terms of semantics and information volume and density, (4) interobject distances, due to patterns of objects, (5) intraspace definition of objects, (6) interspace definition of objects, and (7) transformations of objects and object patterns between/among the different spaces.

Then, the different styles of interaction, including DMI, VR, and IMI, could be put to interesting tests. For example, it would be useful to develop detailed case studies in which patterns of objects, and tasks to be performed on them, are defined within and across the different spaces behind the interface. They could be rendered visible and accessible to users via different interaction styles. Experimental measurement and evaluation methodology (Parts II and III) could be invoked to determine the most synergistic as well as efficient and effective style available for each category of users and for each type of application considered.

Exercises

11.1. Consider a "data analysis and display" type of application. Use it to formulate and describe a hybrid interaction technique that involves elements of each of DMI, VR, and IMI. Define the constituent components of the application, as you envision it, and discuss how the hybrid interaction would accommodate them effectively and in what pattern.

11.2. Repeat Exercise 11.1 for "computer-aided instruction and learning."

11.3. Repeat Exercise 11.1 for a "home-based shopping" application.

11.4. Does the KEVSI model adequately represent the degree or extent to which a user becomes involved in interaction with a computer? Use it to characterize your involvement with your locally available computer system.

11.5. If you have had the opportunity to experience a VR interface, did it make you feel as though you were in control, or did it give you a sense of being subservient to it? Explain.

11.6. Some people get seasick, carsick, and airsick. Often it helps to orient oneself to something that remains fixed, such as the horizon. The mind seemingly wants to have the certainty and comfort of being able to relate to something that does not move. With reference to Exercise 11.5, is it possible, even likely, for some people to feel less than comfortable when enclosed in special VR headgear and perhaps unsure of exactly what movements cause what computer reactions?

11.7. With regard to the three SEE aspects, where does "conceptual distance" fit in? Why?

11.8. Based on (a) the example of measured real distances within a pattern of cities mentioned in Section 11.7 and (b) the measurements of visual distances between city nodes on a corresponding map displayed on a CRT terminal, can you imagine any use of "conceptual distance" as a true measure (in the sense discussed in Chapters 5 and 7)? Discuss the possibilities.

11.9. Prepare a critique of the use of "conceptual distance" in the design and evaluation of human–computer interfaces, with respect to (a) whether it is only unidimensional, as if representing a linear distance between (parts of) objects, or multidimensional, and (b) whether other factors contributing to a user's mental work in HCI might play greater or lesser roles.

11.10. Read the paper by Woods (1984) to determine whether "visual momentum" might be dependent not only on visual distance and location but also conceptual distance. Describe the results of your analysis.

STRUCTURAL SPECIFICATION AND UTILITY

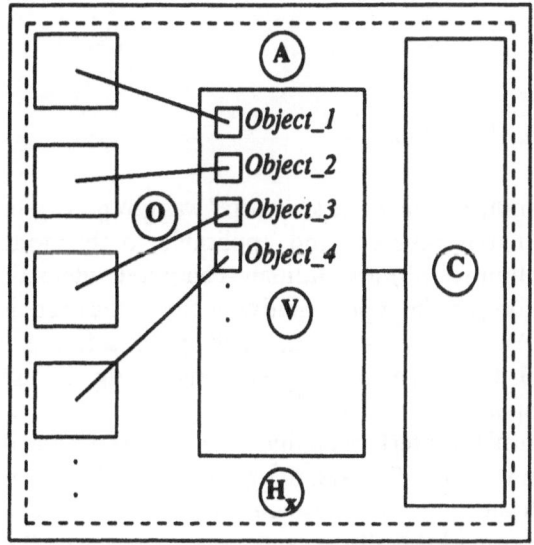

12.1. Overview

Computer science in general and software engineering in particular are very dependent on formal specifications of the elements, structures, and operations of whatever is being designed for implementation on a computer. This dependency also extends to the area of HCI design. The definitions of a variety of interface structures (Chapter 4) and visualizable spaces in which those structures can be instantiated (Chapter 10) have been presented with the assertion that they are useful in designing interfaces. To bear that out, it is essential that the structural paradigms be properly included in the methodology for interface design and evaluation. This means that it must be possible to illustrate both their formal specification and their practical utility once they are specified.

After developing a more formal definition of interface structure in Section 12.2, an example specification is detailed in Section 12.3. Then, the utility question is addressed, in Section 12.4. This is done, first, by outlining several important reasons that can be used to justify the selection of a particular structure. Second, the requirement of taking the identifiable needs of users (the U-factors) into account, as they pertain to interface structures, is characterized.

Experimental testing and analysis of structure-based design and evaluation are advocated in Section 12.5. Finally, Section 12.6 considers whether the set of interface structures defined in Chapter 4 is adequate to accommodate all computer applications, or whether other structures will be needed.

12.2. Formal Definition

The meaning of "interface structure" was given by Definition 4.1. It is a structure that is inherent and applicable to the human–computer interface (Definition 1.5) and human–computer interaction (Definition 1.6). It, therefore, can be representative of any of the user-visible and user-visualizable (1) computer hardware, (2) computer software and data structures, and (3) the information objects constituting the user's computer-supported application.

To be useful for interface engineering, an interface structure must be describable in very specific ways; designers and evaluators must be able to confirm, replicate, and use it through conceptual, logical, and/or physical means. Definition 4.1 is really too general for that purpose. A definition is needed that can encompass the pattern, orientation, operations, and axioms, which are descriptive of such a structure. The graphic symbols for interface structures (displayed in Chapter 4) are similar to the symbols found in textbooks for visual representation of data structures such as arrays, stacks, queues, lists, trees, and graphs. That specialty in computer science can also supply a more formal definition of interface structure.

Consider an interface structure as involving:

1. Any interface object(s), or set(s) of objects (e.g., lines of text, nodes in a logical tree, branches in a real tree, icons on a screen, modules in a program, layers of definition), that may vary significantly in level (volume, size, detail), format (appearance), and type (data)

2. Relationships among those interface objects, or the set of operations that may legally (or safely) be applied to the objects (e.g.,

concatenate into a sequence, traverse a hierarchy, link modules, transition to next layer), and

3. Existence of objects and relationships in any one or more of the R-, L-, and S-spaces, displayable at the interface (I-space), for purposes of user visualization and manipulation in U-space

The user is to visualize, recognize, associate, manipulate, input, and output interface objects, utilizing the operations that are legally available. An abstract definition can be formulated using the algebraic approach (Horowitz and Sahni, 1976; Chi, 1985). That approach is well known, frequently used, and remains valid. Although Chi (1985) also considered other axiomatic specifications of the user interface, those are no more appropriate for our purposes. He defined "interface" to be "all user and machine behavior that is observable by an external observer." That differs from specification of interface structures in at least two respects: (1) interface structures are, in their basic forms, only low-level components of a complete interface specification and (2) they are expected to represent visualizable objects that are *not* necessarily *observable*, especially when they involve objects that are user-conceived.

Definition 12.1. **Interface structure**: a set of domains of interface objects D, defined relative to partition(s) in the composite space C, using a set of functions F and a set of axioms A. A designated domain of interest d is a member of set D.

Each function in F represents an expressible (in programming terminology) operation that can be performed on the interface objects as they relate within a particular interface structure. The set of axioms, A, are statements that describe the semantics of those operations. Space C identifies one of the R-, L-, S-, and I-spaces, as visualized in U-space. Focus is on user-conceived, -visualized, and -viewed manipulation of the structure. A specific interface structure d can then be simply denoted by the 4-tuple (D, C, F, A).

12.3. Specification Example

With reference to definition 12.1, a specification of a selected interface structure is illustrated below. It assumes the perspective of the target user in defining exactly what the user can do with the V-structure. The target application is the layout of (or the positioning and assignment of space in) the n-story office building depicted in Fig. 10.4. The target user is therefore assumed to be a specialist in that application.

Variable V identifies the current V-structure. Variable i designates the current layer within V, ranging in value from i=1 to n. To prevent null or trivial cases, the value of n should exceed 1. For clarity, the maximum and minimum values of i are also denoted by *top* (= n) and *bottom* (= 1). Variable p is used to pass, or store, a new or removed layer.

The declaration statements (lines 1–18) represent a set of operations or functions (set F) that the user (or user's mind) can perform on a V-structure. It will become clear that the computer can execute these functions as well. The first seven functions pertain to the creation, representation, and single-layer-at-a-time modification of the structure:

CREATE(V): the user conceives (or sets up in his/her mind) a V-structure for the application of interest (the n-story office building layout design); generic meanings are associated with the layers, individually and/or collectively, but the structural layers initially are "empty" (i.e., no interface objects have been assigned to any layer as yet); a separate structure specification (e.g., *H* or *O*) is necessary to deal with objects assigned to and contained in layers.

ELIM(V): the user eliminates (deletes or destroys) the current V-structure from his/her mind; separate versions of this function could instead inactivate V or place it on hold, subject to future recall by the user; this would be like scheduling a mental return to V.

APPD_LAYER(i,p,V): the user appends the V-structure by adding a layer to either end (top or bottom); for example, a high-level, penthouse meeting room floor or an entry-level reception/cafeteria floor is to be added.

ABBRV_LAYER(i,p,V): same as APPD_LAYER(i,p,V) but to abbreviate or remove top or bottom layer; optionally, layer i could be "saved" in layer variable p.

INSRT_LAYER(i,p,V): the user inserts layer p, just above layer i, within the existing sequence of n layers (with n>2); for example, as a result of intermediary level refinement or expansion to accommodate some client company's office needs.

DELET_LAYER(i,p,V): opposite of INSRT_LAYER(i,p,V); optionally, layer i → layer p.

RPLAC_LAYER(i,p,V): the user decides to replace or modify a layer, or its meaning.

Other functions, e.g., SWAP_LAYERS(i,j) might be added to this set, depending on whether they make sense to the application and are conceptually convenient for the user. The second set of functions (lines 8–11) exemplifies operations on an entire n-layer structure, or on two such structures combined:

INVERT(V): the user reorients the entire structure by inverting it, placing the previous bottom layer to the top and the top layer to the bottom; this is analogous to having the most specific level, or the last in alphabetical order, appear at the top rather than the bottom; this function may not be meaningful for the office building example.

PARTITION(i,V): the user breaks one large V-structure into two smaller V-structures, one with layers 1 to i, the other with layers i+1 to n; this operation can be repeated depending on the size of n and the user's application-specific logic for carrying out the partition; perhaps each partition represents office space dedicated to a different company.

MERGE(V1,V2): the user merges two V-structures, sized n and m, respectively, into a single structure, consisting of at most m+n layers; the same organizational criterion (e.g., contiguous physical location for similar office functions) must be used on both V1 and V2 to perform the merger.

ABUT(V1,i,V2): instead of merging, the user simply abuts (or joins) structure V1 to the top or bottom of V2.

Again, more complicated functions might be added, e.g., total rearrangement (within vertical pattern) of all layers of V, using a different organizational criterion or key. For example, an association pattern (O-structure) might be used to cause offices of companies that do business with each other to be located in close proximity. Such arrangement, e.g., based on searching an association matrix or linked list for business associates, is very easy to do by a computer. But, depending on how many layers (n) are in V and the nature of the organizational, associative criterion, it may be unduly complex and/or time-consuming for the user's mind. Use of such a function may therefore depend on the application and whether the user actually participates in the manipulation of V or is willing to delegate such a transformation to the computer.

The third set of functions (lines 12–18) in the example of Fig. 12.1 are those that pertain to the user's conceptual movement within the layers of a V-structure, after it has been created and modified. These operations are analogous to the traversal of a data structure (e.g., a tree) in some order, visiting and examining the nodes, and taking any action on their data contents if desired.

FOCUS(i,V): the user focuses on (and thinks about) layer i in V; this might lead to user examination of the layer's contents (e.g., individual floor plan in separate display window) via a separately specified structure.

NEXT_UP(i,V): the user decides to move to layer i+1 (with i<n).

```
      structure Vertical_Layering
 1        declare   CREATE() -> V
 2                  ELIM(V) ->
 3                  APPD_LAYER(i,p,V) -> V
 4                  ABBR_LAYER(i,p,V) -> V
 5                  INSRT_LAYER(i,p,V) -> V
 6                  DELET_LAYER(i,p,V) -> V
 7                  RPLAC(i,p,V) -> V

 8                  INVERT(V) -> V
 9                  PARTITION(i,V) -> V1,V2
10                  MERGE(V1,V2) -> V
11                  ABUT(V1,i,V2) -> V

12                  FOCUS(i,V) -> i
13                  NEXT_UP(i,V) -> i
14                  NEXT_DOWN(i,V) -> i
15                  TO_TOP(i) -> i
16                  TO_BOTTOM(i) -> i
17                  TRANS_UP(j,V) -> i
18                  TRANS_DOWN(j,V) -> i

19     for all V,i let
20          APPD_LAYER(top,V) ::= INVERT(APPD_LAYER(bottom,V)
21          ABBRV_LAYER(bottom,V) ::= INVERT(ABBRV_LAYER(top,V)
22          if i-1<1 or i+1>n then
23                  INSRT_LAYER(i,p,V) ::= error
24          if i<1 or i>n then
25                  DELET_LAYER(i,p,V) ::= void
26                  FOCUS(i,V) ::= void
27          if j=1 and i>n then
28                  TRANS_UP(j,V) ::= NEXT_UP(i,V)
29          if j=1 and i>1 then
30                  TRANS_DOWN(j,V) ::= NEXT_DOWN(i,V)
31     end
32  end Vertical_Layering
```

FIGURE 12.1. A specification of the V-structure. [Reprinted from Treu (1992) with kind permission from Academic Press.]

NEXT_DOWN(i,V): the user moves his/her focus to layer i-1 (with i>1).
TO_TOP(i): the user switches focus directly to the top layer (i=n).
TO_BOTTOM(i): same except to bottom layer (i=1).
TRANS_UP(j,V): the user decides to transition or skip from layer i to layer i+j, assuming it does not exceed n.
TRANS_DOWN(j,V): same as TRANS UP(j,V) except with downward movement, not to exceed layer 1.

Once again, this set can be expanded. For example, movement (up or down) might be on the basis of a layer-contents search, or a search for contained interface objects. Depending on complexity of those contents and the size of n, that may or may not be feasible for the user's mind. The computer, however, has little difficulty doing so, if the application calls for it and the search criterion is well defined.

Several axioms, designed to impose semantics and constraints on the above-outlined functions and their relationships, are listed in lines 20–30 of Fig. 12.1. They are not exhaustive. They are indicative of what might be appropriate for certain types of users wanting to employ the V-structure for an application that is conducive to it. Some of the functions could be identified as equivalent and therefore redundant. For example,

$$INSRT\_LAYER(top,V)::= APPD\_LAYER(top,V)$$

But, from the viewpoint of the user, they should both be available. Both are meaningful: insertion implies "between two items"; appending means adding an item to an end.

From the computer's standpoint (or S-space), the specified V-structure can be easily implemented as a linked list of floor objects. Each floor can, in turn, be elaborated by means of an O-structure and/or A-structure that represents the pattern of offices and the associations among them. Using index i to point to the current position (or level) in the floor objects list (or the office area layout graph), upward, downward, and lateral movement is straightforward. It depends of course on the criteria used for any orderings applied to the structures and their contents.

Notice that we started out focusing on the user's perspective in the V-structure specification, but we have naturally progressed to supplementing what the user might and can do with what the computer is very capable of doing. Interesting trade-offs arise. For the computer, great care must be taken not to move past either end of the list (i=1 or i=n). A potentially fatal "error" may result. In the user's mind, on the other hand, conceptual motion beyond the ends of a V-structure, perhaps in an adventuresome mode, is not impermissible. It only leads to a layer that is currently meaningless or "void." The latter is an interesting dilemma (Exercise 12.6).

12.4. Structure Utility

An HCI designer who wants to incorporate interface structures as special features of his/her design, must ensure that the selection of any structure is properly justified. First, according to Chapter 4, the structures chosen should preferably be suitable to both user and computer. In addition, justification can result from the cause-and-effect patterns summarized in Chapter 2. For example, specific U-factors, such as indications that the user prefers a certain arrangement of the data, especially in I-space (Chapter 10) but possibly also relative to the other spaces to be visualized, should have primary influence in a design decision. Likewise, the particular nature of the application (A-factors) may suggest that certain structures are most appropriate.

But, not only design factors but also design principles should influence the design features that are selected. Principles of design were defined and identified in Chapter 2. For our purposes here, two of them are especially relevant to use of interface structures: being *consistent* in the kind of structure used in similar contexts, and causing the interface to be *adaptive* with regard to what structures are used for which users.

To summarize, the following major conditions are particularly important in trying to achieve and evaluate utility of interface structures in HCI design. Note that each one can be treated as a design goal which, in turn, gives rise to designing appropriate measures (Definition 6.11) and having established evaluation criteria (Definition 6.12) for determining whether the goal has been met.

1. *Suitability*: The structure(s) selected for and reflected by interface design should indeed come from the shared set, not from a set that either the user or the computer cannot accommodate well.
2. *Task specificity*: Given 1 above, the structure(s) should be selected in a manner appropriate both to the user and to the user's task, as it relates to the "space" (see Chapter 10) in which the user is trying to visualize and manipulate the task objects.
3. *Consistency*: Given 1 and 2, the utilization (or computer-to-user mapping) of structure(s), for viewing at the interface, should be carried out in a consistent, predictable manner.
4. *Adaptation*: The consistency (of 3) should ultimately be implemented and perform in a way that adapts to individual user capabilities and preferences.

After Condition 1 has been assured, it can be assumed, in general, that the computer can provide the supportive processing for the interface structures selected. Whether or not a particular target computer can accommodate Conditions 2 through 4, all of which are user-oriented, or can accommodate them well, depends on its capabilities (I-factors). With respect to Condition 2, both the user-amenable patterns and the specific tasks for which they are appropriate must be understood and then implemented effectively.

Adaptation and consistency are both listed as user-oriented design principles in Table 2.1 and hence can become couched in evaluation purpose (Definition 6.3), leading to the use of methodology described in Part III. Not everyone agrees that those principles are necessarily desirable. For example, Grudin (1989, 1992) has made a case against consistency, and Polson (1988) has discussed the consequences of (in)consistent interfaces. On the other hand, consistency can be very important, especially when a user is faced with a network of resources in which a great diversity of tasks and functions might be available (Mullins and Treu, 1993). Also, for our interest in utilizing interface structures, consistency seems to be a desirable goal. However, if there are reasons to depart from that consistency, e.g., because of user preferences, the adaptation capability can accommodate such variation.

To gain a practical perspective on what must be accomplished in order to make effective use of interface structures, let us consider the following scenario. As part of the methodology, a conceptual model must be constructed of the needs the user is likely to face and of the actions that the user is likely to want to carry out. These needs and actions are among the U-factors. The example application is the layout of the high-rise office building introduced in Chapter 10. It provides the required A-factors. Now, the designer must be able to envision the user needs and actions and, for each case, take responsibility for identifying and specifying the appropriate, supportive structures. The following scenario is indicative. Inherent to it is a specification–evaluation–iteration cycle that must be repeated as long as necessary.

1. *User Need*: It has been determined that the application-specific user (i.e., working on the layout of an n-story building) wants or needs a V-structure to become oriented to and initiate the required interactive work. At this point, the vertical layers (corresponding to floors in the office building) and the layer boundaries represent the interface objects. Other objects have not as yet been assigned for containment within the layers.

2. *Designer/Evaluator Responsibility*: Generate the specification of the V-structure to be utilized during implementation. This is like the

abstract definition of the structure's shape and what the user can do with it; it does not prescribe exactly how to use it, e.g., with what detailed, interactive commands and devices. The specification only dictates the kind of structure, its orientation, and the abstract functions, or user operations, that must be permissible. It does not attempt to stipulate exactly how the structured object(s) should be displayed and how the user can interact with them. Those are up to the ingenuity and skill of the implementor later on.

3. *User Need*: After the user has (been envisioned to have) completed his/her work within the V-structure representation, e.g., identifying which floors are to be used for what purposes and to be adjacent (vertically) to which other floors, then the user can zero in on any selected layer (i.e., floor) to consider its layout (e.g., of different offices/rooms). This means that some other structure, e.g., the O-structure or the A-structure, becomes necessary.

4. *Designer/Evaluator Responsibility*: With available interactive tools, enable the convenient transition from the V-structure-based interaction mode to interaction with the newly required structure. The latter must also be appropriately specified for subsequent implementation. The two structures might be implemented to be accessible in parallel, in different regions (A-structure) of the visible interface, assuming enough display area is available.

5. *Iterations* on the above: After working on the objects (rooms) of a selected layer, the user may want to proceed to deal with the objects (e.g., items of furniture) to be positioned within a selected room. This again requires a certain structure (e.g., O-structure) to be specified by the designer for implementation. Alternatively, the user may want to return to one of the earlier structures, to work on another floor or room.

The reader will observe that this brief scenario, in effect, shows the designer/evaluator emulating what the user will face in stepping through a sequence of high-level states within a state transition graph. Such a graph (Treu *et al.*, 1991) can represent the various terms and techniques pertaining to dynamic interaction. It confirms clearly that the designer/evaluator, in considering the selection and use of appropriate structures, must look at both (1) the individual, task-specific contexts and (2) their composition into goal-oriented sequences of contexts, as well as the structure-based transitions between them. In general, each state requires a separate specification of its own, locally suitable interface structure. This means that both the state-specific structures and the state transition graph must be specified and evaluated.

12.5. Testing for Utility

Many "measures" are necessarily dependent on structures, as was discussed in Chapter 5. So, structures are certainly useful for that purpose. But what is their utility in attempts to improve HCI? Such utility has been implied throughout the material of Chapters 4 and 10. Yet, it remains a research area. Although many useful bits and pieces on structural utility can be found in the HCI literature (as reviewed in Chapter 4), we need more formal and extensive proof of whether and how the different structures have significant effects on user-oriented design and HCI performance.

Following is a proposed sequence of steps for carrying out experimental work to determine whether and how interface structures contribute to better interface design. For each application (A) selected and sample group of users available to serve as experimental subjects, the experimenter should carry out:

1. *User-oriented analysis of application*, taking both U-factors and A-factors and their interactions into account, to determine
   a. Which interface structures are inherent to the representation of application-specific objects and processes, as reflected in each of the S-, L-, and R-spaces, and
   b. Which of those structures (from a) are likely to be best suited for the users, or different types of users (e.g., novice versus experienced).
   The selection of structures should be restricted to the basic set (Figs. 4.3–4.9) and any meaningful hybrids that can be created (e.g., Figs. 4.10 and 4.11).
2. *Structural composition and mapping*, based on results of 1, to determine
   a. Which of the space-specific structural representations might be necessary and/or desirable for which types of users, and
   b. How to map the resultant representations, in variable combinations, into well-structured layouts of the visible interface (I-space).
   The interface layouts, e.g., sizes and ordered contents of display windows (including which objects are to be represented), and the arrangement of multiple windows on the screen, should also be restricted to the basic set (Figs. 4.3–4.9) and their hybrid combinations (e.g., Figs. 4.10 and 4.11).
3. *Definition of alternative modes*, providing a range of optional modes of structure-based interaction for each application (case study) considered. Each mode must encompass appropriate interaction technique and style. Several options, including at least one for the

novice and one for the relatively experienced user, should be prepared. If feasible, this step can also include *adaptation* to user needs and preferences as they relate to structures.

Adaptation in the third step can be static in nature. User information (e.g., on experience level and preferences) can be predetermined by asking the user and then assigning him/her to the appropriate experimental subgroup. The alternative of adapting dynamically requires use of expert system techniques (e.g., Tyler, 1986; Sanderson, 1991).

Clearly, the determination of which structures and which mappings are "best" should not only be based on designer intuition and indicated user preferences. A user's preference does not necessarily lead to optimal performance. Also, a designer can be mistaken about how a user might like to visualize an object. Empirical evidence about effects on user performance can provide useful additional information to influence interface (re-)design.

As a hypothetical example, the above-listed three steps could result in the following options for the office building layout application. These would then be selectable for inclusion in the design specifications.

1. An A-structure involving three regions: one window containing a V-structure (from L-/R-space) for the entire building, a second window containing an O-structure providing distance data (from L-space) between boundaries of a selected floor, and a third window supporting an L-structure (I-space) for menu-based HCI, together with any cursor-driven interaction through either of the other window channels.
2. A modified version of Option 1, superimposing an O-structure on the A-structure (i.e., A+O), to ensure explicit, visual association between the second window and the currently selected level of the V-structure in the first window; it could also change the structure in the third window in various ways, e.g., for parameter input.
3. Substitute for the contents of the second window (above) some kind of $H_x + H_z$ hybrid, to support the 2-D layout of each floor level, but position it vertically (i.e., to create a top view) using $H_x + V$.
4. Add a fourth window region to one of the above options, to contain a linked (O-structure) representation of the software modules (S-space) corresponding to the (top-down or bottom-up) sequence, or some subsequence, of floors in the building.

The above-listed options are only indicative. They and others would need to be analyzed and tested in detail, to ensure that the most reasonable, user-oriented choices are developed. In addition, interaction modes that are poorly or arbitrarily structured, including deliberate structural mismatches, can be specified for comparison in proposed experimentation. Notice that the actual implementation of the prescribed structural regions, e.g., using window widgets, is left up to the interface implementation.

Experimentation

The major options (in application-specific interface structures) specified must be tested experimentally, to determine which ones do indeed have significant impact on user performance. The prescriptive (or predictive) "type" of evaluation (Chapter 6) would seem most appropriate here. Meaningful tasks must be set up, for each application (case study), requiring the assigned users to carry them out either with or without well-structured support at the interface. The hypothesis is that the user's effort will decrease (by some specified amount), and hence the performance will generally improve, as more user-conducive structural support is provided at the interface, and is provided in consistent and predictable ways.

The groups of subjects must be chosen properly, according to experimental design methodology (Chapter 3). Example selection criteria might be:

a. All subjects should be knowledgeable in computer software (in S-space) and relevant structures.
b. Half of them should be familiar with the application (implying reasonable knowledge about relevant L-space considerations), while the other half should be relative novices.
c. For each of the two groups resulting from b, subjects should be asked to carry out interactive sessions, both *with* and *without* well-structured support (in I-space).

Then, using measures such as *task completion time, number of errors* committed, and others (Chapters 5 and 7), data about interactive sessions can be collected and analyzed. Intragroup and intergroup comparisons can then be made. Also, the fact that the same persons get an opportunity to utilize both options (i.e, with and without well-structured support), assigned in either order, enables the asking of questions about respective advantages and disadvantages observed by the users.

Interaction Scenarios

Besides attention to state- or context-specific usage of interface structures, the goal-oriented sequence of structures and interstructure transitions should be considered. This suggests representing an application-specific and goal-oriented path (through a state transition graph) as a "structural signature." Such a signature is a sequence of basic and hybrid structures employed, relative to different visualizable spaces involved. An interesting related question involves the number of interstructure transitions imposed on (or demanded of) the user, while he/she tries to complete a task.

For example, suppose a user is currently set up with a double-window display interface, one window for menu selection (V-structure) and the other window to output and manipulate information in response to each selected menu command or function. In other words, the latter window is for carrying out the substantive work. For simplicity, let us assume that the user only needs to visualize representations in L-space. Also, we ignore the menu window and focus only on what happens in the work window. Then the user might have to transition through the following scenario, as mapped to I-space:

$$SEQ1 = [V(\text{L-space})] \rightarrow [O+V(\text{L-space})] \rightarrow [S(\text{L-space})] \rightarrow [O(\text{L-space})]$$

It denotes that the user must reorient his/her mind, in order to deal with each of the following, in turn: (1) a vertically (V) organized, alphabetized list of names, e.g., of different animals (or species), (2) a hierarchically structured (O+V) sort tree of those names, (3) a display of arbitrarily positioned sets (S) or clusters of animal names, each set representing some particular species, and (4) a schematic (O) display of the relationships among members of any one set.

Now, to take the menu window into account within the signature notation, we can use the above SEQ1 to easily compose the following. The menu is assumed to be vertically arranged:

$$SEQ2 = [SEQ1 \parallel [V(\text{I-space})]] + A$$

This suggests that the above-characterized work window must be used in parallel with the vertically organized menu window (based in I-space), and the two are positioned on the visible interface in a pattern specified by an A-structure.

Much more complicated scenarios and compositions are possible, including numerous iterations and structures (representing different spaces) displayed in parallel. Interest here is not in creating yet another terminology. The purpose of developing any such notation is to enable description and determination of the number of transitions involved, and whether such compositions and transitions have a bearing on the amount of mental work expended by the user. They surely are expected to impose a transformation in the user's mental framework for visualizing the information objects. If an effect is measurable and significant, the designer should attempt to minimize the structure-dependent mode changes and/ or make the use of interface structures as consistent and predictable as possible. This topic also relates to interaction style and the extent of mental involvement it demands of the user (Chapter 11).

A corollary question is how some arbitrary or inconsistent structures, through which the user is forced to transition, compare with carefully structured alternatives. The expectation is that they should compare quite unfavorably, that is, the user should expend more effort (and make more mistakes, etc.) if he/she has to transition between unstructured (or illogically structured) I-space presentations.

Comparative Analysis

Using the above-outlined kind of experimentation, interesting patterns, commonalities, and differences should emerge for different target users working on different target applications. Useful design guidelines can be among the products. The ability to generate structure-based signatures for interaction scenarios, and the relevant notation, could become useful in characterizing comparative results. For example, it may be possible to observe whether the number of transitions (or cognitive switches) between/among different structural patterns has a bearing on the levels of difficulty experienced by users in carrying out different applications.

A prioritized list of guidelines on how to select the best structures could be useful to HCI designers. The inherent nature of the application (A-factors) and the type of user (U-factors) are expected to have dominating effects on choices of structure. In addition, the selection criteria are likely to be dependent on answers to a number of difficult questions. For example, if no particular structure seems uniquely applicable, on what basis does the designer decide? Under what conditions is consistency (i.e., presenting the same structure for the same purposes) more important than use of the most appropriate structure? Do circumstances exist under which an unstructured alternative may be preferable and/or necessary?

12.6. Structure Adequacy

Finally, it must be emphasized that the interface structures defined in Chapter 4 and supportive of visualization in Chapters 10 and 11 may not be adequate to represent all interactive applications. Some may have to be altered or refined; others may have to be added. It is clear that HCI does not merely involve interaction with static structures, or structures that do not move or change orientation. The basic interface structures have to be properly extended and adapted to handle off-angle views (with direction of user viewing not coincident with the z-axis). They must also support the more dynamic visual actions in HCI.

Examples are the major transformations of graphical objects. A user's mind can see and perceive a *translating* object on the screen, as moving from one (finely grained) layer to the next in the V-, H_x-, or C-structures. *Scaling* the object to appear nearer to or farther away from the viewer can be associated with the H_z-structure. Its size compared with another object (as perceived by the user) depends on whether it is located in the same layer or in an imaginary layer in front or behind. *Rotation* is more difficult. One interpretation is to position an object within a layered structure so that two of its most prominent extreme constituents (surfaces, edges, points) lie in two adjacent (parallel) boundary planes of the structure. For a cube, the two elements are simply parallel planes. Then, whether a V-structure or an H-structure is used, the user's mind seems receptive to rotating the object along with the attached structural layers. That imaginary attachment can aid in providing mental orientation and comfort. It relates to the way an airline passenger, experiencing uncomfortable turbulence, can use a horizontal plane (e.g., defined by the wing tips and nose point of the airplane) to orient him/herself with reference to the horizon. It may also relate to the apparent reality produced by "virtual reality" interfaces and whether or not a user can feel comfortable within it (Chapter 11).

Much more research and experimentation are necessary. Perhaps it can be proven that a certain subset of basic interface structures constitutes a "minimal set," or a basis. Then, all other (hybrid) structures could be created using members of that set. Structures-based HCI design and evaluation could thereby be greatly facilitated.

Exercises

12.1. Compare Definitions 4.1 and 12.1 Besides being more formal and thereby more specific, does Definition 12.1 seem to be an extension of Definition 4.1? Explain. (Note: Recall the assertion in Chapter 4 that knowledge representation involves two parts: a declarative structure part and a process part.)

12.2. Specification of the V-structure in Section 12.3 could be done generically, i.e., without regard to the application mentioned. Would that make it more or less useful to the (a) designer, (b) user? Why?

12.3. What other functions could be added to each of the three subsets in Fig. 12.1? Why? What additional axioms could be added?

12.4. Read the paper by Chi (1985). Identify the other axiomatic specification approaches he described and discuss whether they could be more effective for the V-structure example (Fig. 12.1).

12.5. Write a specification of the O-structure in a manner analogous to the V-structure example (Fig. 12.1). Relate it to the same application, but focus on any part of it that may require the O-structure pattern and logic.

12.6. To reinforce the differences in freedom of movement (or imagination) within an interface structure, such as in the V-structure of Fig. 12.1, should the designer enable the user to create imaginary additional floors (in the office building) even though they are not part of the official, computer-internal representation? How might that be done? In general (not relating to the topic of interface structures), are such facilities for temporary, exploratory work by users already available in some computer applications? Explain.

12.7. Students in programming courses, especially introductory versions, typically dislike specifying and diagramming (e.g., flowcharting) their programs; they prefer delving immediately into writing the programs. As a result, they often learn the hard way that careful planning and organization at the outset tends to prevent problems later on. Analogously, the specification of interface structures may seem to be yet another miscellaneous chore imposed on the interface designer. When considering the need to provide different structures in the states of a state transition graph representative of an application, is it realistic to expect the designer to "specify" each of those structures? Is it important? Explain. Are there any ways for facilitating the task of specifying interface structures? (Note: Remember that this kind of specification is only a component of the total interface design that must be specified by the designer.)

12.8. Using the structure-based signature terminology indicated in Section 12.5, construct a signature for a fairly complex, multiwindow application. Explain each component. Can you suggest an algorithm for counting the number of interstructure transitions that might be required of the user (or user's mind) in a typical interactive session (e.g., one hour)?

12.9. Do you think it is feasible to prove that a "minimal set" of interface structures can accommodate all possible structural patterns needed in HCI? Or does that seem too farfetched? Discuss this prospect, in general terms.

BIBLIOGRAPHY

ABRAMS, M. D., AND TREU, S., 1977, A methodology for interactive computer service measurement, *Commun. ACM* **20**:936–944.

ALLEN, R. B., 1985, The evaluation of text editors: Methodology and empirical results, *Commun. ACM* **28**(3):324–325.

ARNETT, K. P., AND TRUMBLY, J., 1991. Performance relationship considerations for user interface design, in *Human Factors in Information Systems: An Organization Perspective* (J. M. Carey, ed.), Ablex Publishing Corp., Norwood, N.J., pp. 105–116.

ASTERITA, M. F., 1985, *The Physiology of Stress*, Human Sciences Press, New York.

BAECKER, R. M., AND BUXTON, W. A. S., (eds.), 1987, *Readings in Human–Computer Interaction—A Multidisciplinary Approach*, Morgan Kaufmann Publishers, San Mateo, Calif.

BALLAS, J. A., HEITMEYER, C. L., AND PEREZ, M. A., 1992, Evaluating two aspects of direct manipulation in advanced cockpits, *Human Factors in Computing Systems, CHI'92 Conference Proceedings*, ACM, pp. 127–134.

BENBASAT, I., AND TODD, P., 1993. An experimental investigation of interface design alternatives: Icon vs. text and direct manipulation vs. menus, *Int. J. Man-Mach. Stud.* **38**: 369–402.

BENNETT, J. L., 1986, Observations on meeting usability goals for software products, *Behav. Inf. Techno.* **5**:183–193.

BIERMAN, A. W., FINEMAN, L., AND HEIDLAGE, J. F., 1992, A voice- and touch-driven natural language editor and its performance, *Int. J. Man-Mach. Stud.* **37**:1–21.

BISHOP, Y. M. M., FIENBERG, S. E., AND HOLLAND, P. W., 1975, *Discrete Multivariate Analysis: Theory and Practice*, MIT, Cambridge, Mass.

BLANKENBERGER, S., AND HAHN, K., 1991, Effects of icon design on human–computer interaction, *Int. J. Man-Mach. Stud.* **35**:363–377.

BLY, S. A., AND ROSENBERG, J. K., 1986, A comparison of tiled and overlapping windows, *Human Factors in Computing Systems, CHI'86 Conference Proceedings*, ACM, pp. 101–106.

BORENSTEIN, N. S., 1985, The evaluation of text editors: A critical review of the Roberts and Moran methodology based on new experiments, *CHI'85 Conference Proceedings*, ACM, pp. 99–106.

BOURNIQUE, R., 1981, User-Oriented Features and Language-Based Agents—A Study of Graphical Interaction Language Specification, Ph.D. dissertation, Department of Computer Science, University of Pittsburgh, Pittsburgh, Pa.

BOURNIQUE, R., AND TREU, S., 1985, Specification and generation of variable, personalized graphical interfaces, *Int. J. Man-Mach. Stud.* **22**:663–684.

BOX, G. E. P., AND DRAPER, N. R., 1987, *Empirical Model-Building and Response Surfaces*, Wiley, New York.

BOX, G. E. P., HUNTER, W. G., AND HUNTER, J. S., 1978, *Statistics for Experimenters: An Introduction to Design, Data Analysis, and Model Building*, Wiley, New York.

BROWN, C. M., 1988, *Human–Computer Interface Design Guidelines*, Ablex Publishing Corp., Norwood, N.J.

BUXTON, B., 1993, HCI and the inadequacies of direct manipulation systems, *SIGCHI Bull.* **25**:21–22.

CALLAHAN, J., HOPKINS, D., WEISER, M., AND SHNEIDERMAN, B., 1988, An empirical comparison of pie vs. linear menus, *Human Factors in Computing Systems, CHI'88 Conference Proceedings*, ACM, pp.95–100.

263

CARBONELL, J. R., ELKIND, J. I., AND NICKERSON, R. S., 1968, On the psychological importance of time in a time sharing system, *Hum. Factors* 10(2):135–142.

CARD, S. K., MORAN, T. P., AND NEWELL, A., 1980, The keystroke model for user performance time with interactive systems, *Commun. ACM* 23(7):396–410.

CARD, S. K., MORAN, T. P., AND NEWELL, A., 1983, *The Psychology of Human–Computer Interaction*, Lawrence Erlbaum Associates, Hillsdale, N.J.

CARROLL, J. M., KELLOGG, W. A., AND ROSSON, M. B., 1991, The task-artifact cycle, in *Designing Interaction: Psychology at the Human–Computer Interface* (J. M. Carroll, ed.), Cambridge University Press, London, pp. 74–102.

CHANG, S. K., 1987, Visual languages: A tutorial and survey, *IEEE Software*, pp. 29–39.

CHANG, S. K., 1989, *Principles of Pictorial Information Systems Design*, Prentice–Hall, Englewood Cliffs, N.J.

CHANG, S. K., 1990, Visual reasoning for information retrieval from very large databases, *J. Visual Languages Comput.* 1:41–58.

CHANG, S. K., ICHIKAWA, T., AND LIGOMENIDES, P. A., (eds.), 1986, *Visual Languages*, Plenum Press, New York.

CHAPANIS, A., 1975, Interactive human communication, *Sci. Am.* 232(3):36–43.

CHI, U. H., 1985, Formal specification of user interfaces: A comparison and evaluation of four axiomatic approaches, *IEEE Trans. Software Eng.* SE-11(8):671–685.

CHIN, J. P., DIEHL, V. A., AND NORMAN, K. L., 1988, Development of an instrument measuring user satisfaction of the human–computer interface, *Human Factors in Computing Systems, CHI'88 Conference Proceedings*, ACM, pp. 213–218.

COCHRAN, W. G., AND COX, G. M., 1957, *Experimental Designs*, 2nd ed., Wiley, New York.

COFER, C. N., 1967, Does conceptual organization influence the amount retained in immediate free recall, in *Concepts and the Structure of Memory* (B. Kleinmuntz, ed.), Wiley, New York, pp. 181–214.

COOPER, B. E., 1969, *Statistics for Experimentalists*, Pergamon Press, Elmsford, N.Y.

COX, T., AND MACKAY, C. J., 1981, A transactional approach to occupational stress, in *Stress, Work Design, and Productivity* (E. N. Corlett and J. Richardson, eds.), Wiley, New York, pp. 91–113.

CURTIS, B., SHEPPARD, S. B., MULLIMAN, P., BORST, M. A., AND LOVE, T., 1979, Measuring the psychological complexity of software maintenance tasks with the Halstead and McCabe metrics, *IEEE Trans. Software Eng.* SE-5(2):96–104.

CUSHMAN, W. H., OJHA, P. S., AND DANIELS, C. M., 1990, Usable OCR: What are the minimum performance requirements? *Human Factors in Computing Systems, CHI'90 Conference Proceedings*, ACM, pp. 145–151.

CZAJA, S. J., AND SHARIT, J., 1988, Aging and the performance of computer-interactive tasks: Job design and stress potential, in *Trends in Ergonomics/Human Factors V* (F. Aghazadeh, ed.), North-Holland Elsevier Science Publishers, Amsterdam, pp. 185–190.

DAINOFF, M., 1984, A model for human efficiency: Relating health, comfort and performance in the automated office workstation, in *Human–Computer Interaction* (G. Salvendy, ed.), North-Holland Elsevier Science Publishers, Amsterdam, pp. 355–360.

DAMON, R. A., AND HARVEY, W. R., 1987, *Experimental design, ANOVA, and Regression*, Harper & Row, New York.

DOW, C.-R., SOFFA, M. L., AND CHANG, S. K., 1993, Program visualization for parallelized code with the aid of visual transformation specifications, in *Software Automation* (D. Cooke, ed.), World Scientific Publishing Co., Singapore.

DRAPER, S. W., AND NORMAN, D. A., 1985, Software engineering for user interfaces, *IEEE Trans. Software Eng.* SE-11(3):252–258.

DUFFY, T. M., PALMER, J. E., AND MEHLENBERGER, B., 1993, *Online Help: Design and Evaluation*, Ablex Publishing Corp., Norwood, N.J.

EBERTS, R. E., AND BITTIANDA, K. P., 1993, Preferred mental models for direct manipulation and command-based interfaces, *Int. J. Man-Mach. Stud.* 38:769–785.

ENGELBART, D. C., 1963, A conceptual framework for augmentation of man's intellect, in *Vistas in Information Handling*, Vol. 1 (P. W. Howerton and D. C. Weeks, eds.), Spartan Books, Washington, D.C., pp. 1–29.

ENGELBART, D. C., AND ENGLISH, W. K., 1968, A research center for augmenting human intellect, *Proceedings of Fall Joint Computer Conference*, AFIPS, Montvale Press, Montvale, N.J., pp. 395–410.

ERICSSON, K., AND SIMON, H., 1984, *Protocol Analysis: Verbal Reports as Data*, MIT Press, Cambridge, Mass.

FISHER, R. A., 1951, *The Design of Experiments*, 6th ed., Oliver & Boyd, Edinburgh.

FISHMAN, G. S., 1978, *Principles of Discrete Event Simulation*, Wiley, New York.

FOLEY, J. D., 1979, The structure of interactive command languages, in *Methodology of Interaction* (R. A. Guedj, P. J. W. ten Hagen, F. R. A. Hopgood, H. A. Tucker, and D. A. Duce, eds.), North-Holland, Amsterdam, pp. 227–234.

FOLEY, J. D., 1987, Interfaces for advanced computing, *Sci. Am.* **257**(4):126–135.

FOLEY, J. D., AND WALLACE, V. L., 1974, The art of natural graphic man–machine conversation, *Proceedings of the IEEE*, Special Issue on Computer Graphics, **62**(4):462–471.

FOLEY, J. D., VAN DAM, A., FEINER, S. K., AND HUGHES, J. F., 1990, *Computer Graphics—Principles and Practice*, 2nd ed., Addison–Wesley, Reading, Mass.

FRANKENHAEUSER, M., 1980, Psychoneuroendocrine approaches to the study of stressful person–environment transactions, in *Selyes Guide to Stress Research Volume 1* (H. Selye, ed.), Van Nostrand–Reinhold, Princeton, N.J.

FRANKISH, C., JONES, D., AND HAPESHI, K., 1992, Decline in accuracy of automatic speech recognition as a function of time on task: Fatigue or voice drift? *Int. J. Man-Mach. Stud.* **36**:797–816.

FRESE, M., 1987, A concept of control: Implications for stress and performance in human–computer interaction, in *Social, Ergonomic and Stress Aspects of Work with Computers* (G. Salvendy, S. L. Sauter, and J. J. Hurrell, Jr., eds.), North-Holland Elsevier Science Publishers, Amsterdam, pp. 43–50.

FULLER, F., 1976, *The Use of Polygraphs and Similar Devices by Federal Agencies: Hearings before a Subcommittee of the Committee on Government Operations, House of Representatives*, 93d Congress, 2d Session.

GAINES, B. R., AND SHAW, M. L. G., 1986, From timesharing to the sixth generation: The development of human–computer interaction, Part I, *Int. J. Man-Mach. Stud.* **24**:1–27.

GAIT, J., 1985, An aspect of aesthetics in human–computer communications: Pretty windows, *IEEE Trans. Software Eng.* SE-**11**:714–717.

GASEN, J. B., AND AIKEN, P., 1993, Report on the CHI'92 Workshop on Lessons Learned from Teaching HCI: Challenges, innovations and visions, *SIGCHI Bull.* **25**:5–7.

GOLDBERG, A., AND ROBSON, D., 1983, *Smalltalk-80 The Language and its Implementation*, Addison–Wesley, Reading, Mass.

GOLDBERG, D., AND RICHARDSON, G., 1993, Touch-typing with a stylus, *Human Factors in Computing Systems, INTERCHI'93 Conference Proceedings*, ACM, pp. 80–87.

GORDON, G., 1978, *System Simulation*, 2nd ed., Prentice–Hall, Englewood Cliffs, N.J.

GOULD, J. D., AND LEWIS, C., 1985, Designing for usability: Key principles and what designers think, *Commun. ACM* **28**(3):300–311.

GRAF, W., AND KRUEGER, H., 1989, Ergonomic evaluation of user-interfaces by means of eye-movement data, in *Work with Computers: Organizational, Management, Stress and Health Aspects* (M. J. Smith and G. Salvendy, eds.), North-Holland Elsevier Science Publishers, Amsterdam, pp. 659–665.

GRAY, W. D., JOHN, B. E., AND ATWOOD, M. E., 1992, The precis of Project Ernestine or an overview of a validation of GOMS, *Human Factors in Computing Systems, CHI'92 Conference Proceedings*, ACM, pp. 307–312.

GRUDIN, J., 1989, The case against user interface consistency, *Commun. ACM* **32**:1164–1173.

GRUDIN, J., 1992, Consistency, standards, and formal approaches to interface development and evaluation, *Trans. Inf. Syst.* **10**:103–111.

GUGERTY, L., 1993, The use of analytical models in human-computer-interface design, *Int. J. Man-Mach. Stud.* **38**:625–660.

GUILLEMETTE, R. A., 1991, The usability criterion for designing information systems: A conspectus, in *Human Factors in Information Systems: An Organization Perspective* (J. M. Carey, ed.), Ablex Publishing Corp., Norwood, N.J., pp. 65–87.

GUYNES, J. L., 1988, Impact of system response time on state anxiety, *Commun. ACM* **31**(3):342.

HALSTEAD, M. H., 1977, *Elements of Software Science*, Elsevier North-Holland, Amsterdam.

HANEY, T. L., AND BLUMENTHAL, J. A., 1985, Stress and the type A behavior pattern, in *Stress: Psychological and Physiological Interactions* (S. R. Burchfield, ed.), Hemisphere Publishing Corp., Washington, D.C.

HANUSA, H., 1983, Tools and techniques for the monitoring of interactive graphics dialogues, *Int. J. Man-Mach. Stud.* **19**:163–180.

HART, S. G., BATTISTE, V., CHESNEY, M. A., WARD, M. W., AND McELROY, M., 1987, Response of type A and type B individuals performing a supervisory control simulation, in *Social, Ergonomic and Stress Aspects of Work with Computers* (G. Salvendy, S. L. Sauter, and J. J. Hurrell, Jr., eds.), North-Holland Elsevier Science Publishers, Amsterdam, pp. 67–74.

HAYES, P. J., AND REDDY, D. R., 1983, Steps toward graceful interaction in spoken and written man–machine communication, *Int. J. Man-Mach. Stud.* **19**:231–284.

HEBB, D. O., 1949, *The Organization of Behavior*, Wiley, New York.

HICKS, C. R., 1964, *Fundamental Concepts in the Design of Experiments*, Holt, Rinehart & Winston, New York.

HOBDAY, S. W., 1988, A keyboard to increase productivity and reduce postural stress, in *Trends in Ergonomics/Human Factors V* (F. Aghazadeh, ed.), North-Holland Elsevier Science Publishers, Amsterdam, pp. 321–330.

HOROWITZ, E., AND SAHNI, S., 1976, *Fundamentals of Data Structures*, Computer Science Press, Washington, D. C.

HUNT, E. B., 1962, Memory and concept learning, in *Concept Learning*, Wiley, New York.

HUTCHINS, E. L., HOLLAN, J. D., AND NORMAN, D. A., 1986, Direct manipulation interfaces, in *User Centered System Design: New Perspectives on Human–Computer Interaction* (D. A. Norman and S. W. Draper, eds.), Lawrence Erlbaum Associates, Hillsdale, N.J., pp. 87–124.

ITOH, Y., HAYASHI, Y., TSUKUI, I., AND SALTO, S., 1989, Heart rate variability and subjective mental workload in flight task: Validity of mental workload measurement using H.R.V. method, in *Work with Computers: Organizational, Management, Stress and Health Aspects* (M. J. Smith and G. Salvendy, eds.), North-Holland Elsevier Science Publishers, Amsterdam, pp. 209–216.

JACOB, R. J. K., AND SIBERT, L. E., 1992, The perceptual structure of multidimensional input device selection, *Human Factors in Computing Systems, CHI'92 Conference Proceedings*, ACM, pp. 211–218.

JACKSON, P., 1986, *Introduction to Expert Systems*, Addison-Wesley, Reading, MA.

JEFFRIES, R., AND ROSENBERG, J. K., 1987, Comparing a form-based and a language-based user interface for instructing a mail program, *Proceedings of CHI + GI 1987 Conference*, ACM, Toronto, pp. 261–266.

JEFFRIES, R., MILLER, J. R., WHARTON, C., AND UYEDA, K. M., 1991, User interface evaluation in the real world: A comparison of four methods, *Human Factors in Computing Systems, CHI'91 Conference Proceedings*, ACM, pp. 119–124.

JOHN, B. E., AND VERA, A. H., 1992, A GOMS analysis of a graphic, machine-paced, highly interactive task, *Human Factors in Computing Systems, CHI'92 Conference Proceedings*, ACM, pp. 251–258.

KACMAR, C. J., 1991, An experimental comparison of text and icon menu item formats, in *Human Factors in Information Systems: An Organization Perspective* (J. M Carey, ed.), Ablex Publishing Corp., Norwood, N.J., pp. 27–41.

KANT, K., 1992, *Introduction to Computer System Performance Evaluation*, McGraw–Hill, New York.

KARAT, C.-M., CAMPBELL, R., AND FIEGEL, T., 1992, Comparison of empirical testing and walkthrough methods in user interface evaluation, *Human Factors in Computing Systems, CHI'92 Conference Proceedings*, ACM, pp. 397–404.

KIERAS, D., 1992, Diagrammatic displays for engineered systems: Effects on human performance in interacting with malfunctioning systems, *Int. J. Man-Mach. Stud.* **36**:861–895.

KIERAS, D., AND POLSON, P. G., 1985, An approach to the formal analysis of user complexity, *Int. J. Man-Mach. Stud.* **22**:365–394.

KIRK, R. E., 1982, *Experimental Design: Procedures for the Behavioural Sciences*, 2nd ed., Wadsworth Publishing Co., Belmont, Calif.

KOSSLYN, S. M., 1980, *Image and Mind*, Harvard University Press, Cambridge, Mass.

KOSSLYN, S. M., AND SCHWARTZ, S. P., 1978, Visual images and spatial representations in active memory, in *Computer Vision Systems* (E. M. Riseman and A. R. Hanson, eds.), Academic Press, New York, pp. 223–241.

KUMASHIRO, M., KAMADA, T., AND MIYAKE, S., 1989, Mental stress with new technology at the workplace, in *Work with Computers: Organizational, Management, Stress and Health Aspects* (M. J. Smith and G. Salvendy, eds.), North-Holland Elsevier Science Publishers, Amsterdam, pp. 270–277.

LANSDALE, M. W., SIMPSON, M., AND STROUD, T. R. J., 1990, A comparison of words and icons as cue enrichers in an information retrieval task, *Behav. Inf. Technol.* **9**:111–131.

LAW, A. M., AND KELTON, W. D., 1991, *Simulation Modeling and Analysis*, McGraw–Hill, New York.

LEABO, D. A., 1972, *Basic Statistics*, Richard D. Irwin, Inc., Homewood, Ill.

LEE, K. S., WAIKAR, A. M., AND OSTBERG, O., 1988, Visual strain evaluation of VDT operators using a laser optometer, in *Trends in Ergonomics/Human Factors V* (F. Aghazadeh, ed.), North-Holland Elsevier Science Publishers, Amsterdam, pp. 305–312.

LEVINE, S., WEINBERG, J., AND URSIN, H., 1978, Definition of the coping process and statement of the problem, in *Pyschobiology of Stress: A Study of Coping Men* (H. Ursin, E. Baade, and S. Levine, eds.), Academic Press, New York, pp. 3–19.

LEWIS, C., POLSON, P., WHARTON, C., AND RIEMAN, J., 1990, Testing a walkthrough methodology for theory-based design of walk-up-and-use interfaces, *Human Factors in Computing Systems, CHI'90 Conference Proceedings*, ACM, pp. 235–242.

LEWIS, T. G., AND SMITH, B. J., 1979, *Computer Principles of Modeling and Simulation*, Houghton Mifflin, Boston.

LICKLIDER, J. C. R., 1960, Man–computer symbiosis, *IRE Trans. Hum. Factors Electron.* 4–11.

LIM, S. Y., ROGERS, K. J. S., SMITH, M. J., AND SAINFORT, P. C., 1989, A study of the direct and indirect effects of office ergonomics on psychological stress outcomes, in *Work with Computers: Organizational, Management, Stress and Health Aspects* (M. J. Smith and G. Salvendy, eds.), North-Holland Elsevier Science Publishers, Amsterdam, pp. 248–255.

LINDQUIST, T. E., 1985, Assessing the usability of human–computer interfaces, *IEEE Software*, pp. 74–82.

MCCABE, D. J., 1976, A complexity measure, *IEEE Trans. Software Eng.* SE-**2**(4):308–320.

MACGREGOR, J. N., 1992, A comparison of the effects of icons and descriptors in videotex menu retrieval, *Int. J. Man-Mach. Stud.* **37**:767–777.

MACK, R., LEWIS, C., AND CARROLL, J., 1983, Learning to use word processors: Problems and prospects, *ACM Trans. Office Inf. Syst.* **1**:254–271.

MACKENZIE, I. S., AND BUXTON, W., 1992, Extending Fitt's law to two-dimensional tasks, *Human Factors in Computing Systems, CHI'92 Conference Proceedings*, ACM, pp. 219–226.

MACKENZIE, I. S., AND WARE, C., 1993, Lag as a determinant of human performance in interactive systems, *Human Factors in Computing Systems, INTERCHI'93 Conference Proceedings*, ACM, pp. 488–493.

MARCUS, R. S., 1983, An experimental comparison of the effectiveness of computers and humans as search intermediaries, *J. Am. Soc. Inf. Sci.* **34**(6):381–404.

MAREK, T., AND NOWOROL, C., 1987, Cumulative fatigue symptoms of dialogue and data entry VDU operators, in *Social, Ergonomic and Stress Aspects of Work with Computers* (G. Salvendy, S. L. Sauter, and J. J. Hurrell, Jr., eds.), North-Holland Elsevier Science Publishers, Amsterdam, pp. 255–262.

MAREK, T., NOWOROL, C., PIECZONKA-OSIKOWSKA, W., PRZETACNIK, J., AND KARWOWSKI, W., 1988, Changes in temporal instability of lateral and vertical phorias of the VDT operators, in *Trends in Ergonomics/Human Factors V* (F. Aghazadeh, ed.), North-Holland Elsevier Science Publishers, Amsterdam, pp. 283–289.

MARTIN, I., AND VENABLES, P. H., (eds.), 1980, *Techniques in Psychophysiology*, Wiley, New York.

MASSARI, A., COSTAGLIOLA, G., CHRYSANTHIS, P. K., AND CHANG, S. K., 1993, Programs as databases: Treating code and comments as first class objects, *Proceedings of 5th International Conference on Software Engineering and Knowledge Engineering*, San Francisco, pp. 78–85.

MEAD, R., 1988, *The Design of Experiments: Statistical Principles for Practical Application*, Cambridge University Press, London.

MILLER, G. A., GALANTER, E., AND PRIBRAM, K., 1960, *Plans and Structure of Behavior*, Holt, New York.

MILLER, R. B., 1968, Response time in man–computer conversational transactions, *Proceedings of Fall Joint Computer Conference*, AFIPS, Vol. 33, Part 1, Montvale Press, Montvale, N.J., pp. 267–277.

MINSKY, M., 1975, A framework for representing knowledge, in *The Psychology of Computer Vision* (P. Winston, ed.), McGraw–Hill, New York, pp. 211–277.

MIYAO, M., ALLEN, J. S., HACISALIHZADE, S. S., CRONIN, S. A., AND STARK, L. W., 1988, The effect of CRT quality on visual fatigue, in *Trends in Ergonomics/Human Factors V* (F. Aghazadeh, ed.), North-Holland Elsevier Science Publishers, Amsterdam, pp. 297–304.

MONK, A., 1986, Statistical evaluation of behavioural data, in *Fundamentals of Human–Computer Interaction* (A. Monk, ed.), Academic Press, New York, pp. 81–87.

MORAN, T. P., 1981, The command language grammar: A representation for the user interface of interactive computer systems, *Int. J. Man-Mach. Stud.* **15**:3–50.

MORGAN, K., MORRIS, R. L., AND GIBBS, S., 1991, When does a mouse become a rat? or . . . comparing the performance and preferences in direct manipulation and command line environments, *Comput. J.* **34**:265–271.

MOSSÉ, D., 1993, Tools for visualizing scheduling algorithms, *Proceedings of IFIP Conference*, Irvine, Calif., July 1993.

MULLINS, P., 1990, The Network User Interface Substrate (NUIS): A Task-Oriented Reference Model, Ph.D. dissertation, Department of Computer Science, University of Pittsburgh, Pittsburgh, Pa.

MULLINS, P., AND TREU, S., 1991, Measurement of stress to gauge user satisfaction with features of the computer interface, *Behav. Inf. Technol.* **10**(4):325–343.

MULLINS, P., AND TREU, S., 1993, A task-based cognitive model for user–network interaction: Defining a task taxonomy to guide the interface designer, *Interact. Comput.* **5**(2):139–166.

MYERS, J. L., 1972, *Fundamentals of Experimental Design*, Allyn & Bacon, Boston.

NEWELL, A., AND SIMON, H. A., 1961, The simulation of human thought, in *Current Trends in Psychological Theory* (W. Dennis et al., eds.), University of Pittsburgh Press, Pittsburgh, pp. 152–179.

NEWELL, A., AND SIMON, H., 1972, *Human Problem Solving*, Prentice–Hall, Englewood Cliffs, N.J.

NICKERSON, R. S., 1977, On conversational interaction with computers, in *User-Oriented Design of Interactive Graphics Systems* (S. Treu, ed.), ACM, New York, pp. 101–113.

NIELSEN, J., 1992, Finding usability problems through heuristic evaluation, *Human Factors in Computing Systems, CHI'92 Conference Proceedings*, ACM, pp. 373–380.

NIELSEN, J., AND LANDAUER, T. K., 1993, A mathematical model of the finding of usability problems, *Human Factors in Computing Systems, INTERCHI'93 Conference Proceedings*, ACM, pp. 206–213.

NIELSEN, J., AND MOLICH, R., 1990, Heuristic evaluation of user interfaces, *Human Factors in Computing Systems, CHI'90 Conference Proceedings*, ACM, pp. 249–256.

NIELSEN, J., AND PHILLIPS, V. L., 1993, Estimating the relative usability of two interfaces: Heuristic, formal, and empirical methods compared, *Human Factors in Computing Systems, INTERCHI'93 Conference Proceedings*, ACM, pp. 214–221.

NORMAN, D. A., 1986, Cognitive engineering, in *User Centered System Design: New Perspectives in Human–Computer Interaction* (D. A. Norman and S. W. Draper, eds.), Lawrence Erlbaum Associates, Hillsdale, N.J., pp. 31–61.

NORMAN, D. A., AND DRAPER, S. W., (eds.), 1986, *User Centered System Design: New Perspectives in Human–Computer Interaction*, Lawrence Erlbaum Associates, Hillsdale, N.J.

NORMAN, K. L., WELDON, L. J., AND SHNEIDERMAN, B., 1986, Cognitive layouts of windows and multiple screens for user interfaces, *Int. J. Man-Mach. Stud.* **25**:229–248.

PAUSCH, R., 1991, Virtual reality on five dollars a day, *Human Factors in Computing Systems, CHI'91 Conference Proceedings,* ACM, pp. 265–270.

PEDHAZUR, E. J., 1982, *Multiple Regression in Behavioral Research,* 2nd ed., Holt, Rinehart & Winston, New York.

POLSON, P. G., 1988, The consequences of consistent and inconsistent user interfaces, in *Cognitive Science and its Applications for Human–Computer Interaction* (R. Guindon, ed.), Lawrence Erlbaum Associates, Hillsdale, N.J., pp. 59–108.

PREECE, J., (ed.), 1993, *A Guide to Usability: Human Factors in Computing,* Addison–Wesley, Reading, Mass.

PRICE, B. A., BAECKER, R. M., AND SMALL, I. S., 1993, A principled taxonomy of software visualization, *J. Visual Languages Comput.* **4**(4), December.

QUILLIAN, M. R., 1968, Semantic memory, in *Semantic Information Processing* (M. Minsky, ed.), MIT Press, Cambridge, Mass.

REISNER, P., 1981, Formal grammar and human factors design of an interactive graphics system, *IEEE Trans. Software Eng.* SE-7:229–240.

REYNOLDS, H. T., 1977, *The Analysis of Cross-Classifications,* Free Press, New York.

ROBERTS, T. L., AND MORAN, T. P., 1983, The evaluation of computer text editors: Methodology and empirical results, *Commun. ACM* **26**(4):265–283.

ROHR, G., 1990, Mental concepts and direct manipulation: Drafting a direct manipulation query language, in *Mental Models and Human–Computer Interaction 1* (D. Ackerman and M. J. Tauber, eds.), North-Holland, Amsterdam, pp. 305–319.

ROSCH, E., 1978, Principles of categorization, in *Cognition and Categorization* (E. Rosch and B. B. Lloyd, eds.), Lawrence Erlbaum Associates, Hillsdale, N.J., pp. 27–42.

ROSENTHAL, R., RIPPY, D. E., AND WOOD, H. M., 1976, *The Network Measurement Machine—A Data Collection Device for Measuring the Performance and Utilization of Computer Networks,* National Bureau of Standards, NBS TN 912.

ROWLEY, D. E., AND RHOADES, D. G., 1992, The cognitive jogthrough: A fast-paced user interface evaluation procedure, *Human Factors in Computing Systems, CHI'92 Conference Proceedings,* ACM, pp. 389–395.

RUMELHART, D. E., AND NORMAN, D. A., 1988, Representation in memory, in *Steven's Handbook of Experimental Psychology,* 2nd ed., Vol. 2 (Atkinson *et al.,* eds.), Wiley, New York, pp. 511–587.

RUMELHART, D. E., AND ORTONY, A., 1977, The representation of knowledge in memory, in *Schooling and the Acquisition of Knowledge* (R. C. Anderson, R. J. Spiro, and W. E. Montague, eds.), Lawrence Erlbaum Associates, Hillsdale, N.J., pp. 99–135.

SACKMAN, H., 1968, Time-sharing versus batch processing: The experimental evidence, *Proceedings of Spring Joint Computer Conference,* pp. 1–10.

SACKMAN, H., 1970, *Man–Computer Problem Solving: Experimental Evaluation of Time-Sharing and Batch Processing,* Auerbach Publishers, Princeton, N.J.

SAINFORT, P. C., AND LIM, S. Y., 1989, A longitudinal study of stress among VDT workers: Preliminary results, in *Work with Computers: Organizational, Management, Stress and Health Aspects* (M. J. Smith and G. Salvendy, eds.), North-Holland Elsevier Science Publishers, Amsterdam, pp. 241–247.

SAINFORT, P. C., AND SMITH, M. J., 1989, Job factors as predictors of stress outcomes among VDT users, in *Work with Computers: Organizational, Management, Stress and Health Aspects* (M. J. Smith and G. Salvendy, eds.), North-Holland Elsevier Science Publishers, Amsterdam, pp. 233–240.

SAITO, S., 1987, Quantitative evaluation of VDT operators through the analysis of spatio-temporal characteristics of eye movements, in *Social, Ergonomic and Stress Aspects of Work with Computers* (G. Salvendy, S. L. Sauter, and J. J. Hurrell, Jr., eds.), North-Holland Elsevier Science Publishers, Amsterdam, pp. 197–202.

SALTHOUSE, T. A., 1985, Speed of behavior and its implications for recognition, in *Handbook of the Psychology of Aging* (J. E. Birren and K. W. Schaie, eds.), Van Nostrand–Reinhold, Princeton, N.J., pp. 400–426.

SANDERSON, D. P., 1991, Structured Design of an Adaptive Human–Computer Interface, Ph.D. dissertation, Department of Computer Science, University of Pittsburgh, Pittsburgh, Pa.

SCHANK, R., AND ABELSON, R., 1977, *Scripts, Plans, Goals, and Understanding*, Lawrence Erlbaum Associates, Hillsdale, N.J.

SEARS, A., AND SHNEIDERMAN, B., 1991, High precision touchscreens: Design strategies and comparisons with a mouse, *Int. J. Man-Mach. Stud.* **34**:593–613.

SELYE, H., 1980, Preface, in *Selye's Guide to Stress Research Volume I*, Van Nostrand–Reinhold, Princeton, N.J.

SHAW, C., LIANG, J., GREEN, M., AND SUN, Y., 1992, The decouple simulation model for virtual reality systems, *Human Factors in Computing Systems, CHI'92 Conference Proceedings*, ACM, pp. 321–328.

SHEPARD, R. N., AND COOPER, L. A., 1982, *Mental Images and Their Transformations*, MIT Press, Cambridge, Mass.

SHNEIDERMAN, B., 1982, The future of interactive systems and the emergence of direct manipulation, *Behav. Inf. Technol.* **1**(3):237–256.

SHNEIDERMAN, B., 1983, Direct manipulation: A step beyond programming languages, *Computer*, 57–69.

SHNEIDERMAN, B., 1992, *Designing the User Interface—Strategies for Effective Human Computer Interaction*, 2nd ed., Addison–Wesley, Reading, Mass.

SIACHI, A. C., AND HIX, D., 1991, A study of computer-supported user interface evaluation using maximal repeating pattern analysis, *Human Factors in Computing Systems, CHI'91 Conference Proceedings*, ACM, pp. 301–305.

SIMON, H. A., AND NEWELL, A., 1964, Information processing in computer and man, *Am. Sci.* **52**:281–300.

SMITH, M. J., 1984a, Human factors issues in VDT use: Environmental and workstation design considerations, *IEEE Comput. Graphics Appl.* **4**(11):56–63.

SMITH, M. J., 1984b, Ergonomic and stress aspects of computerized office technology, in *Human–Computer Interaction* (G. Salvendy, ed.), North-Holland Elsevier Science Publishers, Amsterdam, pp. 337–346.

SMITH, M. J., CARAYON, P., AND MIEZIO, K., 1987, Electronic monitoring and job stress, in *Social, Ergonomic and Stress Aspects of Work with Computers* (G. Salvendy, S. L. Sauter, and J. J. Hurrell, Jr., eds.), North-Holland Elsevier Science Publishers, Amsterdam, pp. 33–42.

SNODGRASS, R., 1983, An object-oriented command language, *IEEE Trans. Software Eng.* **SE-9**:1–8.

SOMBERG, B. L., 1987, A comparison of rule-based and positionally constant arrangements of computer menu items, *Proceedings of CHI + GI 1987 Conference*, ACM, Toronto, pp. 255–260.

SPENCE, R. H., 1985, *Computer Usability Testing and Evaluation*, Prentice–Hall, Englewood Cliffs, N.J.

STASKO, J., BADRE, A., AND LEWIS, C., 1993, Do algorithm animations assist learning? An empirical study and analysis, *Human Factors in Computing Systems, INTERCHI'93 Conference Proceedings*, ACM, pp. 61–66.

SVENDSON, G. B., 1991, The influence of interface style on problem solving, *Int. J. Man-Mach. Stud.* **35**:379–397.

SWEENEY, M., MAGUIRE, M., AND SHACKEL, B., 1993, Evaluating user–computer interaction: A framework, *Int. J. Man-Mach. Stud.* **38**:689–711.

TANENBAUM, A. S., 1988, *Computer Networks*, Second Edition, Prentice–Hall, Englewood Cliffs, N.J.

TAUBER, M. J., 1986, Top-down design of human–computer interfaces, in *Visual Languages* (S. K. Chang, T. Ichikawa, and P. A. Ligomenides, eds.), Plenum Press, New York, pp. 393–429.

TAULBEE, O. E., TREU, S., AND NEHNEVAJSA, J., 1975, User orientation in networking, *Proceedings of National Computer Conference*, pp. 637–644.

TETZLAFF, L., AND SCHWARTZ, D. R., 1991, The use of guidelines in interface design, *Human Factors in Computing Systems, CHI'91 Conference Proceedings*, ACM, pp. 329–333.

THIMBLEBY, H., 1990, *User Interface Design*, ACM Press, New York.

TREU, S., 1967a, Testing and evaluation-literature review, in *Electronic Handling of Information* (A. Kent and O. E. Taulbee, eds.), Thompson Book Co., Washington, D.C., pp. 71–88.

TREU, S., 1967b, Experiments, *Testing and Evaluation of the FTD CIRC System*, Goodyear Aerospace Corp., Final Report under Contract AF 30(602)4039, Restricted Distribution, March 15, 1967, pp. 57–140.

TREU, S., 1971, A conceptual framework for the searcher–system interface, *Interactive Bibliographic Search: The User/Computer Interface* (D. Walker, ed.), AFIPS Press, pp. 53–66.

TREU, S., 1972, *A Computer Terminal Network for Transparent Stimulation of the User of an On-Line Retrieval System*, National Bureau of Standards, TN 732.

TREU, S., 1975a, Interactive command language design based on required mental work, *Int. J. Man-Mach. Stud.* **7**:135–149.

TREU, S., 1975b, On-line student debate: An experiment in communication using computer networks, *Int. J. Comput. Inf. Sci.* **4**(1):39–51.

TREU, S., (ed.), 1977, *User-Oriented Design of Interactive Graphics Systems*, based on ACM/SIGGRAPH Workshop, October 1986, Pittsburgh, ACM.

TREU, S., 1982, Uniformity in user–computer interaction languages: A compromise solution, *Int. J. Man-Mach. Stud.* **16**:183–210.

TREU, S., 1989, Recognition of logical interface structures to enhance human–computer interaction, *Int. J. Pattern Recogn. Artif. Intell.* **3**(2):217–236.

TREU, S., 1990, 'Conceptual distance' and interface-supported visualization of information objects and patterns, *J. Visual Languages Comput.* **1**(4):369–388.

TREU, S., 1992, Interface structures: Conceptual, logical, and physical patterns applicable to human–computer interaction, *Int. J. Man-Mach. Stud.* **37**:565–593.

TREU, S., 1994, *User Interface Design: A Structured Approach*, Plenum Press, New York.

TREU, S., MULLINS, P., AND ADAMS, J., 1989, A network-wide information system: Multi-level context for the user at the workstation interface, *Inf. Syst.* **14**(5):393–406.

TREU, S., SANDERSON, D. P., ROZIN, R., AND SHARMA, R., 1991, High-level, three-pronged design methodology for the *N-CHIME* interface system software, *Inf. Software Technol.* **33**:306–320.

TRUMBLY, J. E., ARNETT, K. P., AND MARTIN, M. P., 1993, Performance effect of matching computer interface characteristics and user skill level, *Int. J. Man-Mach. Stud.* **38**: 713–724.

TYLER, S., 1986, SAUCI: A Self-Adaptive User–Computer Interface, Ph.D. dissertation, Department of Computer Science, University of Pittsburgh, Pittsburgh, Pa.

TYLER, S., AND TREU, S., 1989, An interface architecture to provide adaptive task-specific context for the user, *Int. J. Man-Mach. Stud.* **30**(3):303–327.

VIDAL, J. J., 1973, Toward direct brain–computer communication, *Annu. Rev. Biophys. Bioeng.* **4**:157.

VIDAL, J. J., 1977, Real-time detection of brain events in EEG, *Proc. IEEE* **65**(5):633.

WALKER, N., SMELCER, J. B., AND NILSEN, E., 1991, Optimizing speed and accuracy of menu selection: A comparison of walking and pull-down menus, *Int. J. Man-Mach. Stud.* **35**:871–890.

WATERMAN, D. A., AND HAYES-ROTH, F. (eds.), 1978, *Pattern-Directed Inference Systems*, Academic Press, New York.

WHARTON, C., BRADFORD, J., JEFFRIES, R., AND FRANZKE, M., 1992, Applying cognitive walkthroughs to more complex interfaces: Experiences, issues, and recommendations, *Human Factors in Computing Systems, CHI'92 Conference Proceedings*, ACM, pp. 381–388.

WHITESIDE, J., BENNETT, J., AND HOLTZBLATT, K., 1988, Usability engineering: Our experience and evolution, in *Handbook of Human–Computer Interaction* (M. Helander, ed.), North-Holland, Amsterdam, pp. 791–817.

WINER, B. J., 1971, *Statistical Principles in Experimental Design*, McGraw-Hill, New York.

WOODS, D. D., 1984, Visual momentum: A concept to improve the cognitive coupling of person and computer, *Int. J. Man-Mach. Stud.* **21**:229–244.

WORLD BOOK DICTIONARY, THE, 1975, (C. L. Barnhart, editor-in-chief), Doubleday, New York.

YAMAMOTO, S., MATSUOKA, S., AND ISHIKAWA, T., 1989, Variations in EEG activities during VDT operation, in *Work with Computers: Organizational, Management, Stress and Health Aspects* (M. J. Smith and G. Salvendy, eds.), North-Holland Elsevier Science Publishers, Amsterdam, pp. 225–232.

YOSHINO, K., TAKANO, K., AND NAGASAKA, A., 1989, How human-error probability (is affected) by physiological conditions in the man–machine system, in *Work with Computers: Organizational, Management, Stress and Health Aspects* (M. J. Smith and G. Salvendy, eds.), North-Holland Elsevier Science Publishers, Amsterdam, pp. 636–643.

ZAVALA, A., 1984, Stress and factors of productivity among software development workers, in *Human–Computer Interaction* (G. Salvendy, ed.), North-Holland Elsevier Science Publishers, Amsterdam, pp 365–370.

ZWAHLEN, H. T., AND ADAMS, C. C., JR., 1988, Evaluation of ocular and musculoskeletal subjective discomfort score responses from VDT operators, in *Trends in Ergonomics/ Human Factors V* (F. Aghazadeh, ed.), North-Holland Elsevier Science Publishers, Amsterdam, pp. 267–274.

INDEX

273